Merry Christmas Darli

You're on page 14

SANDBACH, WHEELOCK & DISTRICT

THROUGH TIME

Paul Hurley

Jack
xxxx

AMBERLEY PUBLISHING

Acknowledgements

I would like to thank Colin McLean and his wife Mary for allowing me to use photographs from their archive and providing some interesting history about the town. Their help has been invaluable and we have had some lively discussions. Thanks also to Tom Andrew for his useful advice and to Mike Edison for allowing me access to the photographs in the County Archives. Thanks to Jo from the Ring-O-Roses flower shop in Sandbach for allowing me access to her first-floor window. And, as always, I would like to thank my wife Rose for her unlimited patience during the lengthy compilation of this book.

First published 2011

Amberley Publishing
Cirencester Road, Chalford
Stroud, Gloucestershire, GL6 8PE

www.amberley-books.com

ISBN 978 1 4456 0461 9

British Library Cataloguing in Publication Data.
A catalogue record for this book is available from the British Library.

Typeset in 9.5pt on 12pt Celeste.
Typesetting by Amberley Publishing.
Printed in the UK.

Introduction

Sandbach is a small Cheshire town, but one with quite a lot of interesting history. Unlike other Cheshire towns, it cannot profess to having contributed greatly to the English Civil War. But an interesting occurrence took place here towards the end of it. At the turn of the last century, a momentous change occurred in the way goods and people were carried on the roads of Britain, and the contribution that Sandbach made to that was immense – but we will look at that later. In this book, we look at Sandbach and some of its surrounding villages and hamlets in a way that is intended to make history interesting. It is not for the ardent historian; there are far more learned tomes by such experts as John Parsons Earwaker and Dr George Ormerod. However, there is a dearth of history books dedicated to Sandbach and District. As well as providing us with the excellent and important *History of Cheshire*, Dr Ormerod was also responsible for bringing back the ancient crosses to the town.

But let us start with the English Civil War. The hostilities missed Sandbach, being confined mainly to nearby Nantwich and Middlewich. By 1651, the war was almost over when the Battle of Worcester took place. 16,000 Royalists were well and truly trounced by the 28,000-strong New Model Army of Cromwell. Most of the Royalist army consisted of Scottish soldiers, and after the battle the remnants set off back to Scotland. On Thursday 4 September, they reached Sandbach – it was the day of the September Fair. By now only about 1,000 mounted soldiers remained and they were in a sorry state. Seeing this, the 'honest' men of Sandbach set about them with clubs, stones and wood from their stalls. The battle raged on, with the locals backing off and attacking the rear of the column as it passed. A hundred Scottish prisoners were taken and locked in the church, and about thirty in total from both sides were slain. The common has been called locally 'Scotch Common' and the Sealed Knot Society re-enact the 'battle'.

Now for the Sandbach Crosses. Much has been written about the two famous crosses or obelisks that stand in the old cobbled Market Square, some of it quite contradictory, but with treasures of such antiquity this is to be expected. What we do know is that they are made from millstone grit and covered in carvings depicting biblical and religious scenes. They are believed to have been erected around AD 653, when Christianity was brought to the heathen Mercia from Northumberland. They remained as religious icons for many centuries, but then they were in the shape of Saxon crosses. (Two wooden replica Saxon crosses are on the common showing what such crosses looked like.)

Then along came the seventeenth century and the crosses were smashed up in the Puritan fervour that was obsessed with false idols and the purity of uncluttered faith. Much damage was done to churches and religious establishments in the name of iconoclasm by these fanatics. The bits were carried off across the county to such places as the Oulton Park Estate and Tarporley; they were used as doorsteps and the like until the 1800s, when the renowned historian Dr George Ormerod took the job in hand and sent his team out to scour the county to recover as many pieces as possible. In 1816, under his direction, the crosses were erected on their current site. The cobbles were laid at the same time by John Palmer of Manchester, having been brought from Sandbach Heath.

Now to what has really made Sandbach famous (albeit that it is technically in Elworth). In 1856 a local man, Edwin Foden, joined the heavy engineering company called Plant & Hancock as an apprentice. In 1887 he took over the company and it was renamed Edwin Foden Sons & Co. Ltd. They continued to build static and heavy steam engines and agricultural steam-driven vehicles. At the very end of the 1800s, the company experimented with steam-driven road lorries, introducing them to the market at the turn of the century. The Foden wagons came in all styles, from heavy haulage to light steam vans, and the company prospered, becoming a leader in the world market. Any visit today to one of the popular steam fairs will reveal just how important this company was.

By the early 1930s, Foden were still concentrating on steam traction. Edwin Richard Foden, one of the brothers, had the temerity to suggest that the future lay in diesel engines. For this outrageous suggestion he was pensioned off the board at the age of sixty. With two employees and his son he set up another business building diesel trucks, the first one appearing at the Commercial Motor Show in 1933 under the name Edwin Richard Foden, later renamed ERF to avoid mention of the Foden Company down the road. The ERF plant went by the name Sun Works and became as important to the diesel truck market as Foden were to steam. When the benefits of the internal combustion engine became obvious, Foden followed suit, manufacturing diesel trucks under the Foden name. The last steam vehicle left the works in 1934. The Foden Company went into receivership in 1980 and was bought by Paccar, a US company that also acquired DAF Trucks and Leyland Trucks. As for ERF, they were sold to MAN AG, and in July 2007 the ERF badge ceased to be used. The huge Sun Works had been demolished and the site was used by a doctor's surgery and an Aldi supermarket. Foden's works made way for new houses. One shining star from the days of Foden's is the Foden Motor Works Band, now titled Foden's Band. The band has existed from the very early days and has become one of the best-known brass bands in the world. In fact, it ended 2010 ranked second in the list compiled by World of Brass. It still exists and has its home in Sandbach.

This book contains well-researched captions to accompany the old and new photographs. Included are photograph sets of Wheelock, Warmingham, Elworth and Ettiley Heath – so dip into the past and see what Sandbach has to offer. Peruse what was once there and compare it to what is there today. Most importantly, enjoy the book.

About the Author

Paul Hurley is a freelance writer and member of the Society of Authors. He has a novel, magazine and book credits to his name and lives at Winsford in Cheshire. He has two sons and two daughters.

By the same author:

Fiction

Liverpool Soldier

Non-Fiction

Middlewich (with Brian Curzon)
Northwich Through Time
Winsford Through Time
Villages of Mid Cheshire Through Time
Frodsham & Helsby Through Time
Nantwich Through Time
Chester Through Time (with Len Morgan)
Middlewich & Holmes Chapel Through Time

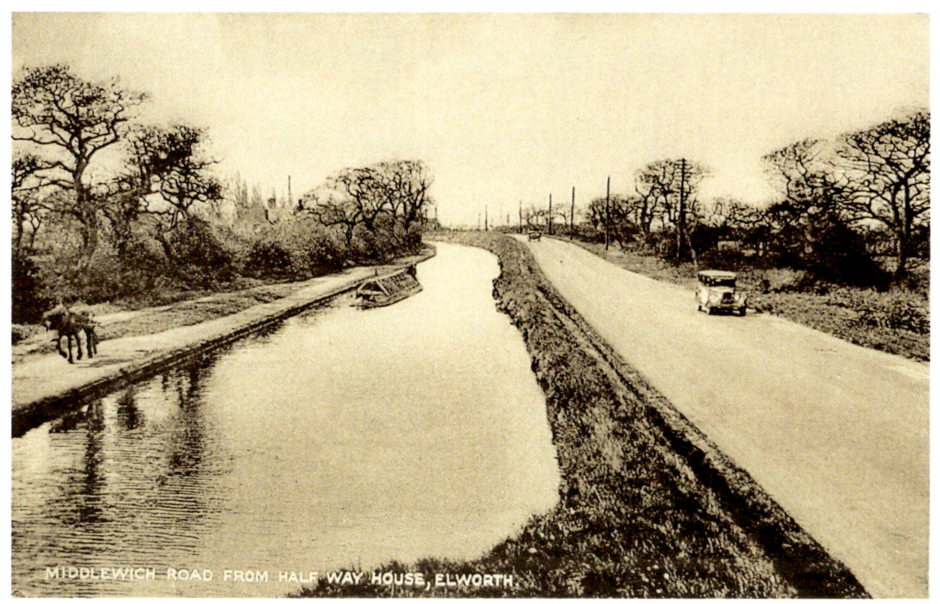

Booth's Lane, 1920s and 2010

This photograph was taken from Lock 69 on the Trent and Mersey Canal and looks back towards Middlewich from Elworth. The old photograph is marked 'Half Way House'; it is believed that a house of that name was on the opposite side of the road in front of Murgatroyd's salt works. At the time of taking the modern photograph in November 2010, extensive works were being carried out on the lock by British Waterways, hence their working boat in the shot. In the old photograph a working boat is being pulled by a horse.

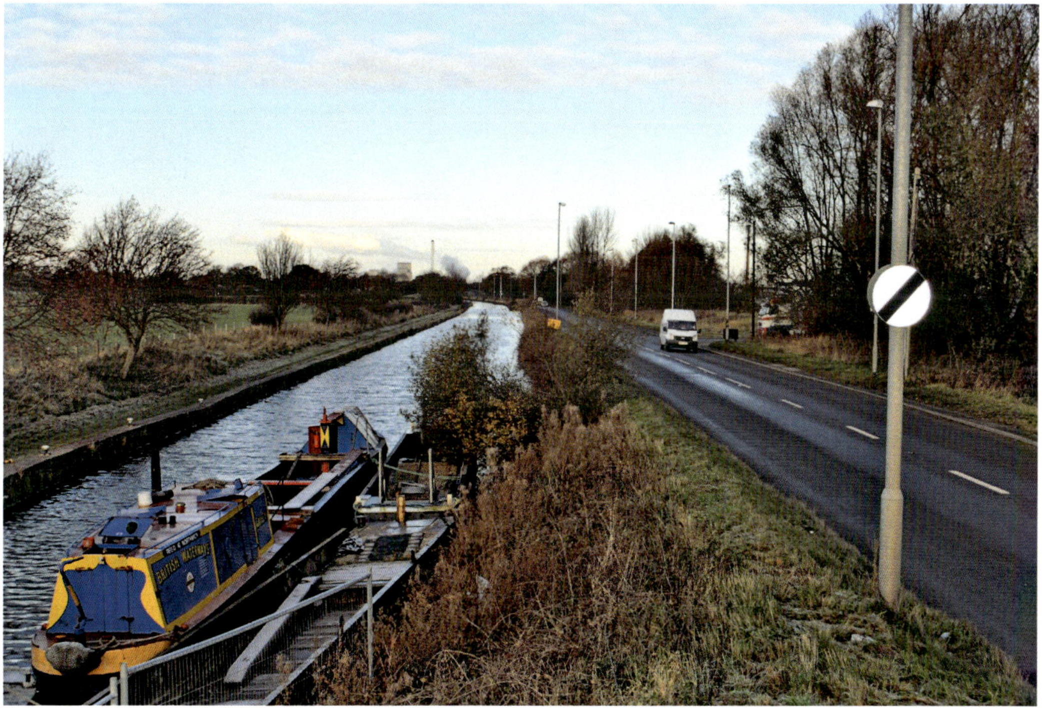

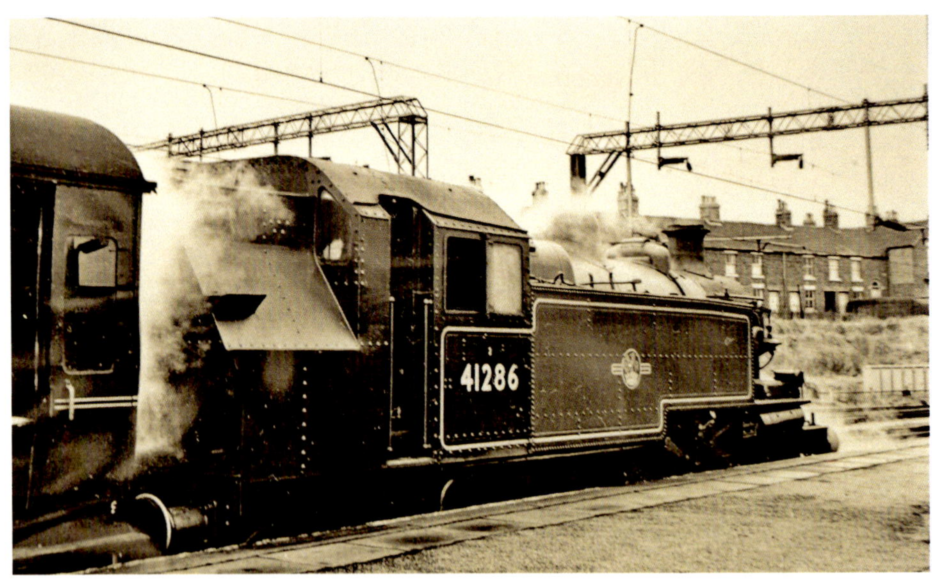

Sandbach Station, 1960s and 2010

Although called Sandbach station, it is in fact in Elworth and was built in the 1840s by the Manchester & Birmingham Railway. It is on the Crewe to Manchester line between Holmes Chapel and Crewe. There is a connection here to Northwich station via Middlewich, but this closed to passengers in 1960 along with Middlewich station. The line still exists though and occasionally sees goods trains and passenger trains when there is work on the West Coast Main Line. The engine in the old photograph is an Ivatt-designed locomotive introduced by the LMS in 1946.

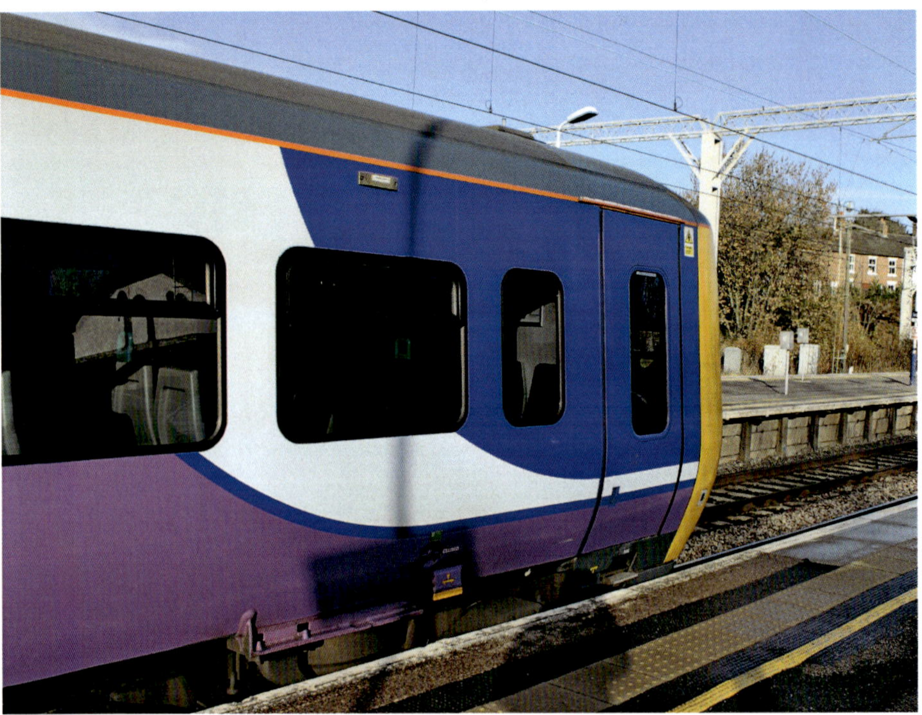

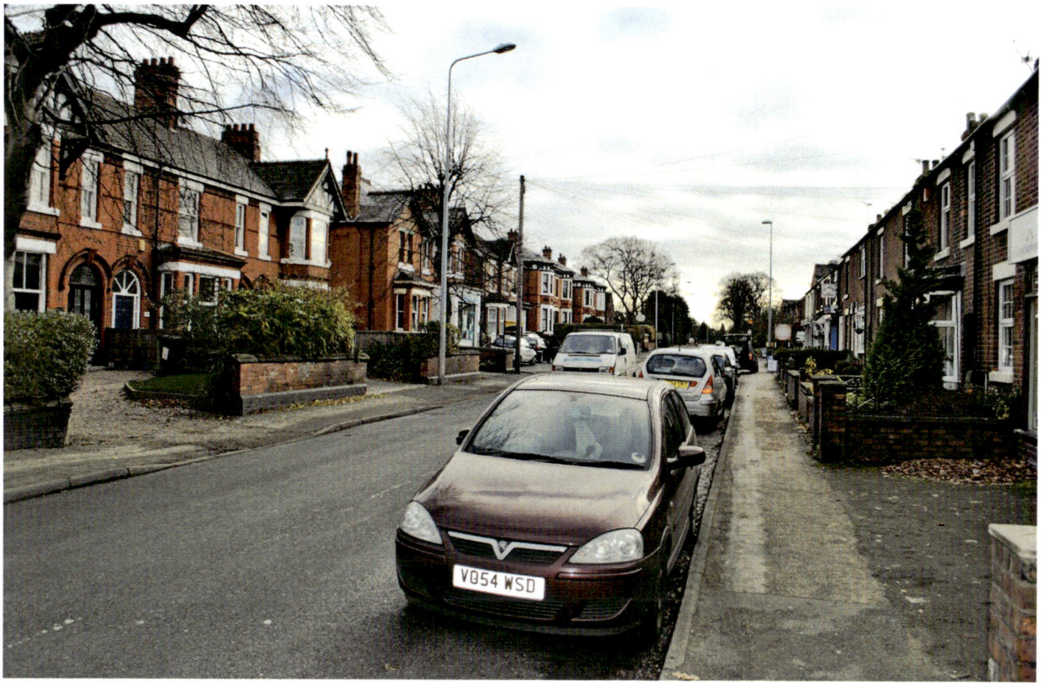

London Road, Elworth, 2010 and 1930s

We now look along London Road in the direction of Sandbach; this is still a busy road stretching from Middlewich to Sandbach town centre. In the old photograph the road is unusually quiet, but at the Foden works on the right a hive of activity would have existed. The road junction on that side is into Hill Street. The entrance to the famous works can be seen on the right with the Foden-owned houses opposite.

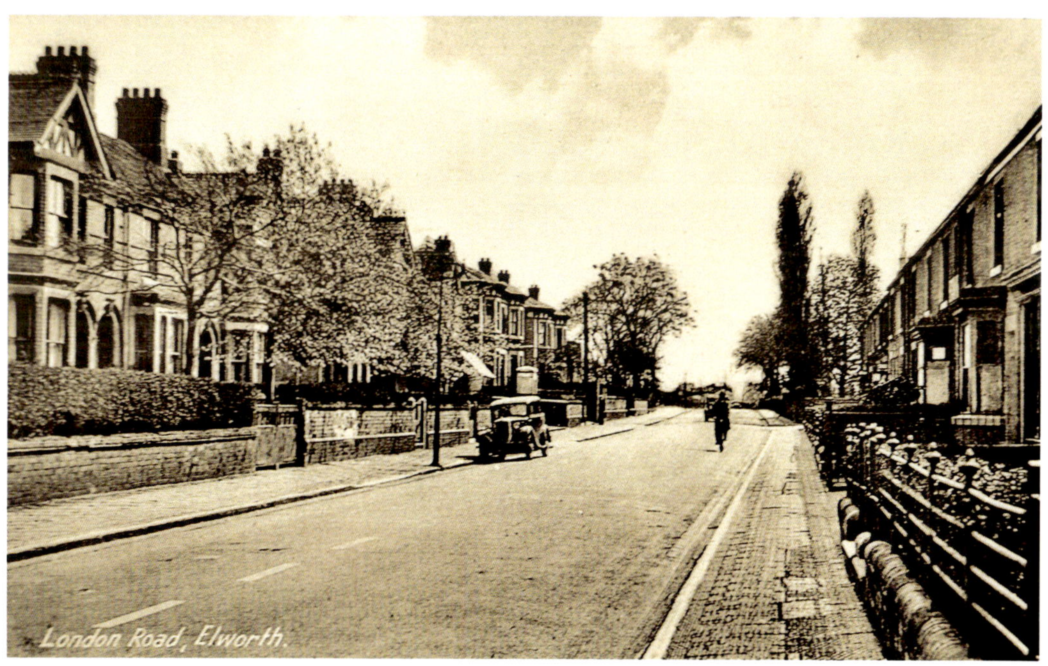

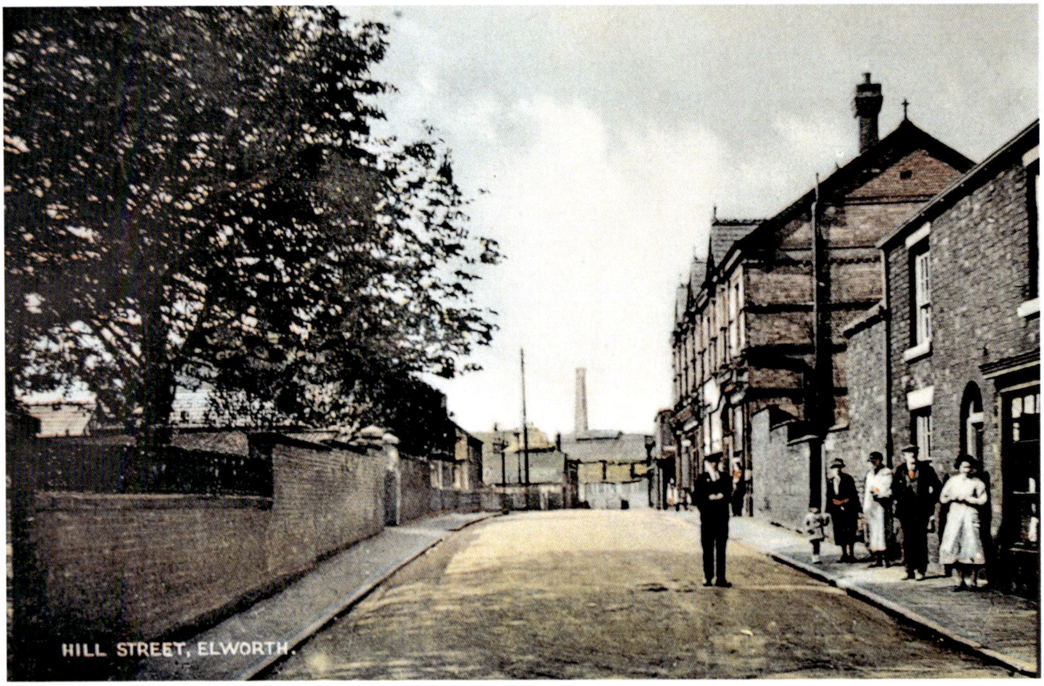

Hill Street, Elworth, 1920s–30s and 2010

This street off London Road once ran up the side of the Foden factory and terminated in Station Road. The large building on the right was owned by the Sandbach Industrial Co-operative Society and it contained a reading room. In 1934, Miss Emmie Jinks was a grocer in the street.

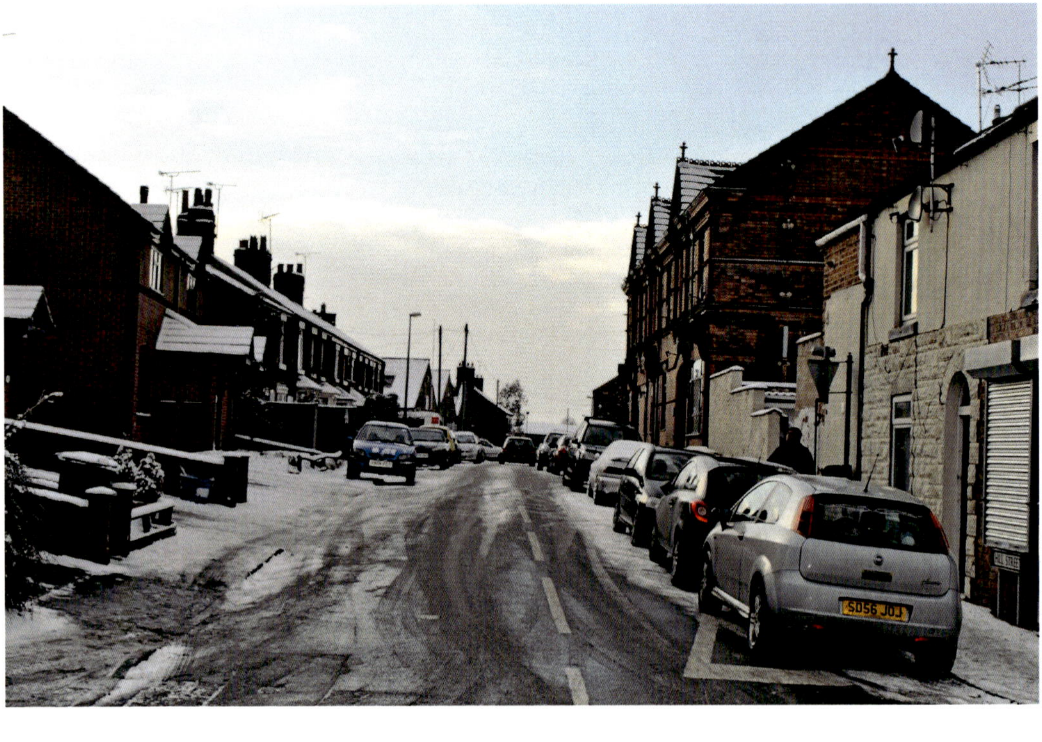

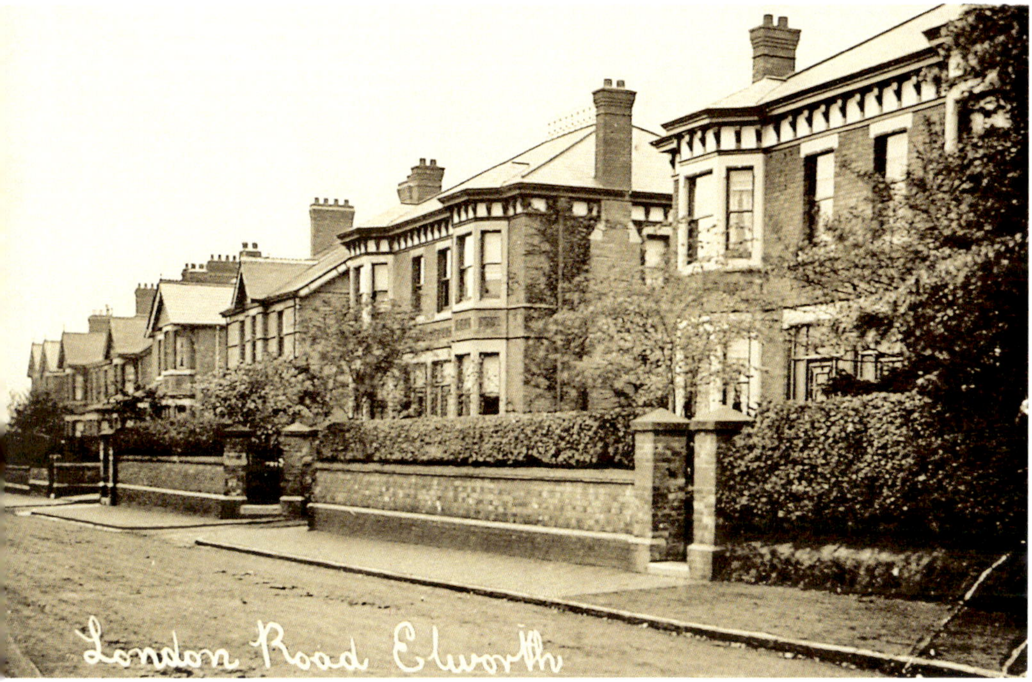

London Road Elworth

Foden Houses, 1920s and 2010

These houses stand almost opposite what was the entrance to the Foden Motor Works. They were built to house members of the Foden family and had names like The Spot, Elworth House and Poplar View. Built as substantial Edwardian semi-detached homes, they have retained their quality over the years.

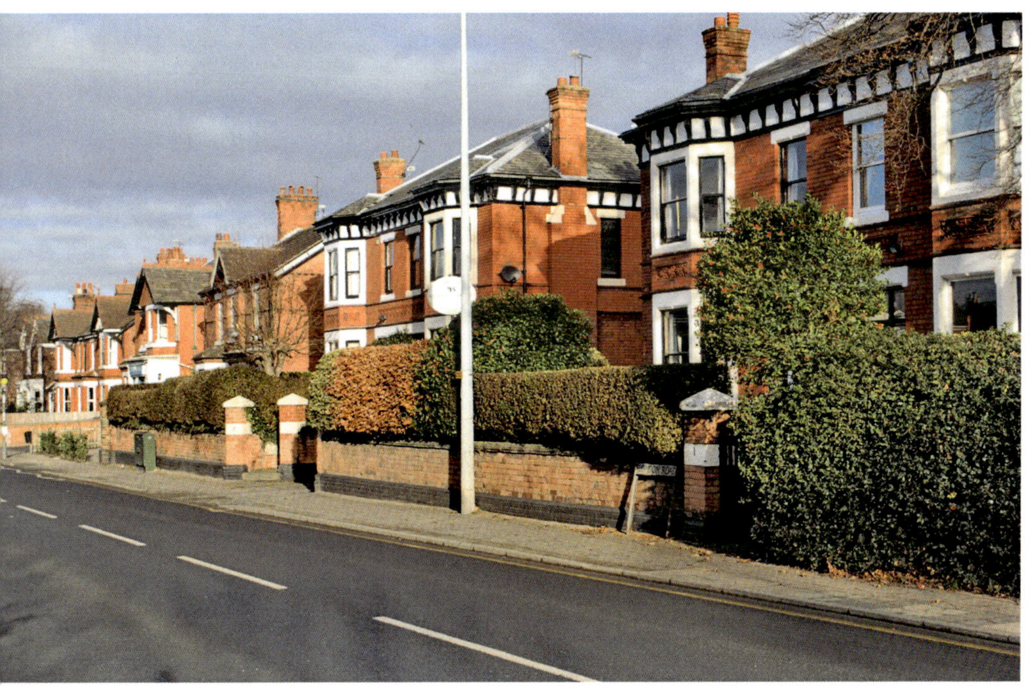

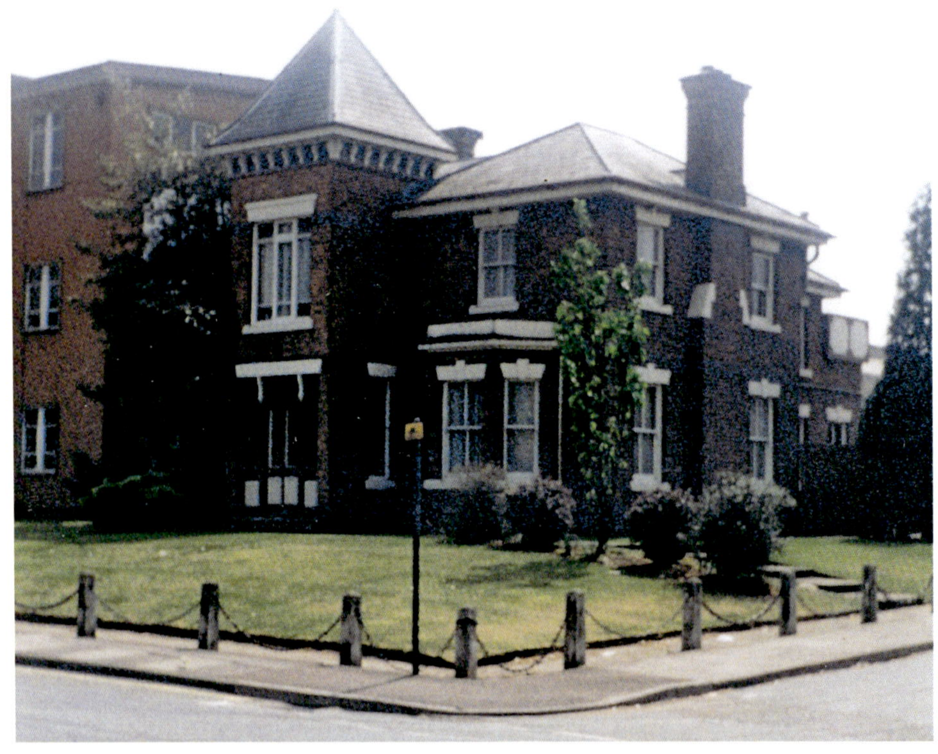

Foden Offices, 2000 and 2010

No book on Sandbach would be complete without a photograph of the Foden works. The image above was taken shortly before demolition. In it the works' offices can be seen on the Hill Street junction. This building was once the home of Mr Foden Snr and when he moved it became offices. This old office block was later joined by the addition of more modern buildings.

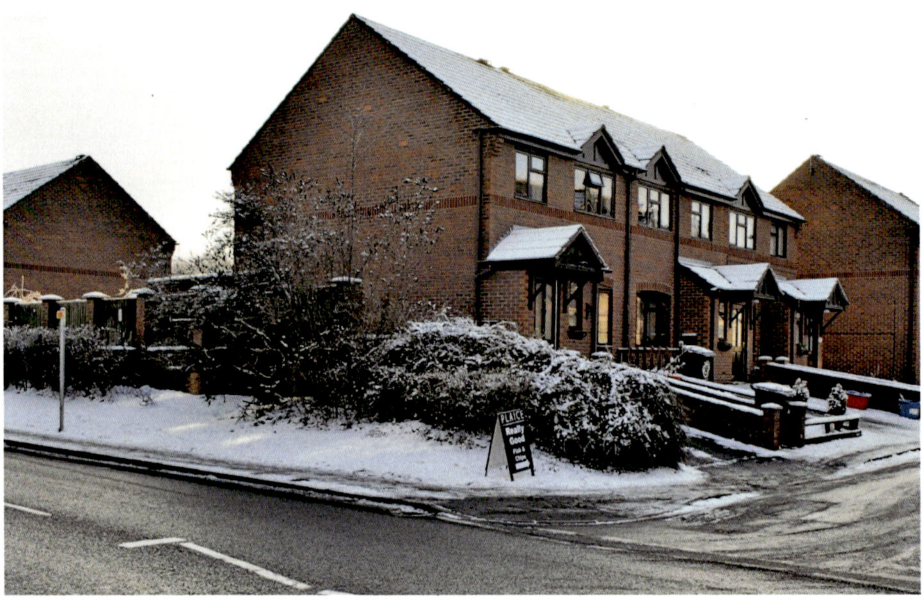

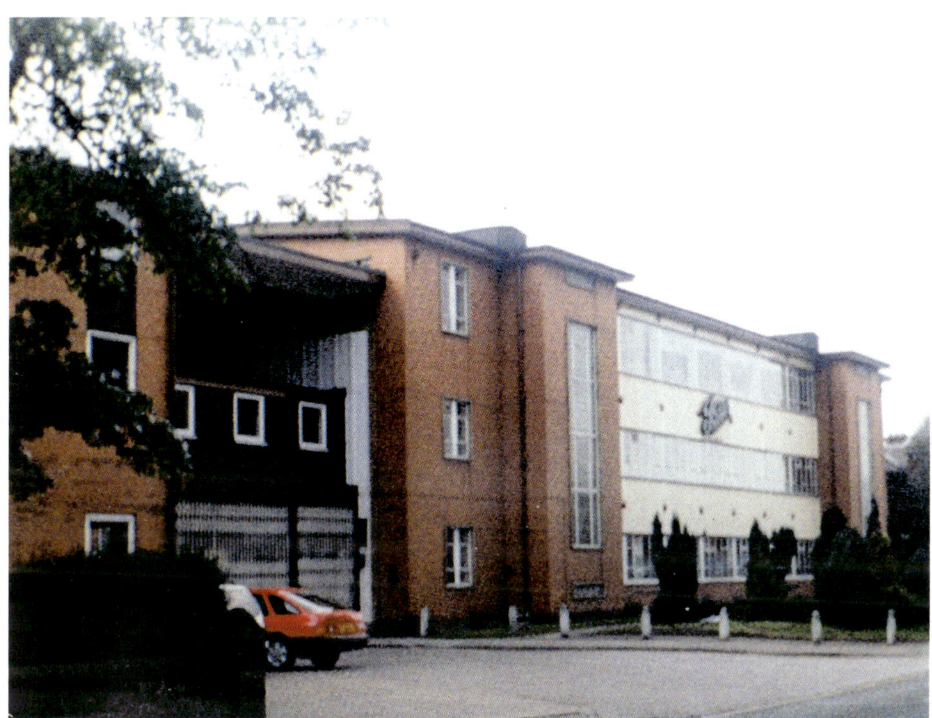

Foden Works, 1990 and 2010

We now carry on along London Road until we reach the original front gate of the Foden works. Through the years, steel was transported into the works to be magically turned into living and breathing steam-driven vehicles of every description. Later, diesel wagons and tractor units would take their place in the catalogue of products produced by this world-famous brand.

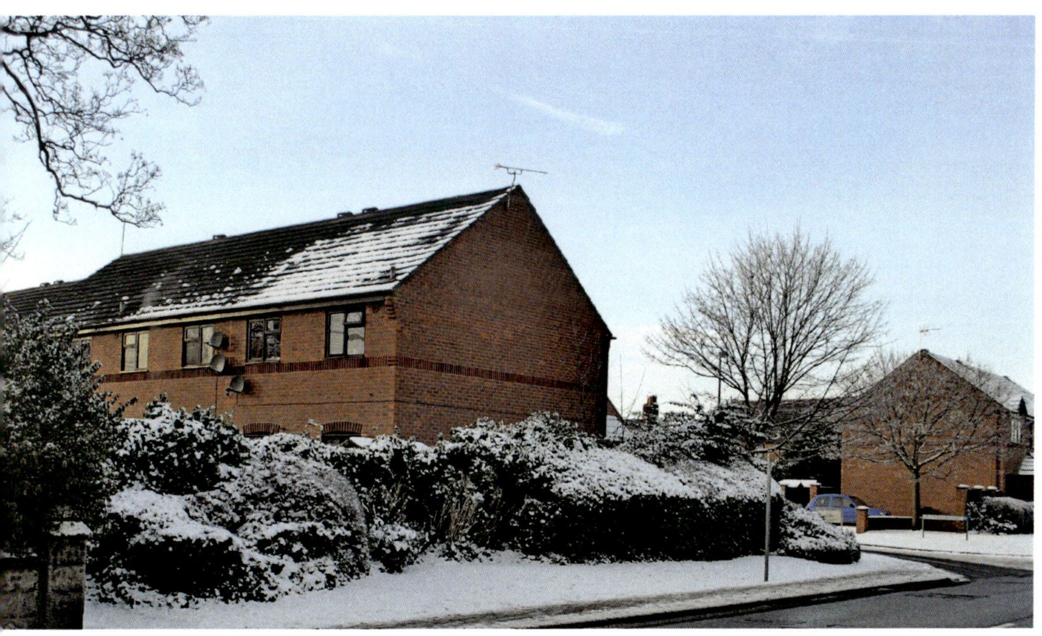

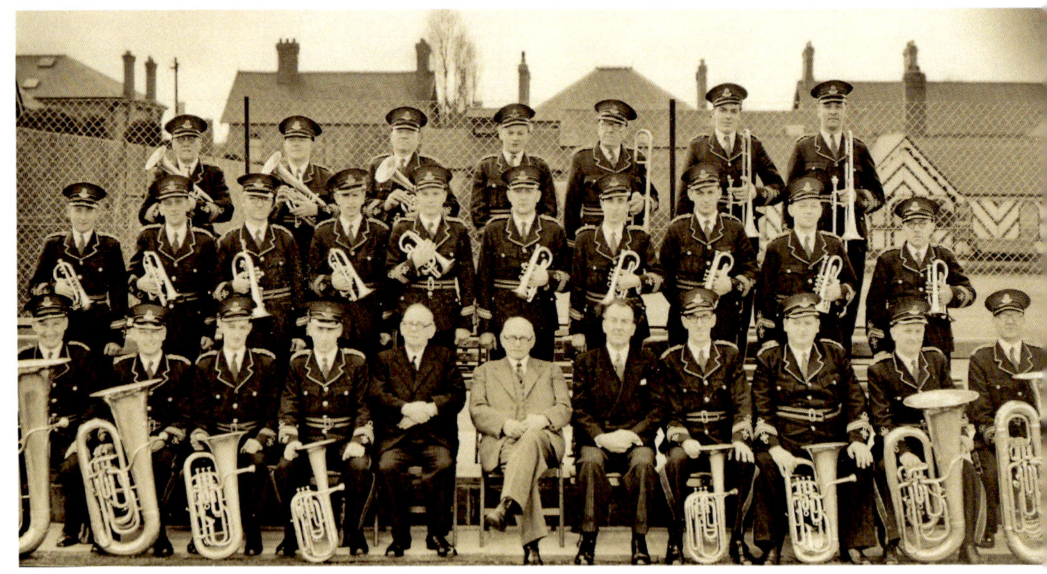

Foden Motor Works Band and Steam Van, 1953 and 1914

A very brief deviation from the usual format of photographs here, as I think that an image of the old Foden Motor Works Band, taken in 1953, is very worthy of inclusion. The photograph was chosen because it is modern enough to show members whose relatives may be perusing this book. I have partnered it with a 1914 publicity photograph of a brand-new Foden steam van. Note the striking lettering on the side of this vehicle, destined for the Boots Company, and also note that it had a top speed of 12 mph!

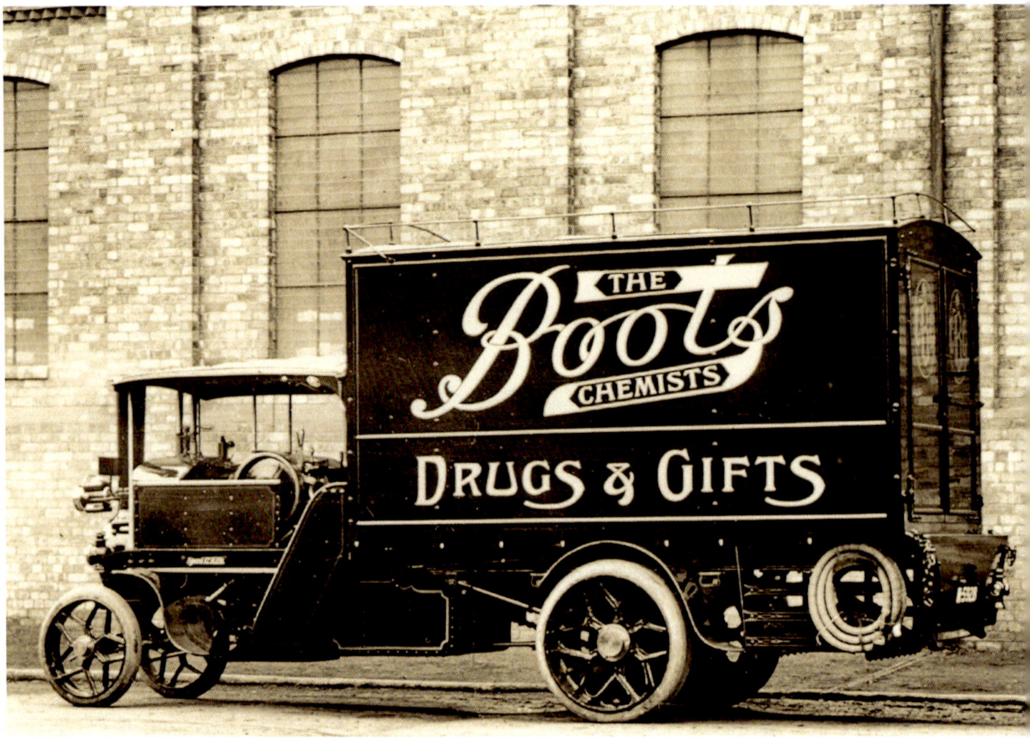

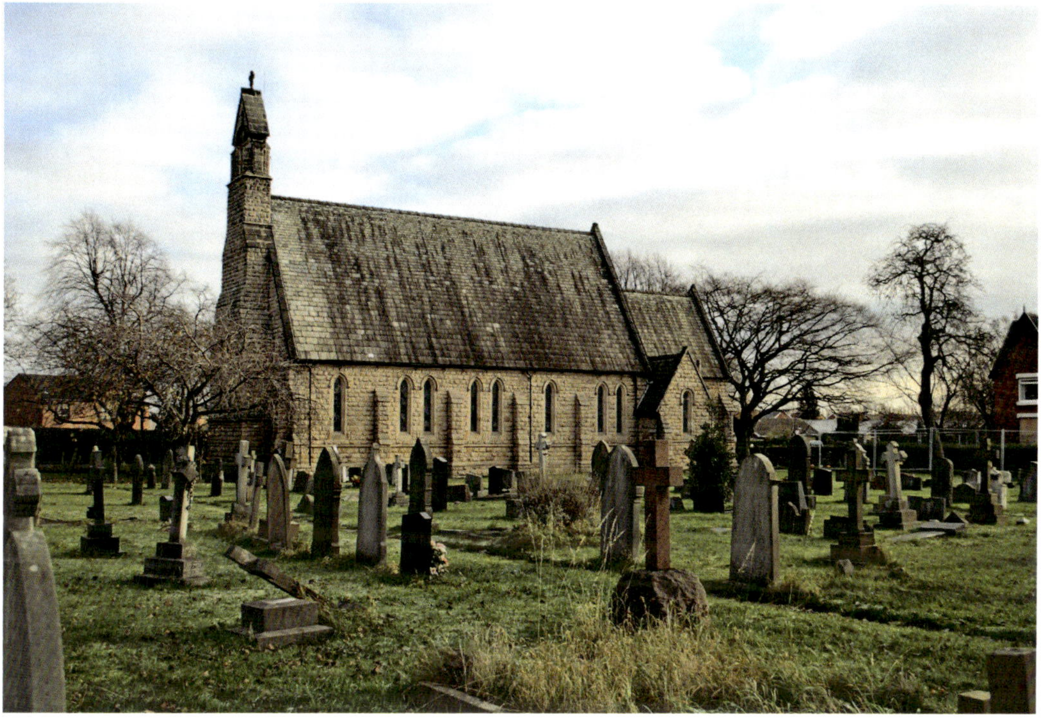

Elworth Church, 2010 and Undated

St Peter's church in Elworth was built in the Gothic style in 1846 and these photographs show the rear from the churchyard. Unfortunately, on 1 February 2010, the large church hall at the side was gutted by fire.

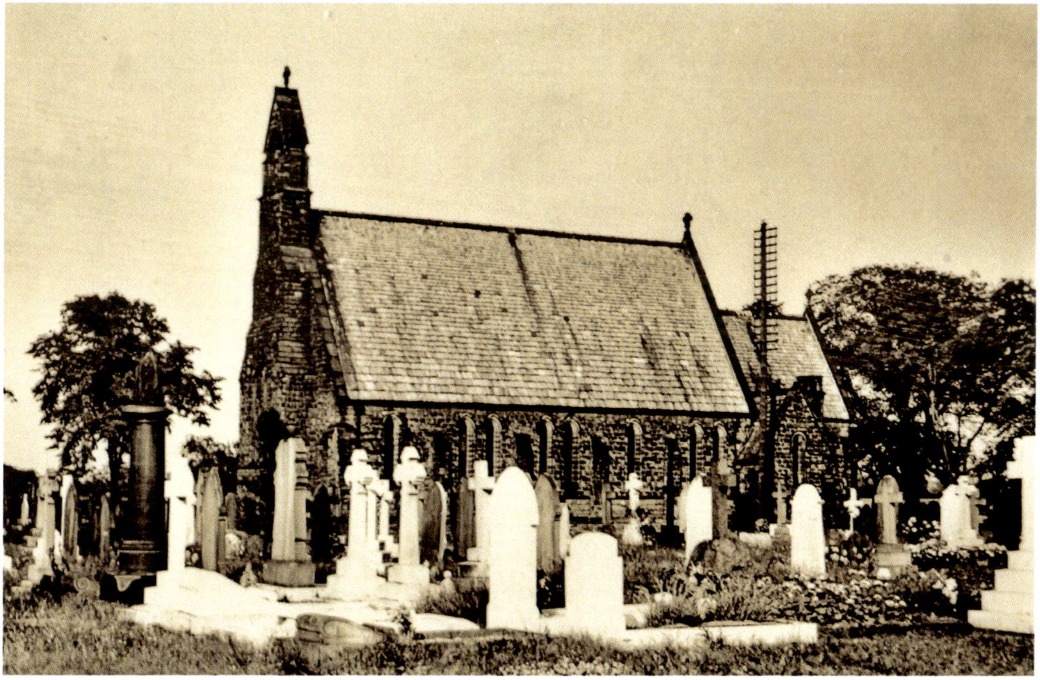

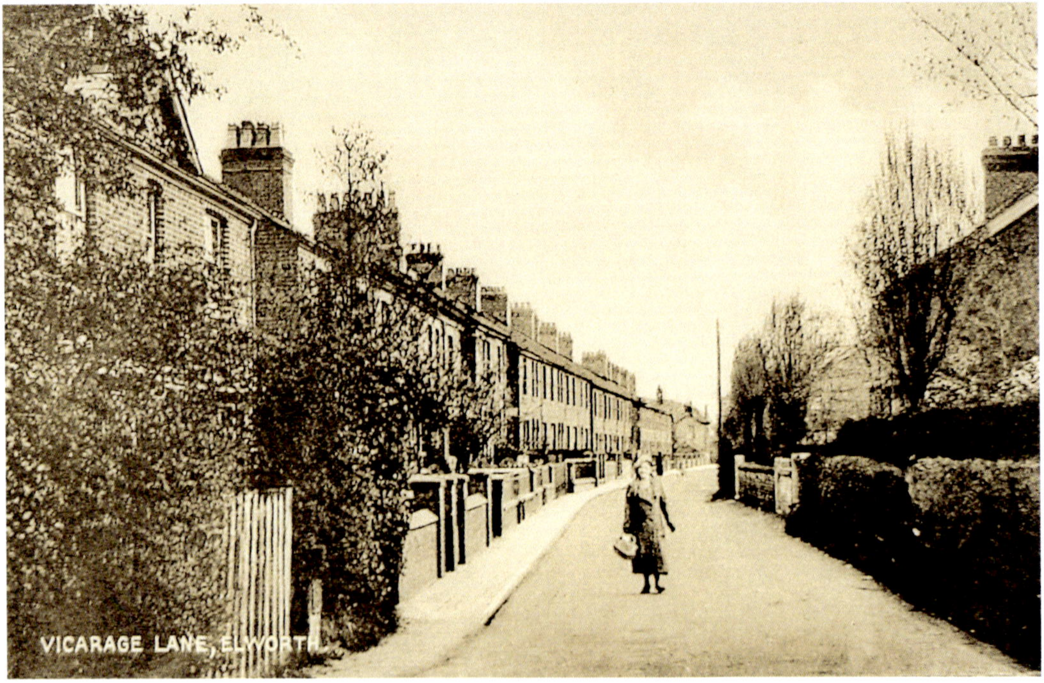

VICARAGE LANE, ELWORTH

Vicarage Lane, Elworth, 1940s–50s and 2010

We are now opposite the church in Elworth, looking into the aptly named Vicarage Lane as a smiling woman heads into town for her daily shop. Hedges and shrubbery have been cut back and cars now line the footpath; but other than that, little has changed in the area.

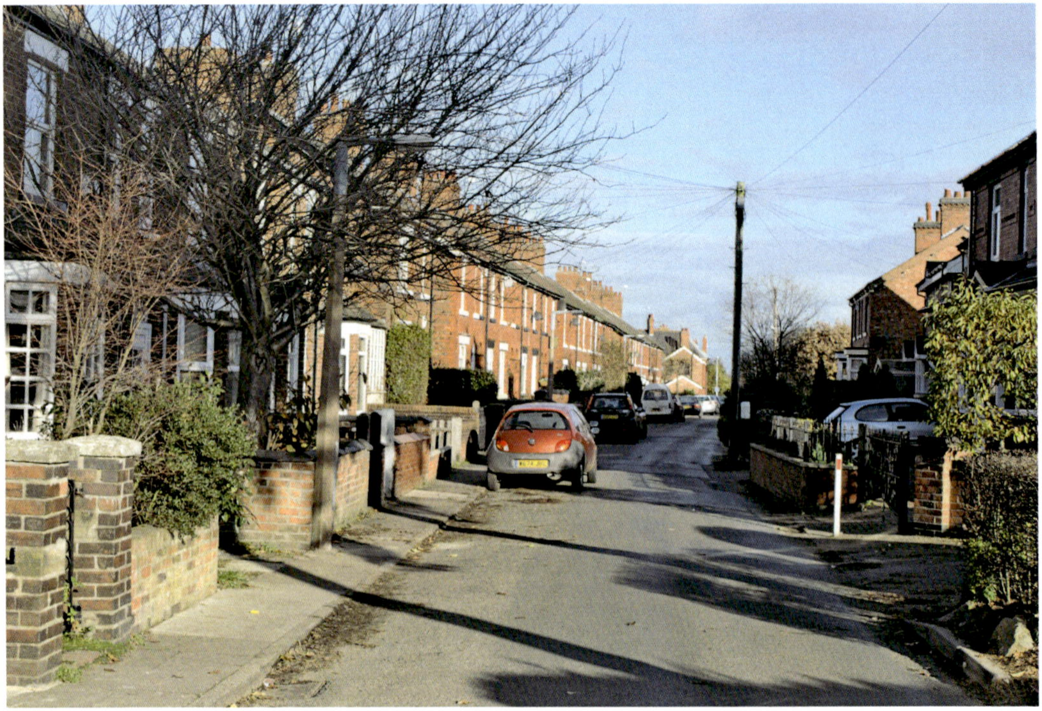

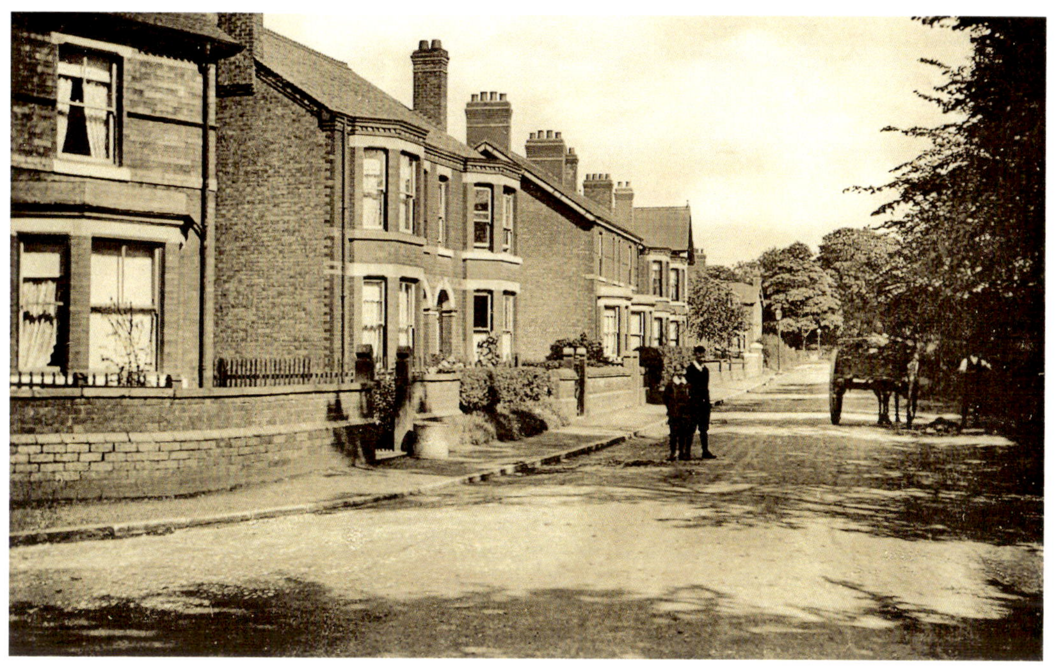

The Avenue, Early 1900s and 2010

This road can be found further along Vicarage Lane. The modern photograph was taken in the deep midwinter of December 2010. The horse and light cart in the old image are being used by a man either working on the road or more likely collecting horse manure from it. Across from him, two boys in their smart Victorian or Edwardian Sunday best watch the cameraman, wondering no doubt what he is doing photographing this ordinary residential street. You can see by the comparison that it has not changed much over the intervening century or so.

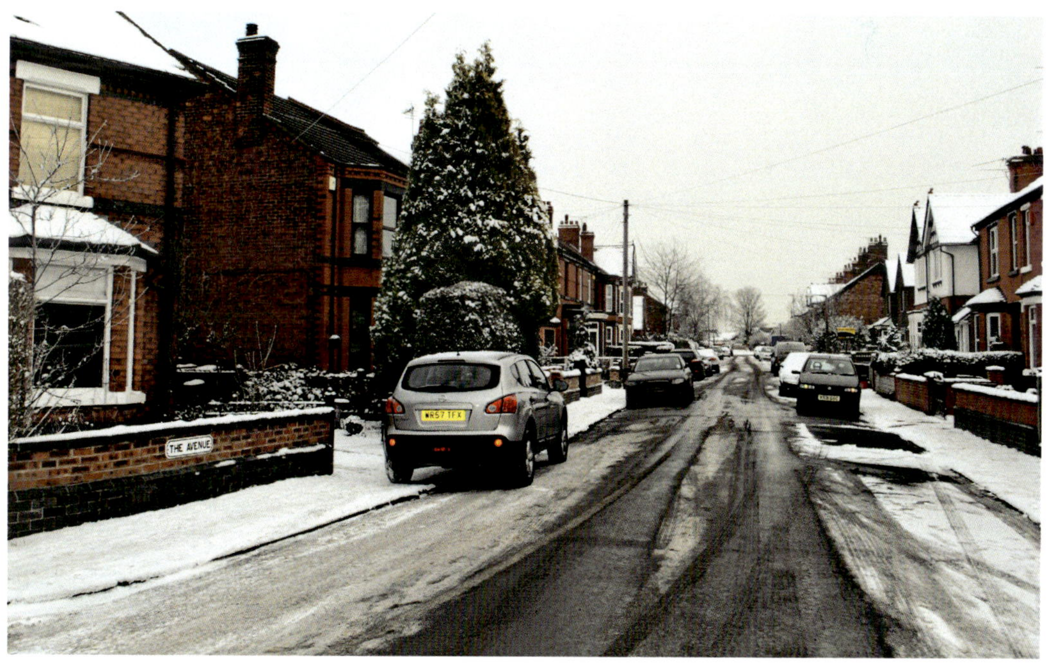

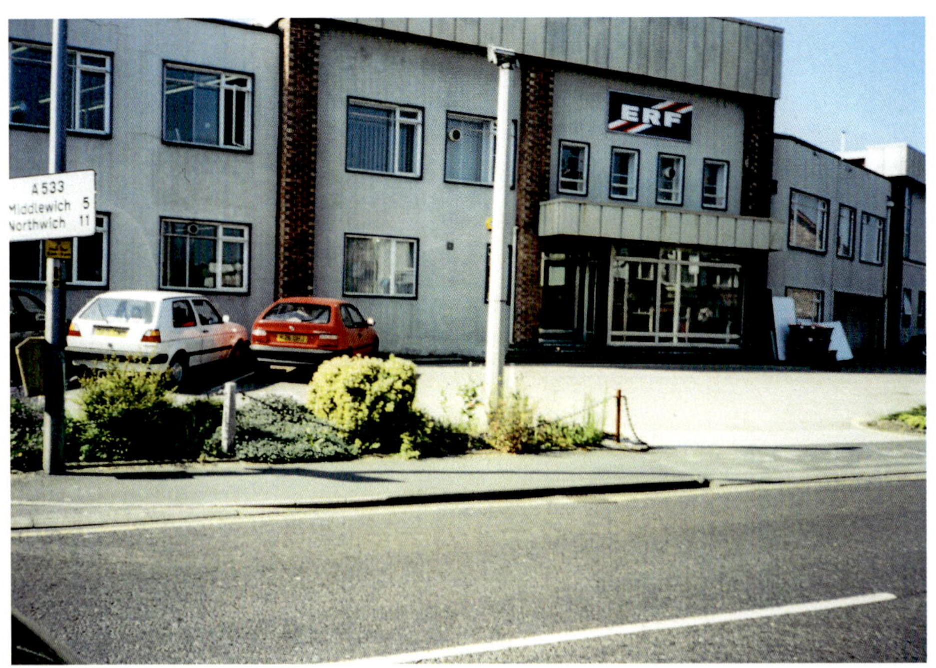

Sun Works, 2000 and 2010

Further along Middlewich Road we come to another famous name, the ERF motor works that bore the name 'Sun Works Sandbach' and the home since the 1930s of the ubiquitous ERF truck that can be found in its many forms around the world. The top photograph is of the ERF works just before it closed in 2000. The offices have now gone and been replaced by a doctor's surgery (below) and, among other things, an Aldi supermarket.

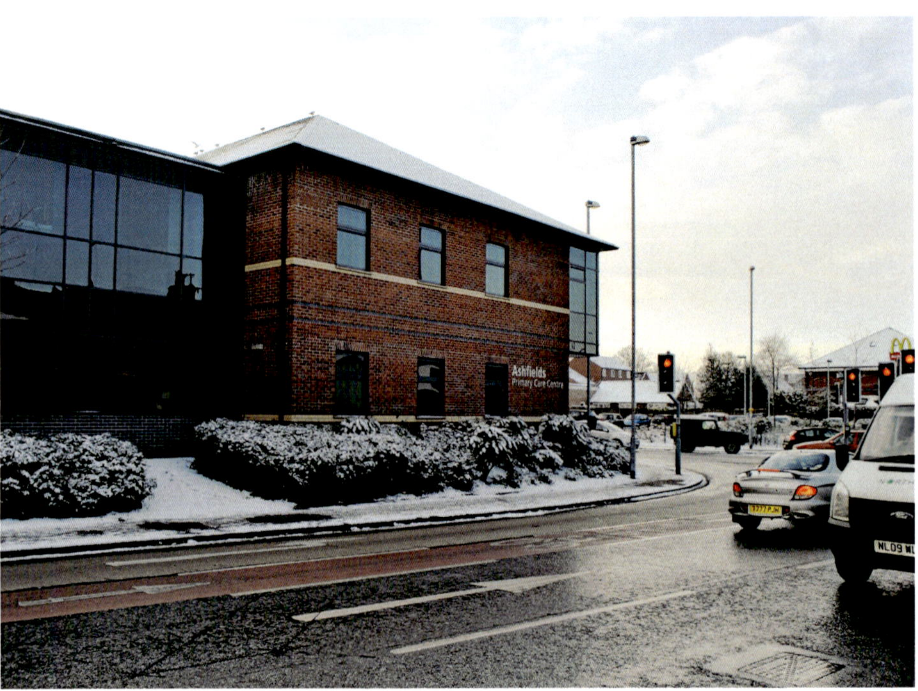

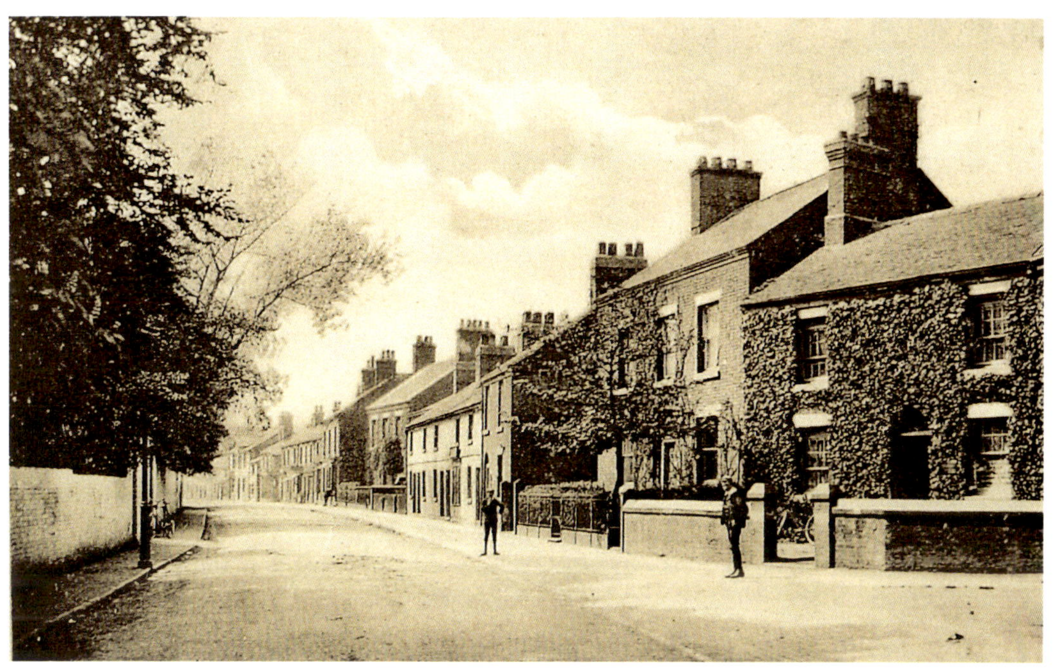

Middlewich Road, Sandbach, Early 1900s and 2010

The photograph above, looking from the Sandbach end of Middlewich Road back towards Middlewich, was taken just off the town centre. Horse manure is spread liberally upon the road, adding to the early twentieth-century ambience! In the modern photograph the ivy has gone, together with the iron railings. The building with the ivy has been, over the years, converted into a shop and is now a dentist's. Again the photographer is watched by two boys in their starched collars and stockings.

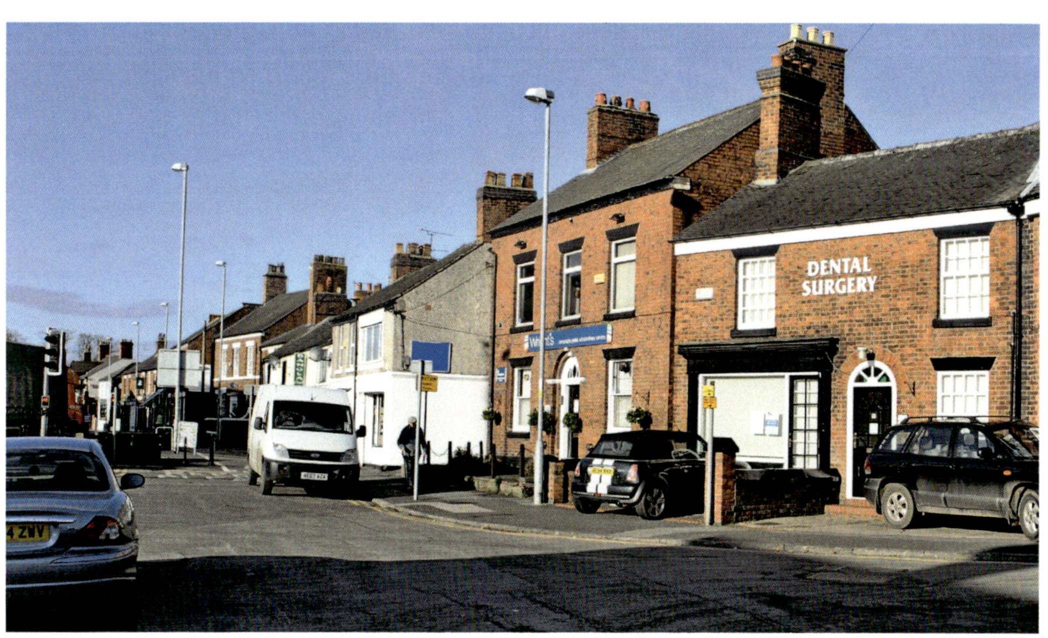

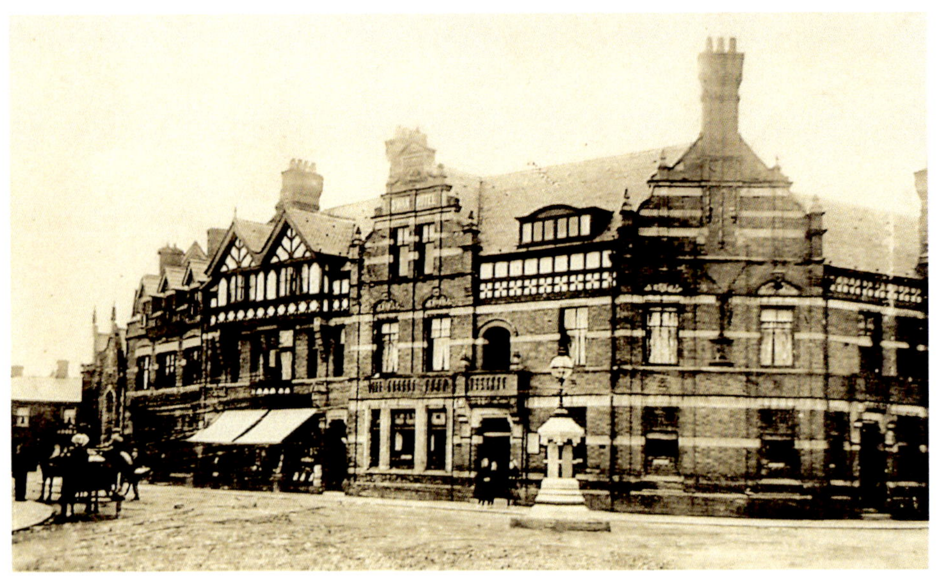

Swan Hotel, Hightown, Sandbach, Early 1900s and 2010

This large hotel, formerly known as simply the Swan Hotel, is on the site of an earlier thatched building of the same name. It was demolished in 1895 and the current building was built to replace it. Far bigger than its predecessor, the builder John Stringer did well to fit it in the limited space that was available to him. The architects were Bird & Whitenbury of Manchester. The lamp in the foreground is a memorial to Dr Charles Latham, a well-loved local doctor. We will look at this memorial again later.

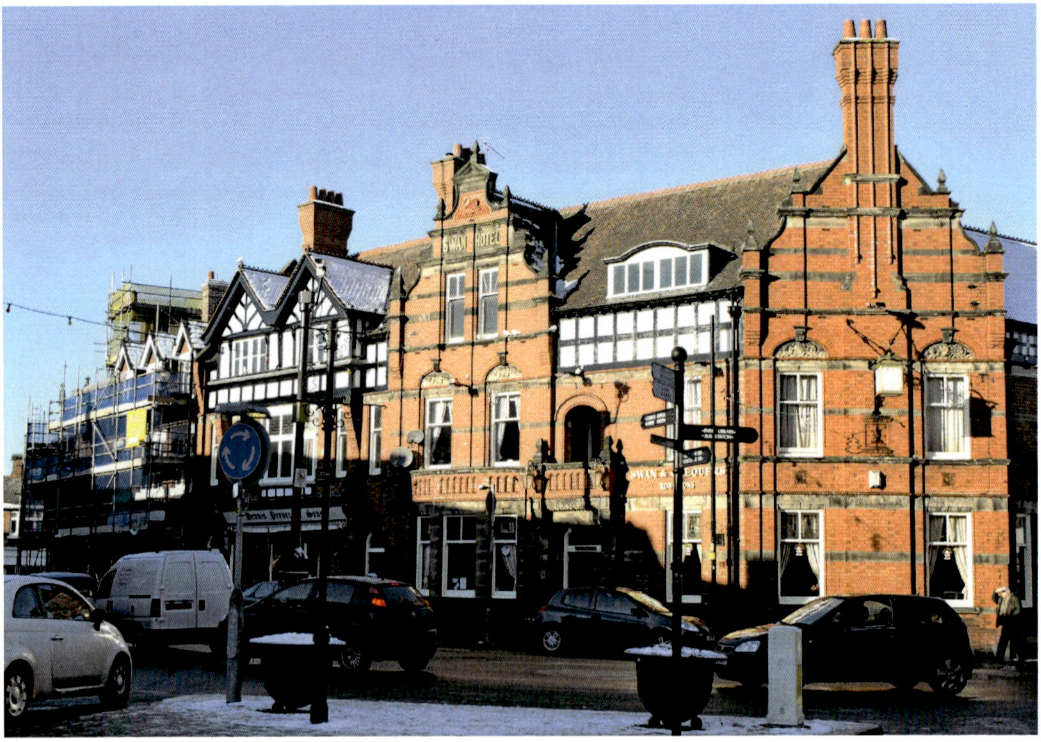

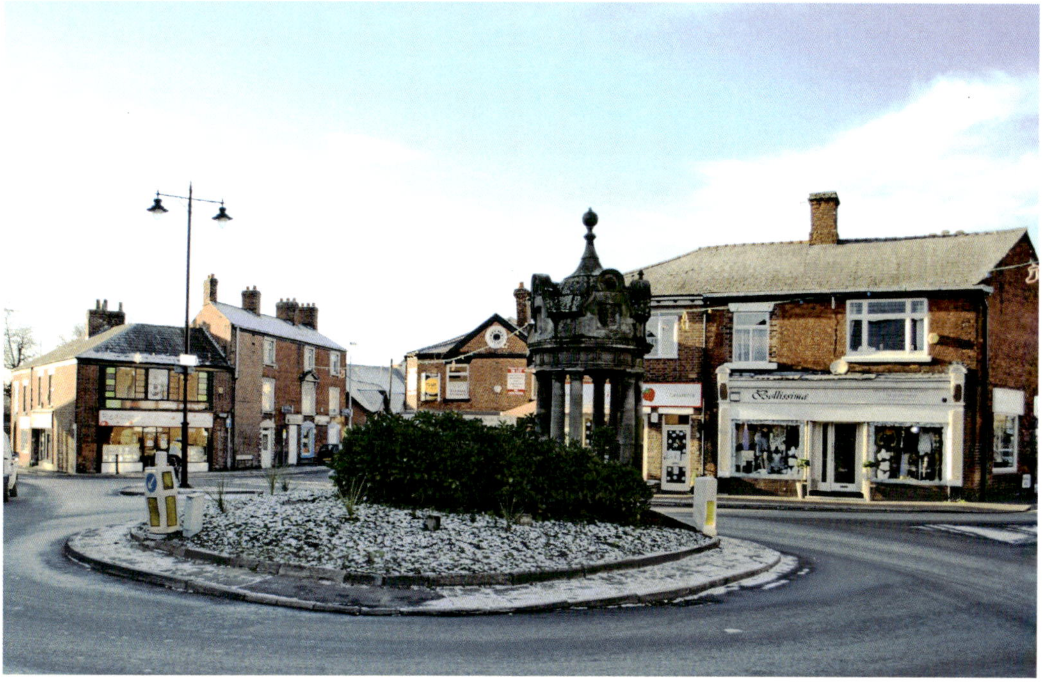

Hightown Fountain, 2010 and Early 1900s

Still in Hightown, we see the drinking fountain – now a listed building that stands in the centre of the road, where there is a roundabout today. The fountain was built in 1897 by John Stringer with design by Thomas Bower (the architect of the town hall) in order to quench the thirst of animals and humans alike. Edwin Lunt's grocer's shop can be seen on the far left; we will also look at this shop again later in the book. Miss M. J. Jones' stationer's shop is also on view, as is B. Porthouse, milliner's.

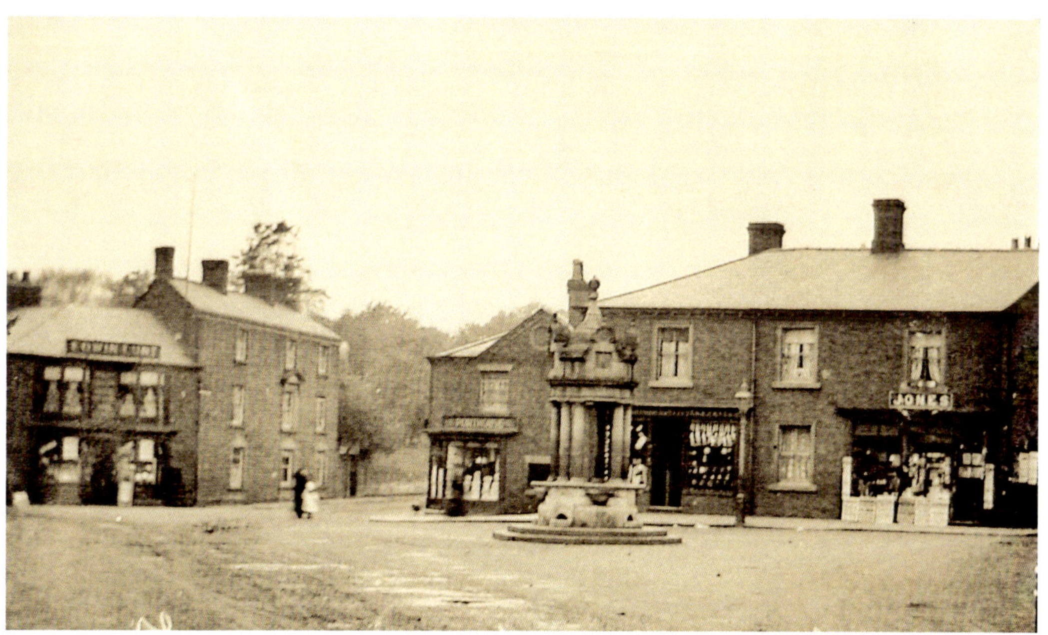

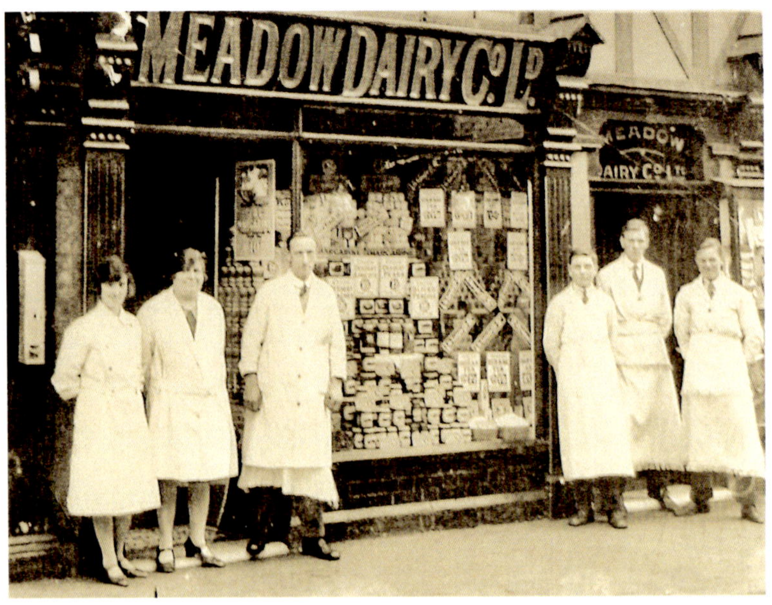

Meadow Dairy, Hightown, 1920s–30s and 2010

This impressive shop was situated at 11B Hightown and in the old photograph you see the many staff in their smart white coats. This shop was typical of so many town centre shops of the time. No cash and carry here – everything was served with the personal touch. All this went with the coming of the faceless albeit efficient self-service stores that followed. Unfortunately, as can be seen in the photograph below, the Meadow Dairy has been demolished, only to be replaced by an eyesore of a building.

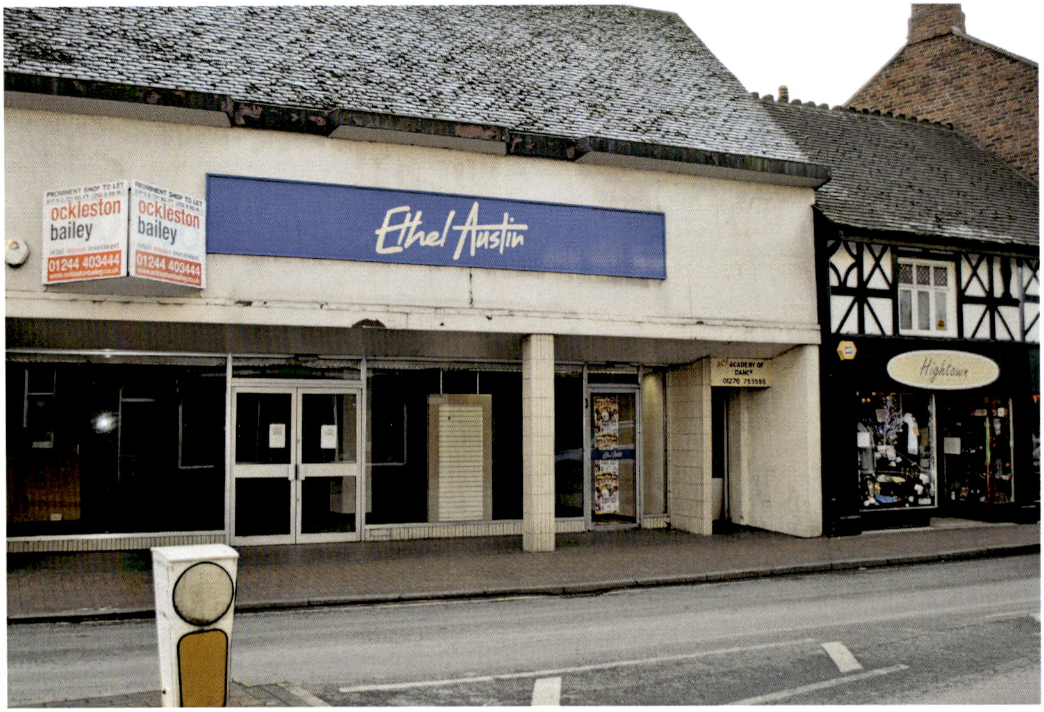

Lunt's Grocers, High Town, 1920–30 and 2010

As promised earlier, we now take a closer look at Edwin Lunt's grocer's in Hightown at the junction with Old Middlewich Road. Imagine the myriad of smells in that store from the molasses in the animal food as well as from other medications, fresh bacon, cheeses, bread and cakes. The old photograph is a true snapshot in time that tells a story and takes the viewer back to those slower, calmer days of old. The estate agent's in the modern photograph serves its purpose well, but just doesn't have the same antiquarian appeal.

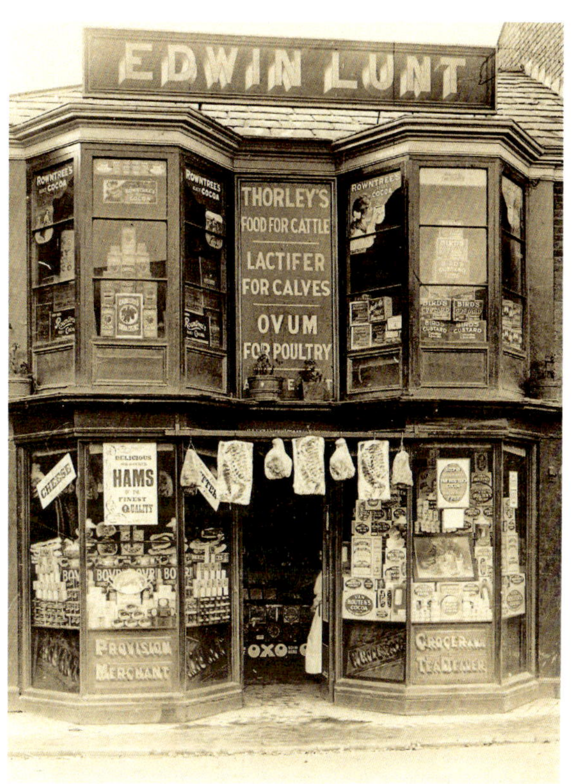

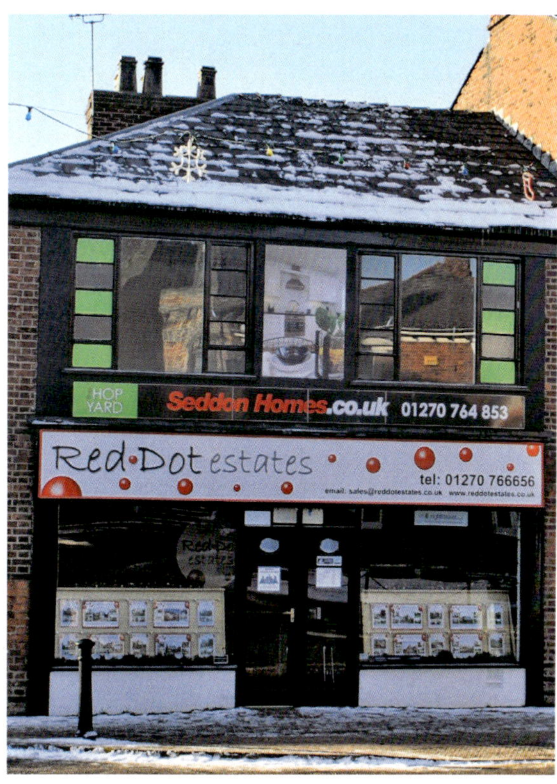

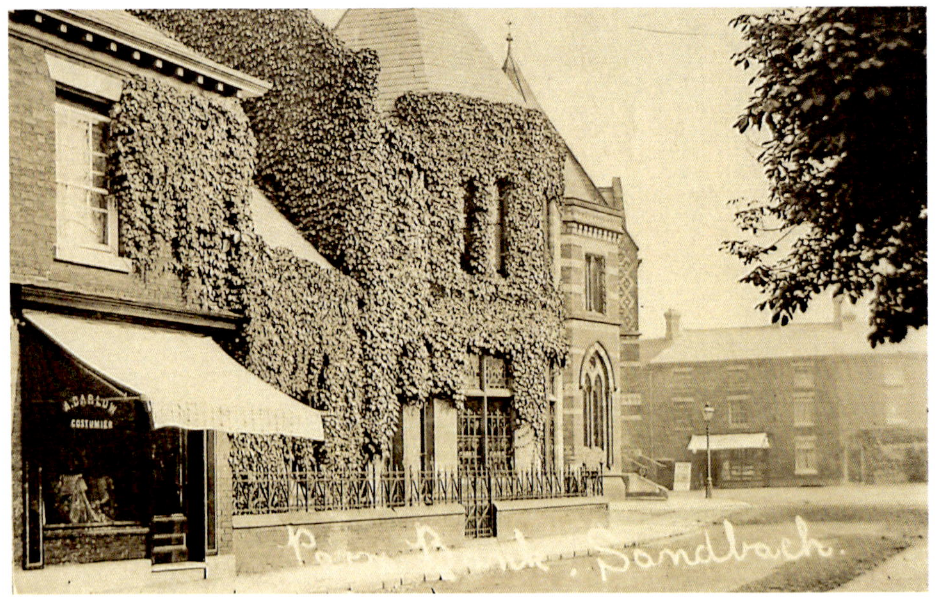

Parr's Bank, Early 1900s and 2010

Parr's Bank was founded in Winwick Street, Warrington, in 1788 by Joseph Parr, a sugar refiner. Many small banks were taken over by Parr's, initially in Cheshire and the North West but later nationwide. By 1918 there were 235 branches and 94 sub-branches. This was the Sandbach branch around the turn of the century, when Arthur Edgar Slade was the manager. The name went through many changes over the years, becoming the National Westminster and finally ending up as part of The Royal Bank of Scotland.

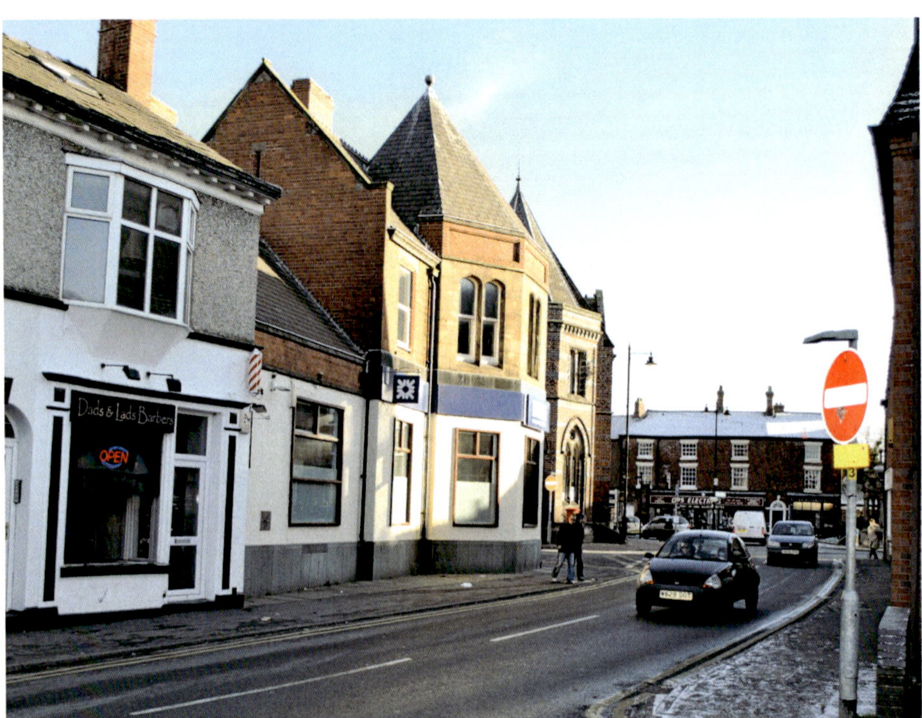

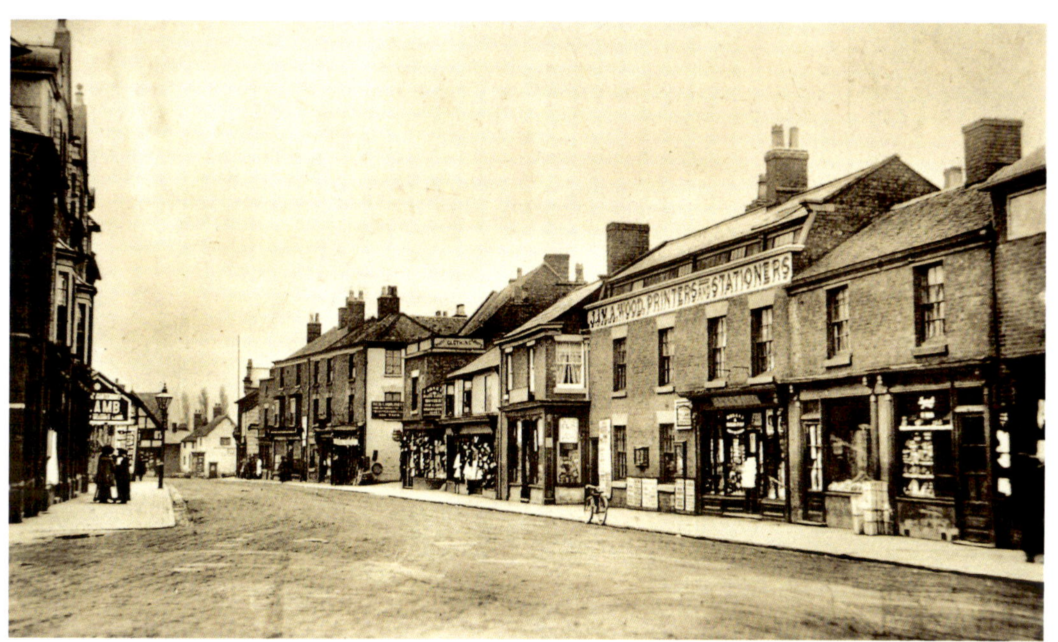

Sandbach High Street, 1920s and 2010

No. 7 High Street predominates here in the old photograph in the form of J. & M. A. Wood, stationer's and printer's. This building has been considerably altered or rebuilt, but in the same footprint as the stationer's. Note the Nationwide building in the right foreground; the front elevation is virtually the same. Beyond the stationer's little has changed, although the HSBC building has been extended and rebuilt.

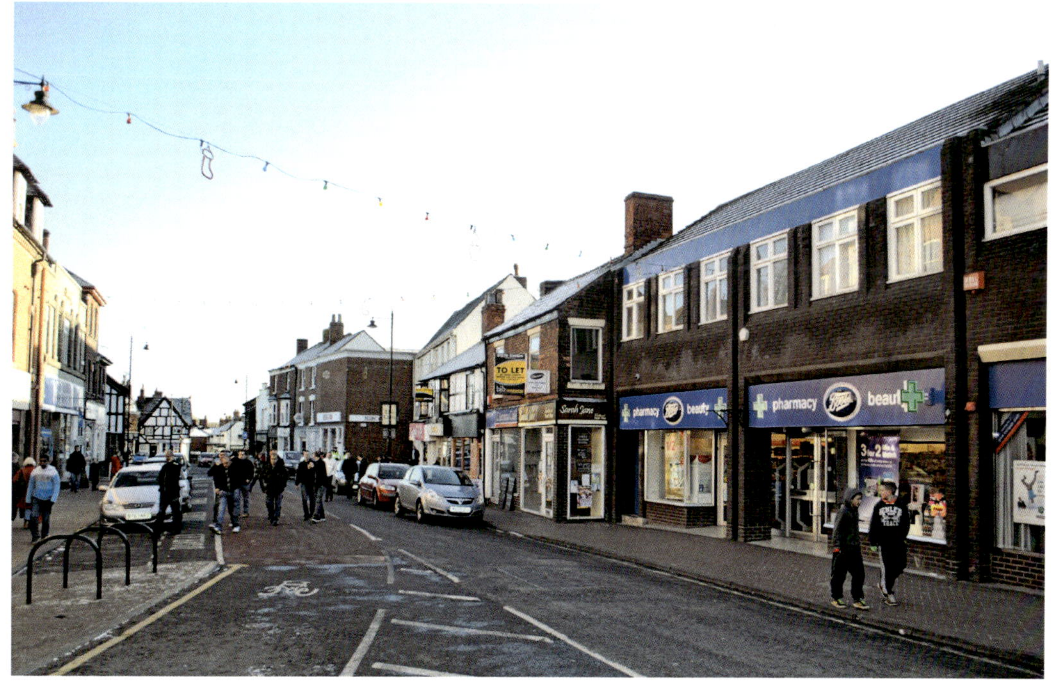

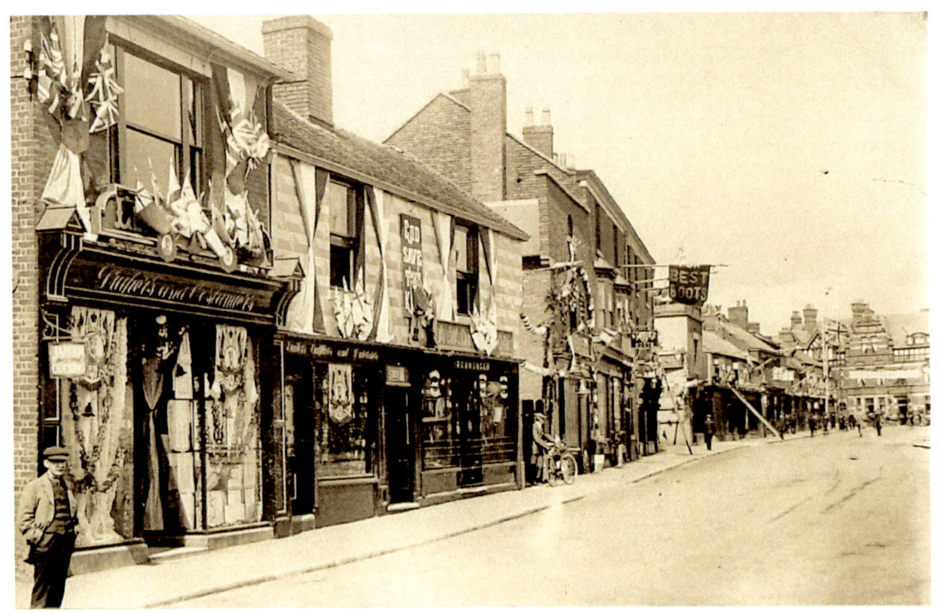

Upper High Street, 1930s and 2010

Here we walk down the High Street and turn to look back opposite the Black Bear. In the distance is the Swan Hotel. The date of the old photograph will be 1936 since the bunting was erected to celebrate the coronation of King George VI. The ladders in use show that it was still being applied to the shops. The shop on the left is Alfred W. Dickinson, ironmonger's. In the modern photograph, nearest the camera, is the unlovely New Ruby takeaway building, which is hardly preferable to its predecessor, the milliner's and clothier's store.

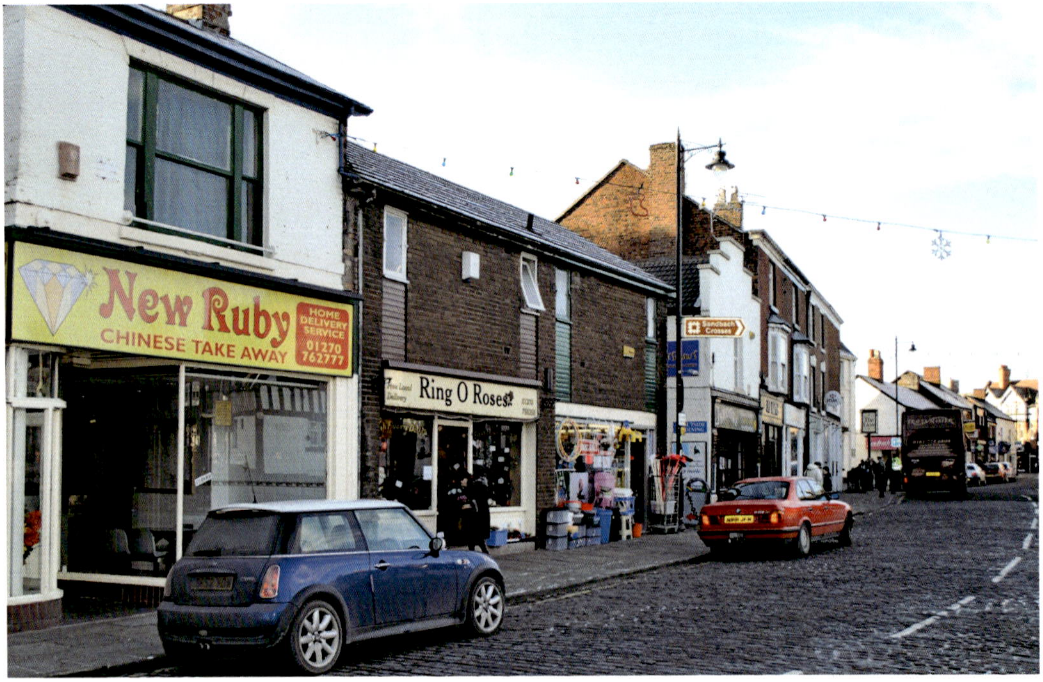

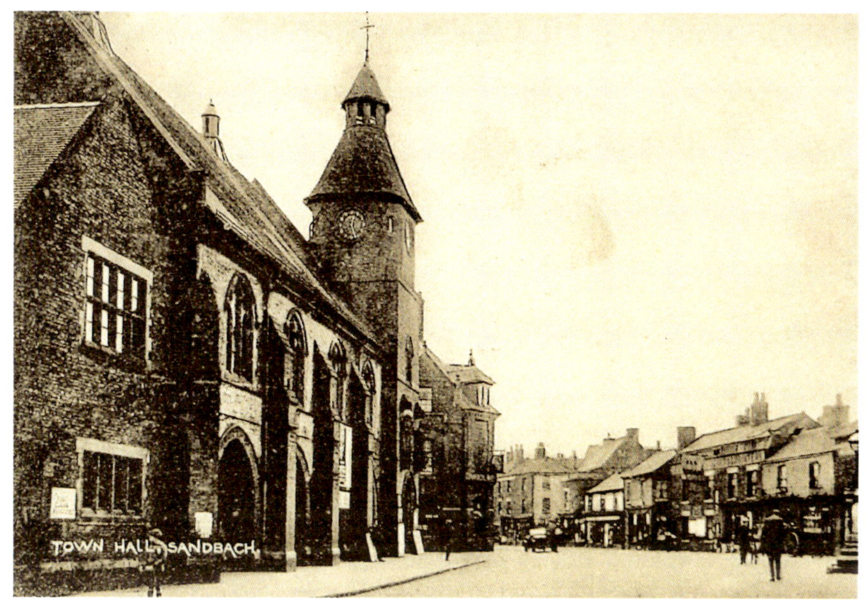

Town Hall Building, 1930s and 2010

Sandbach town hall and market hall were built in 1889 at a cost of £2,700, using bricks that were handmade locally. The clock in the tower was presented by Mrs Jane Court, late of Wheelock House. The foundation stone was laid by Lord Crewe, who presented the land and the market tolls to the town; he also built the Wheatsheaf Hotel opposite. The town hall was beautifully built in the Gothic style. Sandbach market can be traced back to 1578, when it took place on the square.

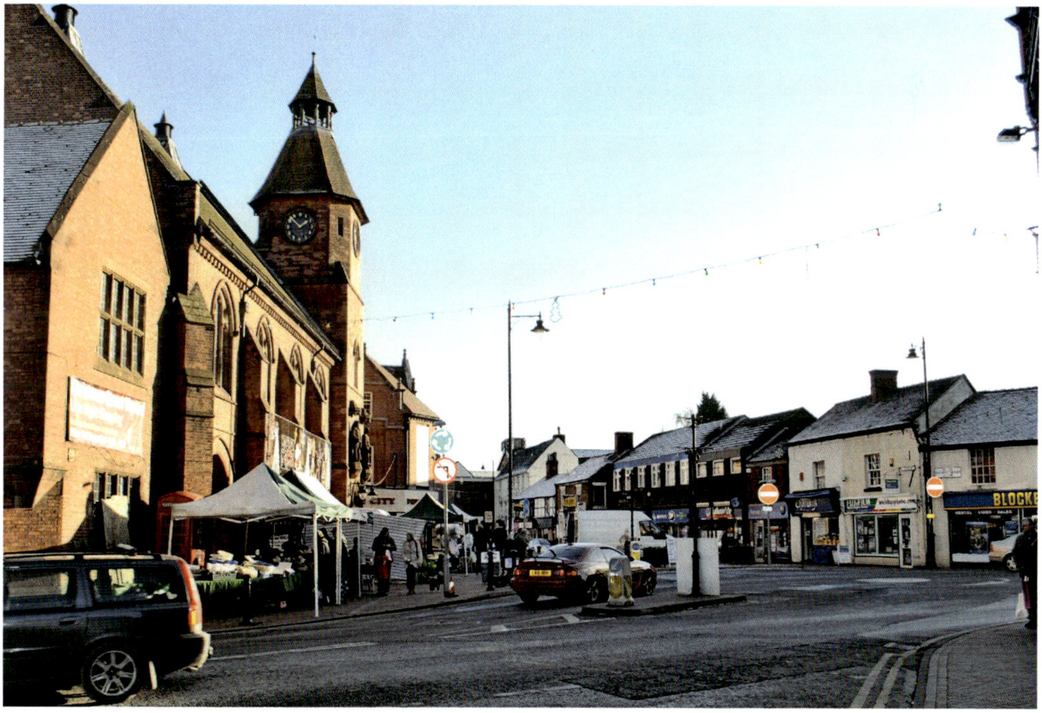

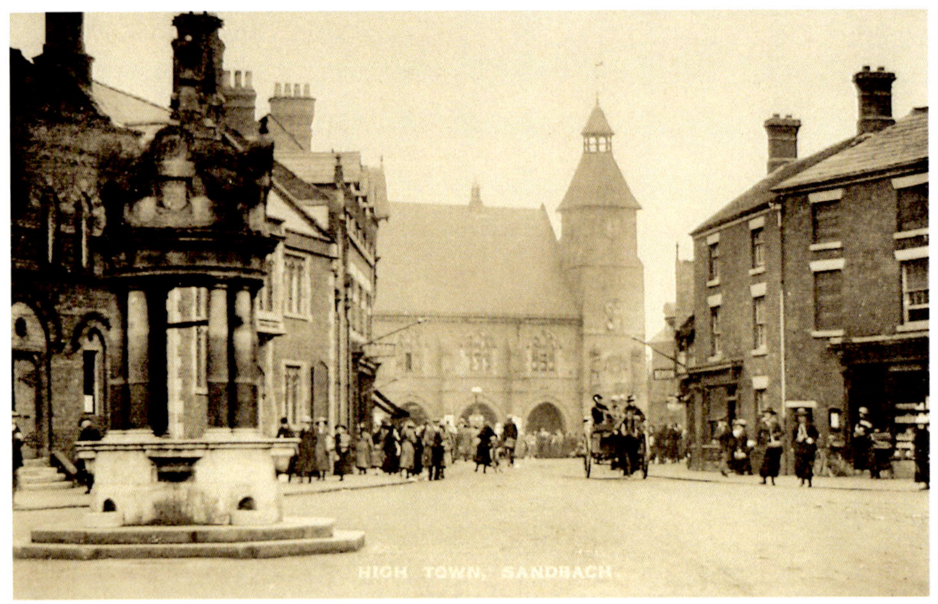

Hightown to Market Hall, Early 1900s and 2010

We now look at the town hall from another angle in Hightown. The bane of photographers compiling 'Then and Now' books is in plain view in the modern image: scaffolding and its blue curtains. Here we see the same scene through the years across the two pages. The date of this old photograph is around 1900, the crowds of people suggesting a ceremony of some sort, or even a busy market day.

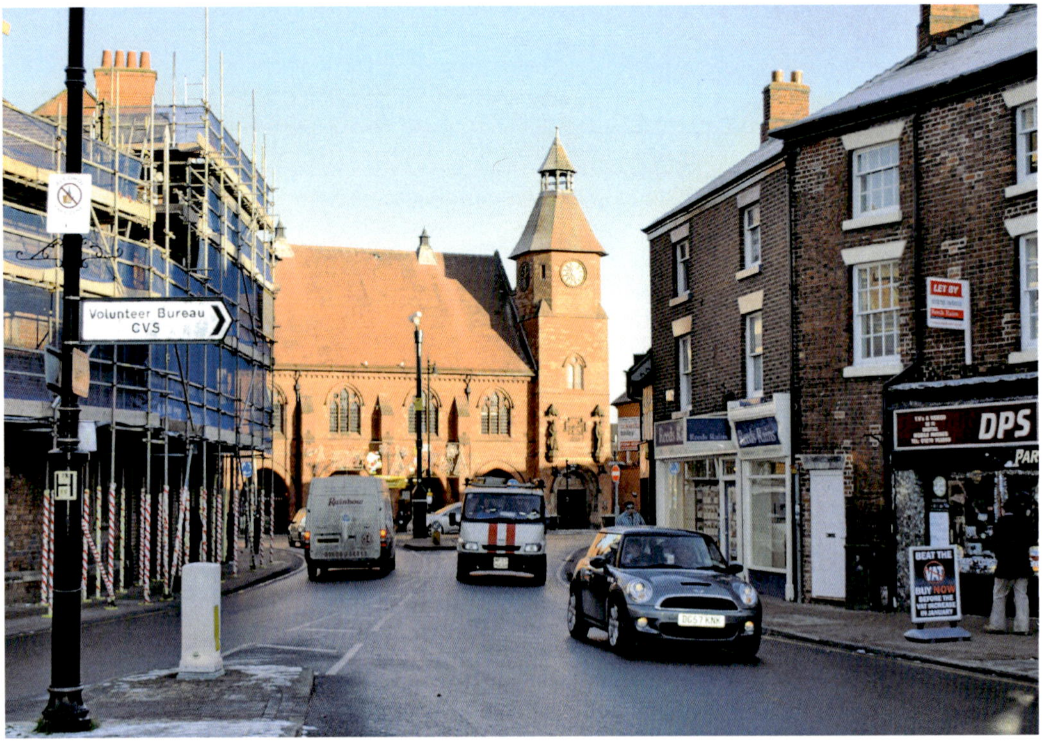

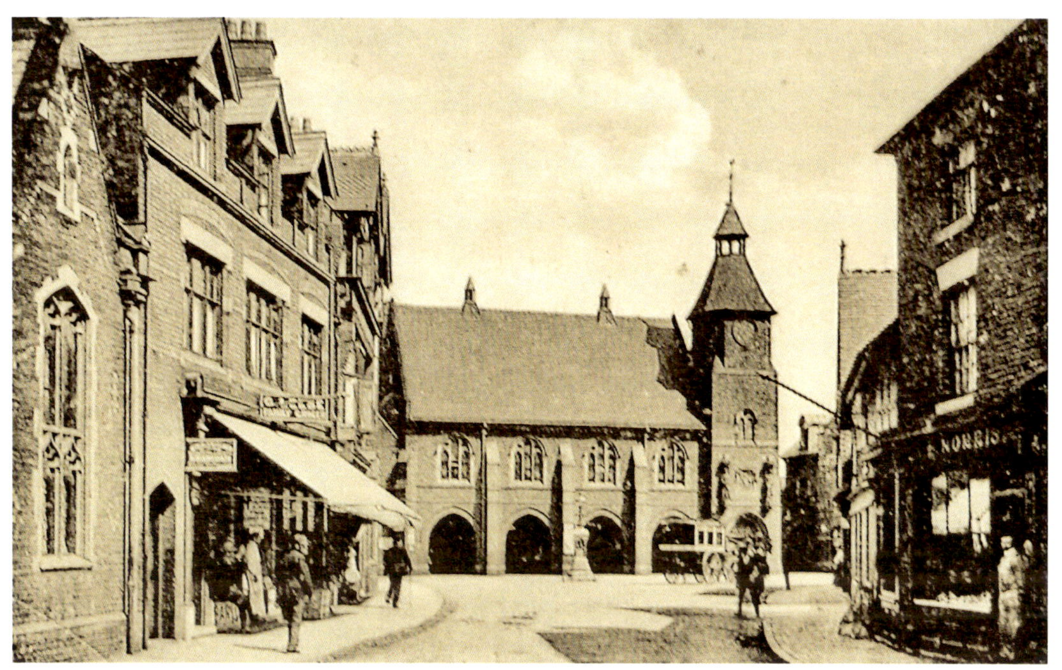

Hightown to the Market Hall, Early 1900s and 1950s

The earlier photograph is from the turn of the last century and we see a horse-drawn omnibus that will have collected passengers from the Wheatsheaf, Swan and George hotels to convey them to the town's railway stations. The image below is from the 1950s and shows period Morris and Ford cars. The quality of photographs started going downhill at this point, unless professionally taken or using expensive equipment. This state of affairs lasted until digital cameras arrived. George Leese grocer's can be seen on the left, in what was Middlewich Road.

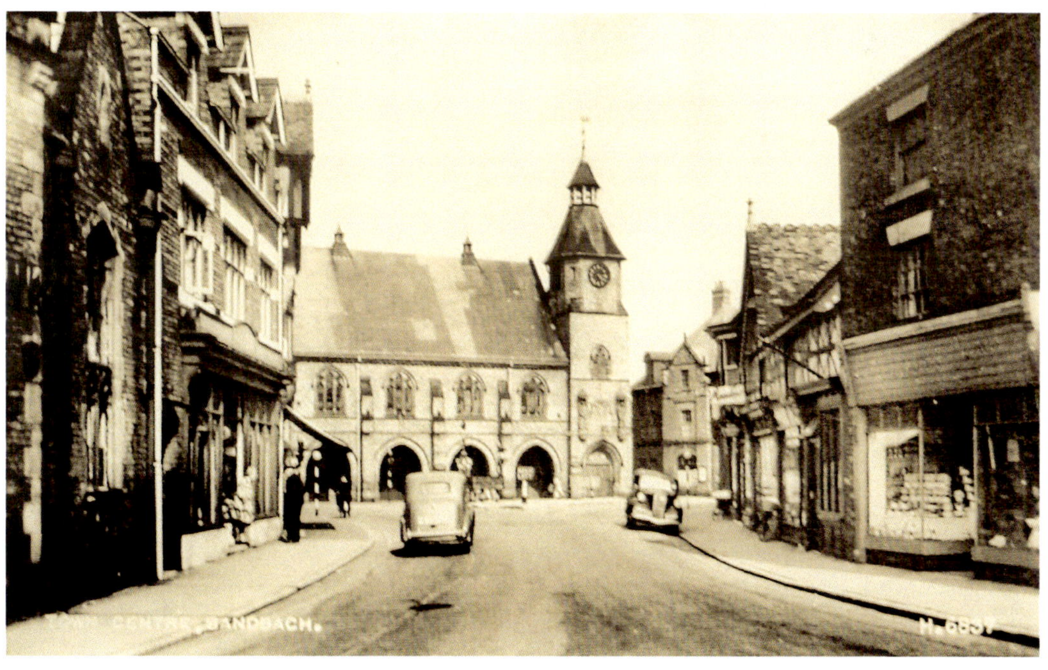

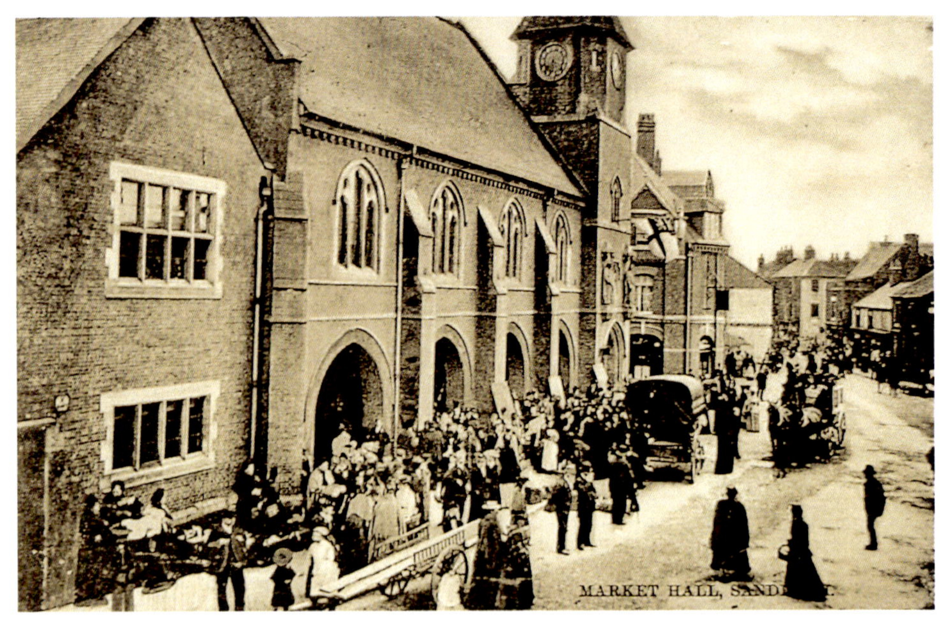

Market Hall to High Street, Early 1900s and 2010

We now have a full-on view of the town/market hall. The old photograph will have been taken from the balcony of the Swan and Chequers Hotel, but unfortunately the present landlord declined to allow me access to replicate it. The 1900s photographer *was* granted permission and has provided us with a photograph filled with the period charm of horse buses and traffic. There is a total lack of the mechanical transport that would soon start to appear in larger numbers.

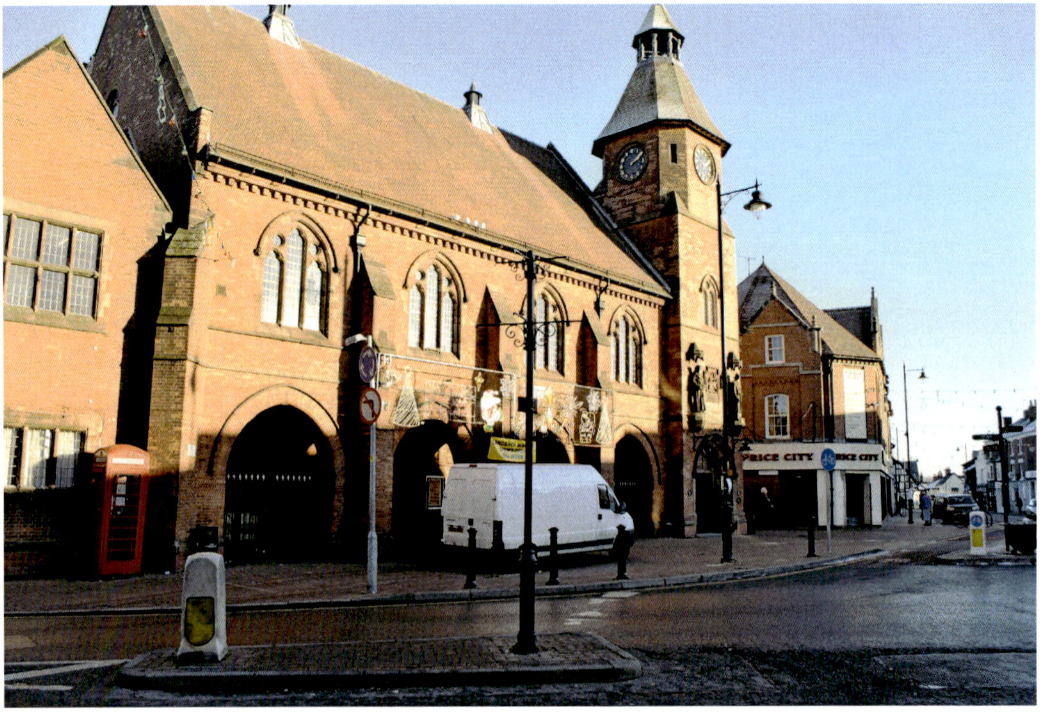

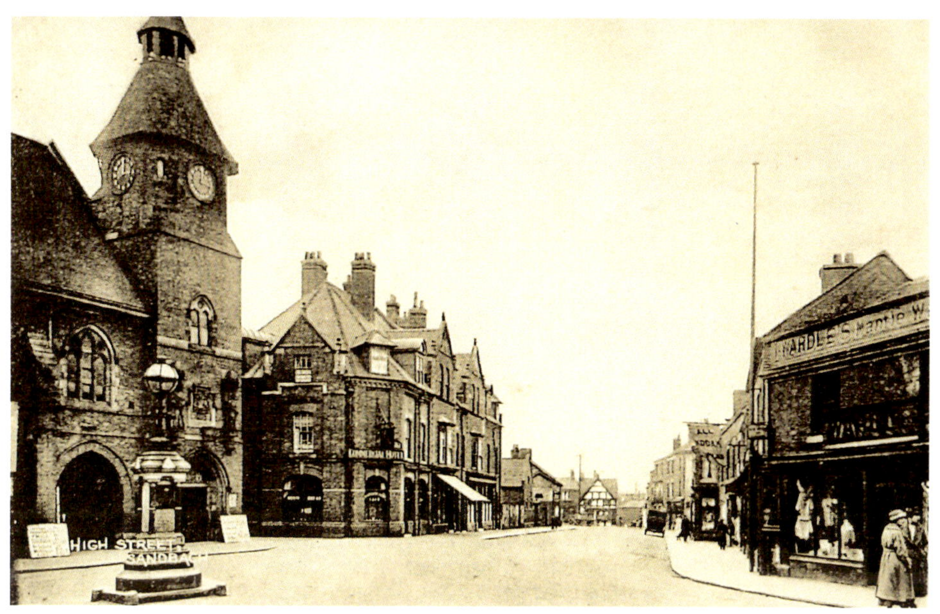

High Street, 1920s and 2010

Another look down Sandbach High Street: Price City in the modern photograph was previously the Commercial Hotel, and on the right of the old image Charles Wardle's draper's can be seen. The two statues above the door of the town hall are of Bigot, the first Norman to hold the manor of Sandbach, and Sir Randolph Crewe, ancestor of Lord Crewe, who gave the site to the town.

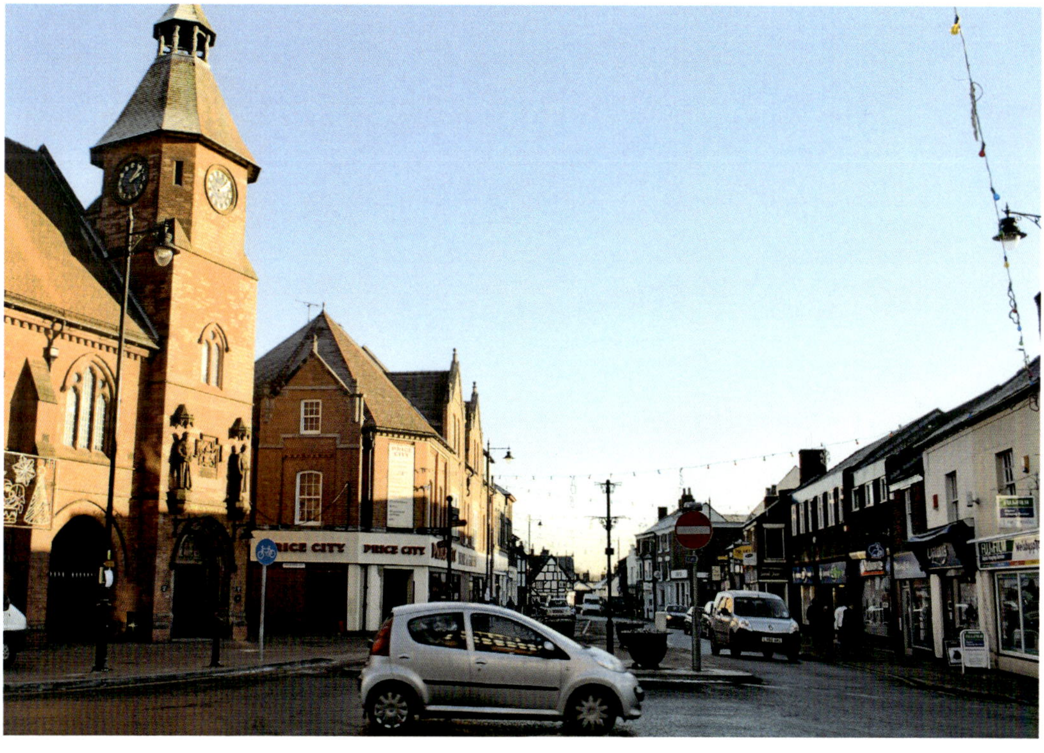

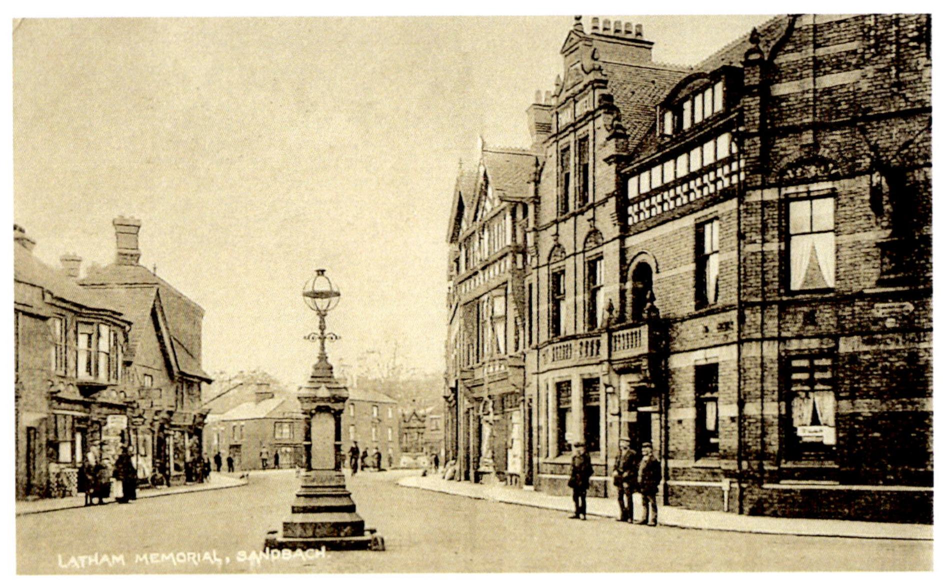

Latham Memorial, 1920s and 2010

Here we look into Hightown. In the centre of the view is the Latham Memorial, which was erected by public subscription in honour of Dr Charles Latham (1816–1907), a long-standing general practitioner in Sandbach whose good works were many. The Latham family is a distinguished Sandbach (Bradwall) family with roots going back to 1578; the parish church also has stained-glass windows in memory of various family members. When the roads were redeveloped, the memorial was moved to Sandbach Park and then to the new Ashfield's health centre, once the ERF factory on Middlewich Road.

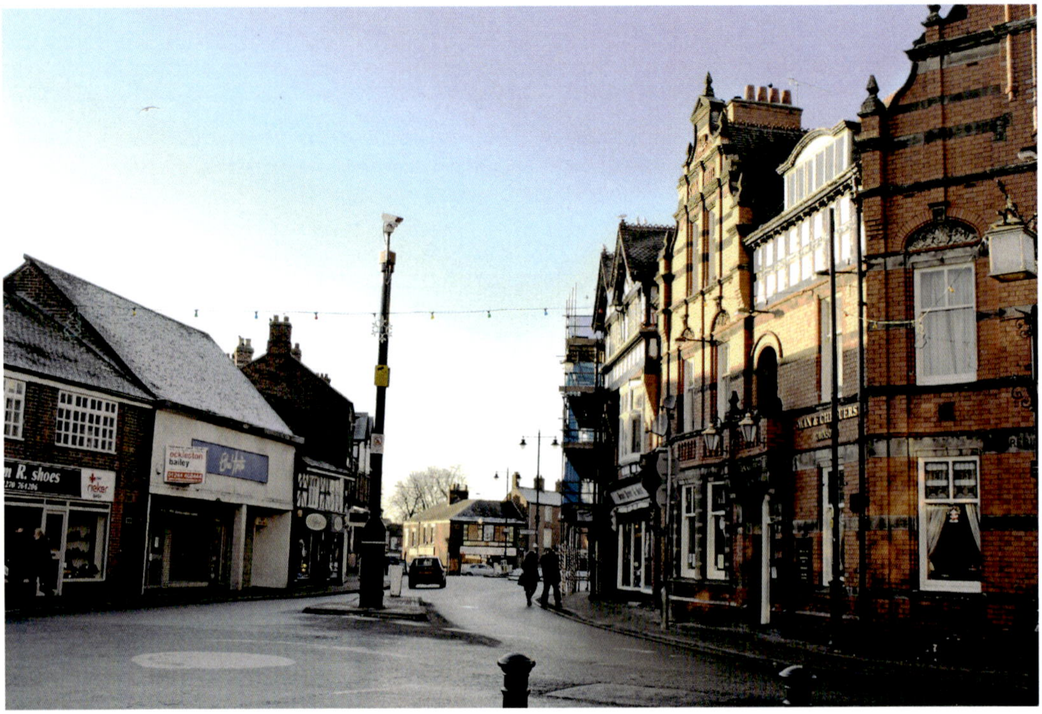

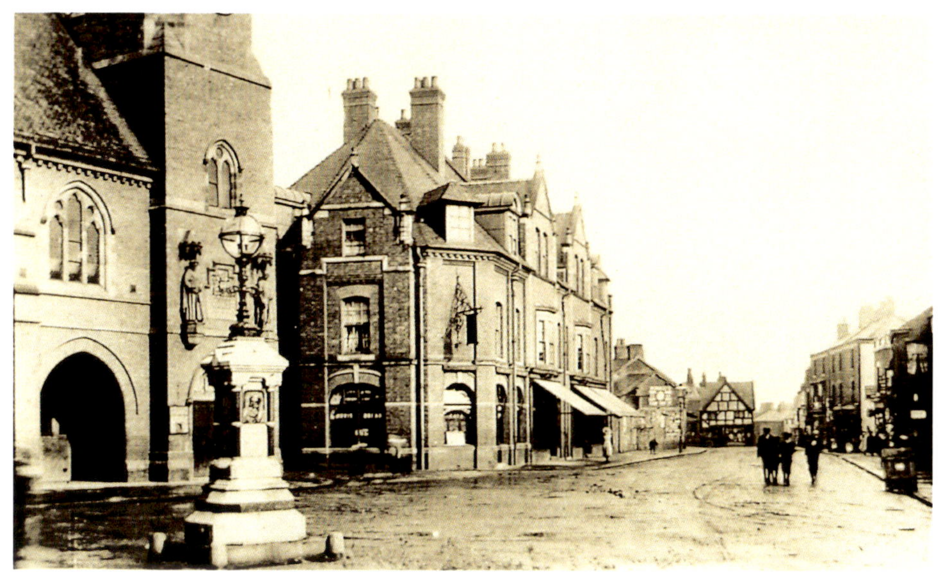

Into High Street, Early 1900s and 2010

Here we take a last look into the High Street towards the Black Bear public house. This set of photographs shows just how the traffic congestion has changed over the years. In the old photograph the boys in their smart clothes walk comfortably up the centre of the muddy road. In the modern photograph, the Commercial Hotel sign has gone from the Price City store, while traffic congestion is clear to see.

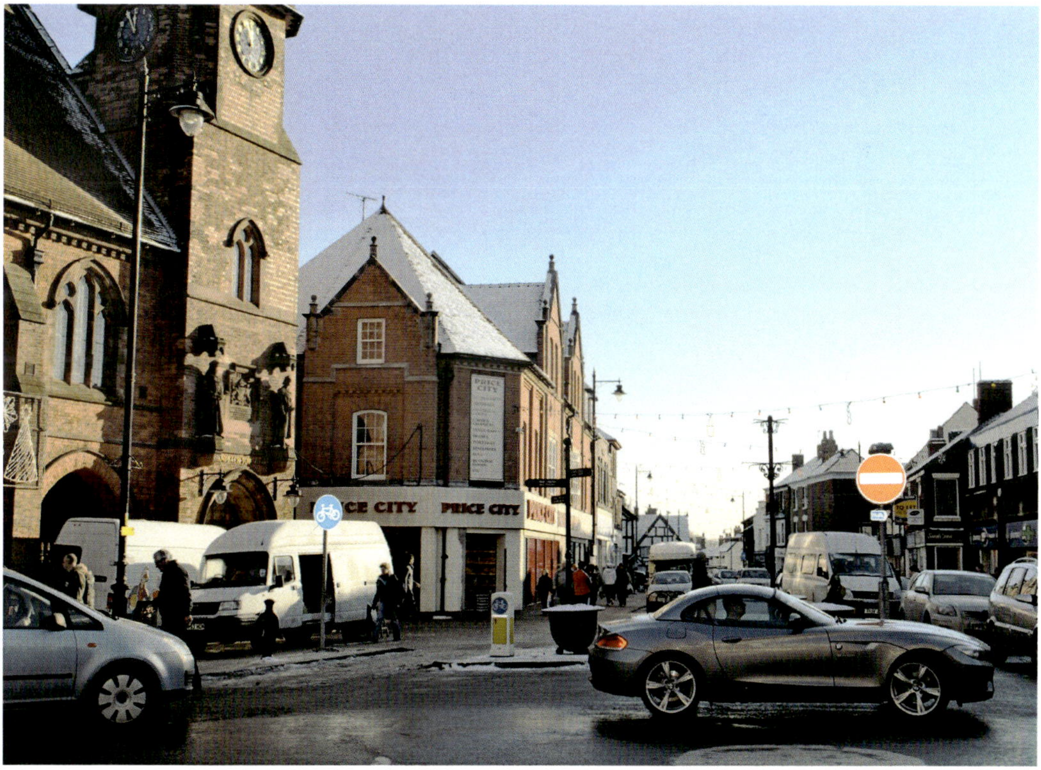

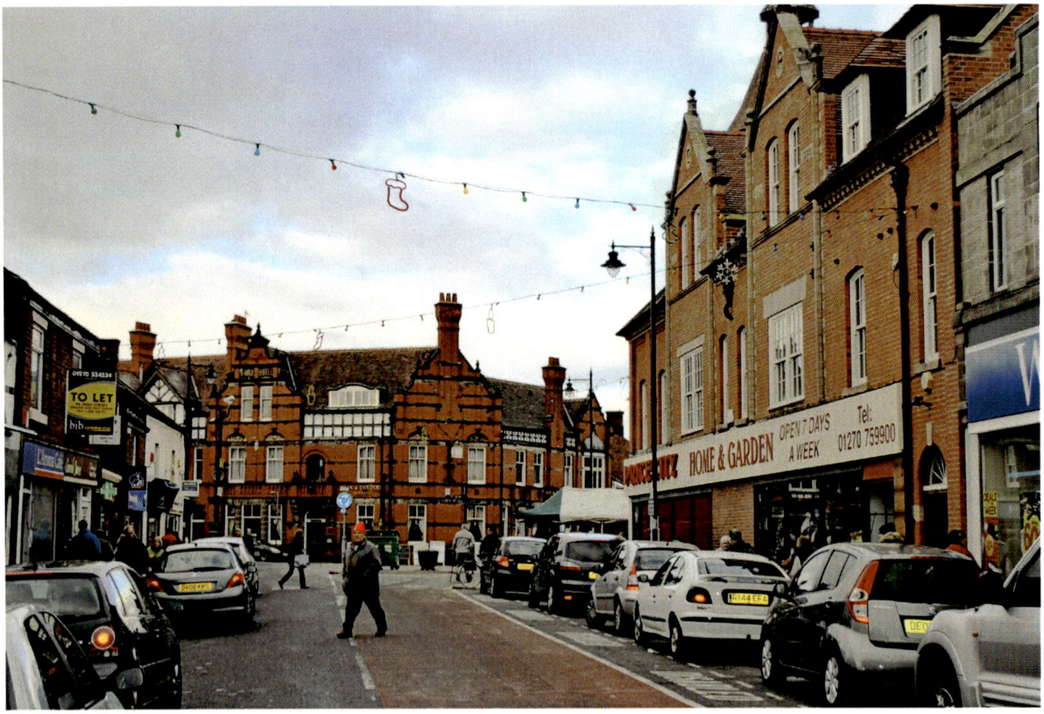

Top of High Street, 2010 and 1910–20

Taken around the time of the First World War, the old photograph exudes antiquarian charm with the early motor car moving away from the camera, its hood down and the ladies in their fine hats sitting in the back. The bay windows in the shops on the right have been removed and the car shares the road with only pedestrians and a pedal cycle.

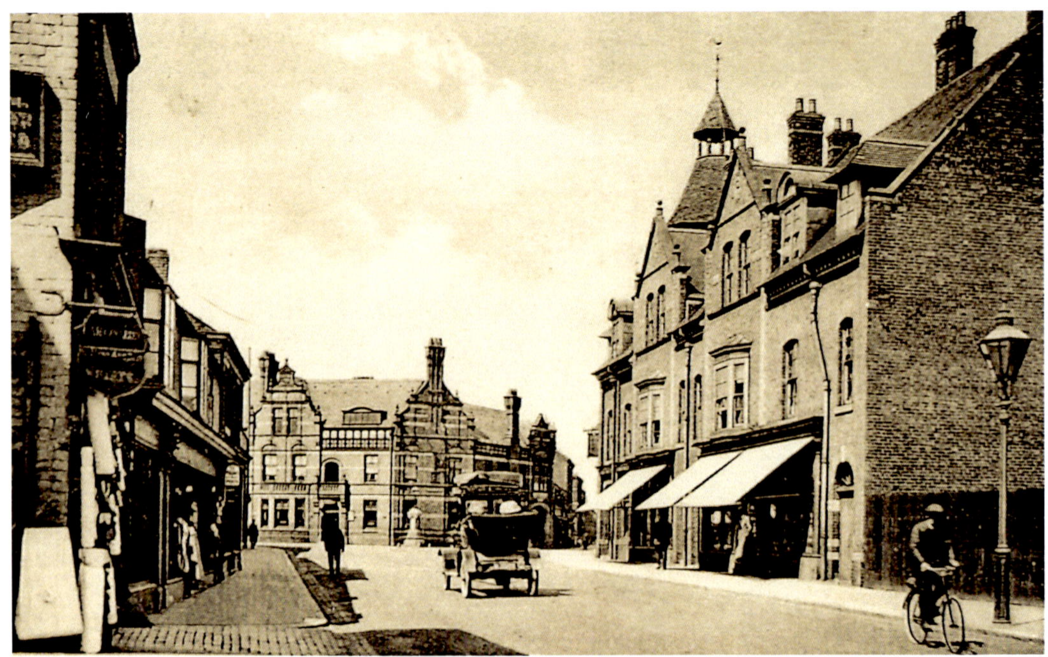

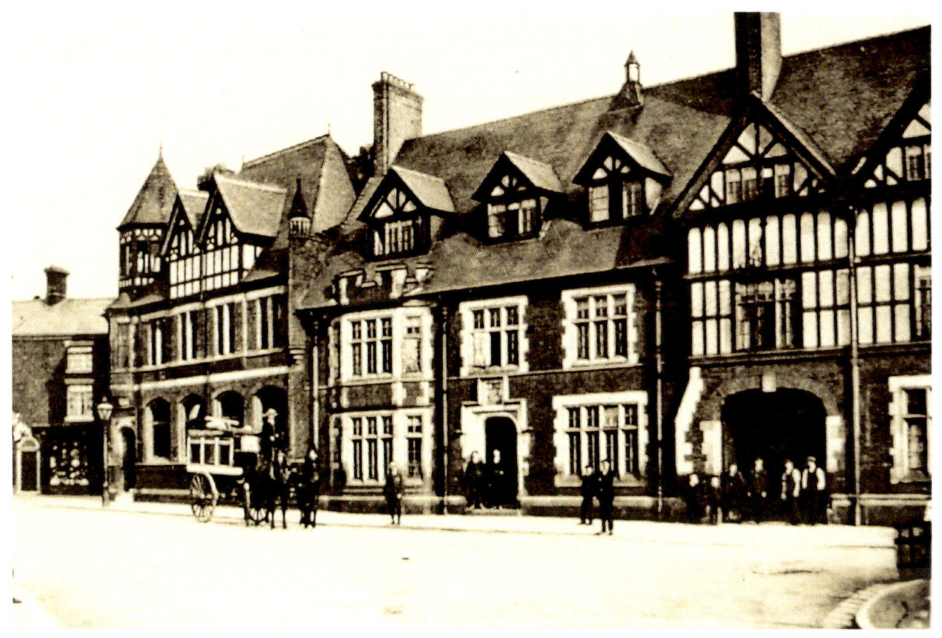

The Wheatsheaf, Early 1900s and 2010

Now let us compare today's impressive hotel with how it looked at the turn of the twentieth century. The hotel was built around 1889 by the Rt. Hon. Hungerford Crewe (3rd Baron Crewe) at the same time as he built the town hall. It too was built in locally handmade bricks and the architect was Mr Thomas Bower of Nantwich. In the old photograph, a horse-drawn omnibus awaits its passengers – many have gathered, not to have a smoke as today but to watch the photographer at work.

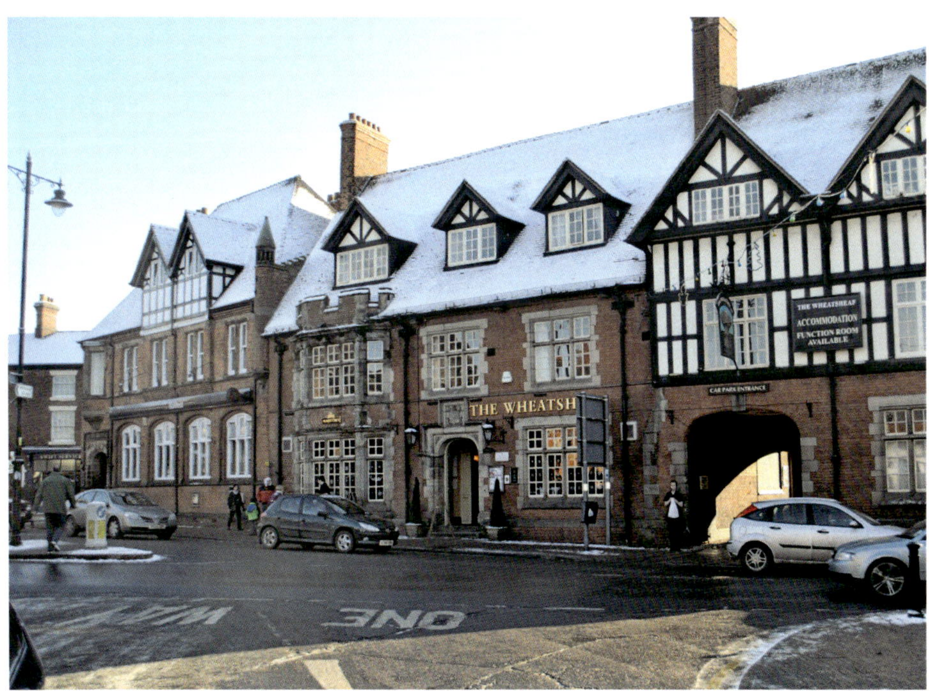

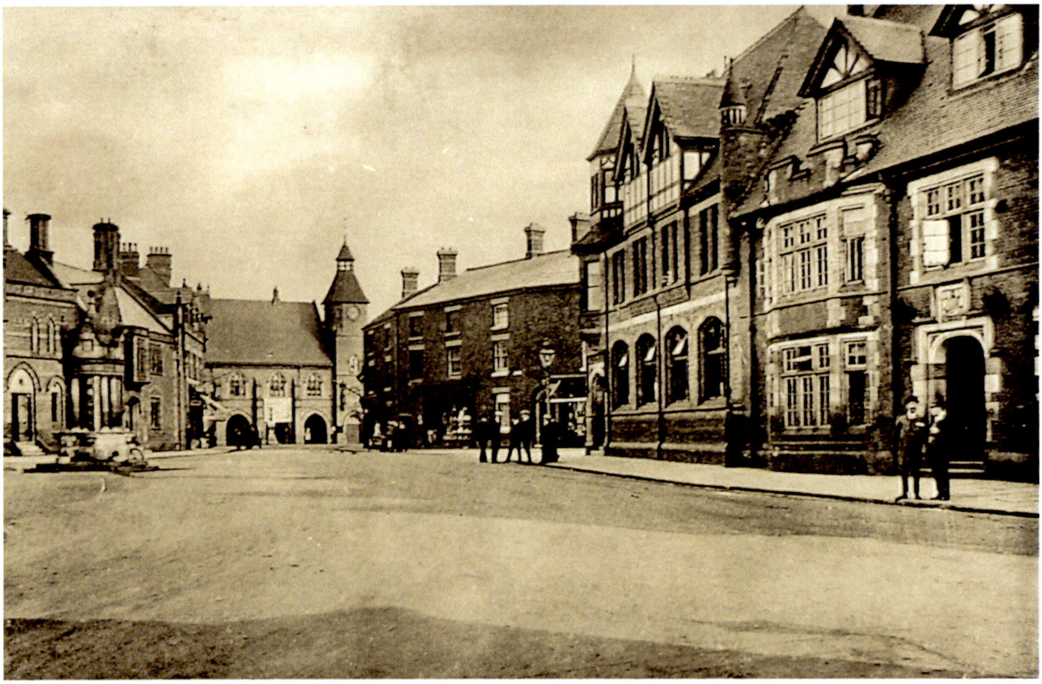

Hightown, 1920s and 2010

A last look past the Wheatsheaf Hotel towards the town/market hall. Note the position of the fountain and the uncluttered road. This was not the case when celebrations in Sandbach took place, usually in this area.

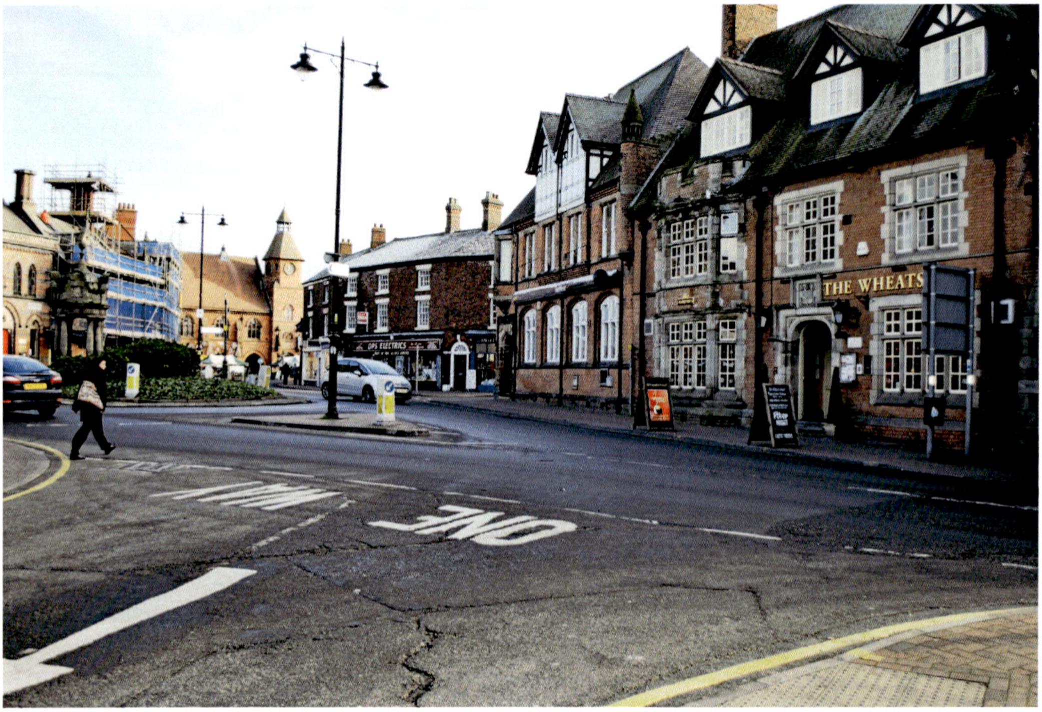

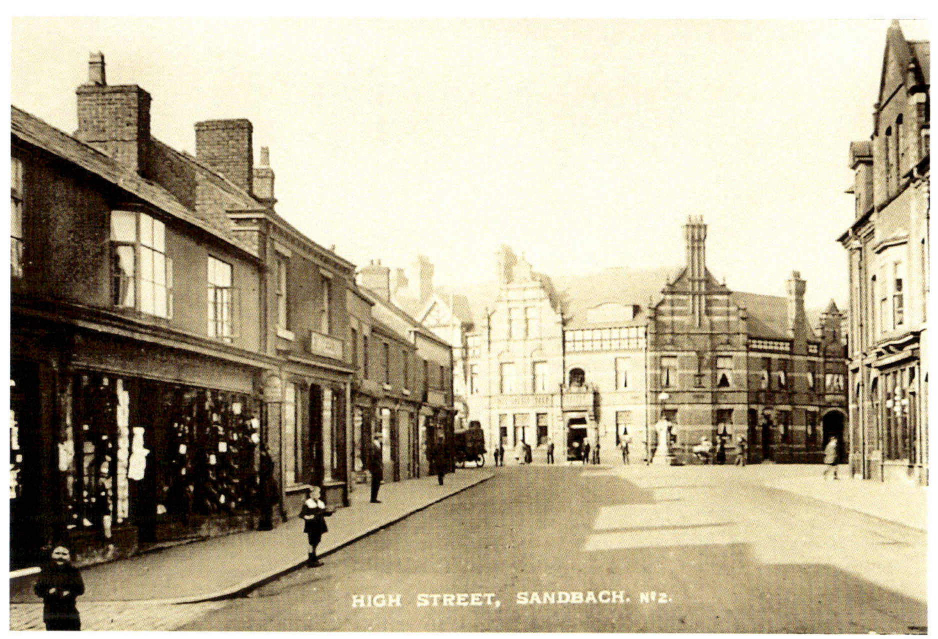

High Street to The Swan, early 1900s and 2010

Here we take another look at the top of the High Street towards The Swan and Chequers. In 1860 The Old Swan and Chequers Posting and Commercial Hotel is shown as being in High Street; the landlady was Mary Ann Whittingham. When the new pub was built in 1895, the name was initially The Swan, although there was another Swan in Crown Bank. It later reverted to The Swan and Chequers.

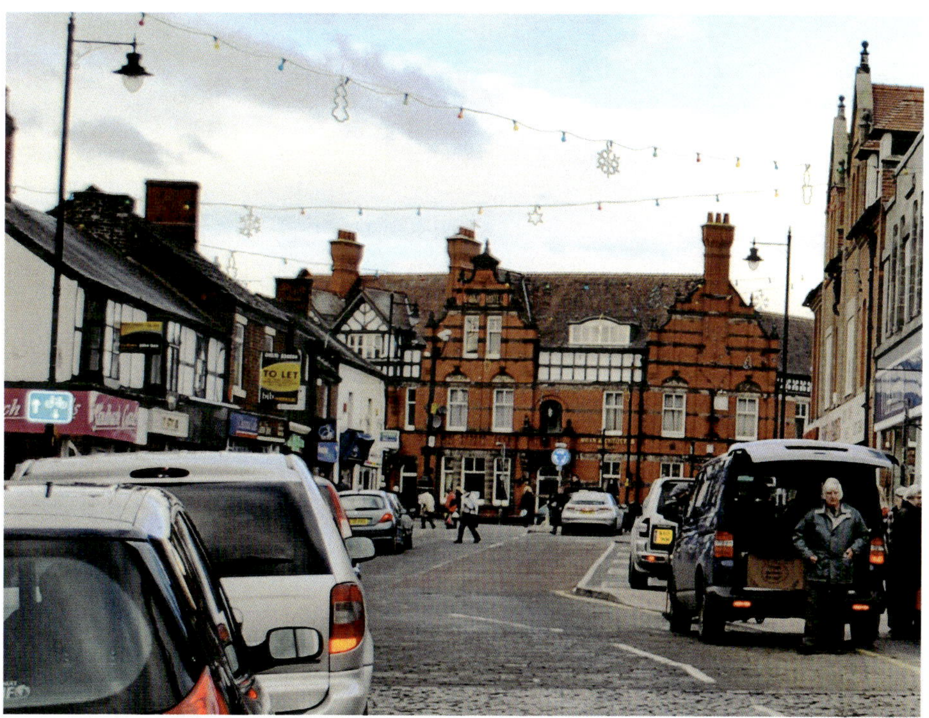

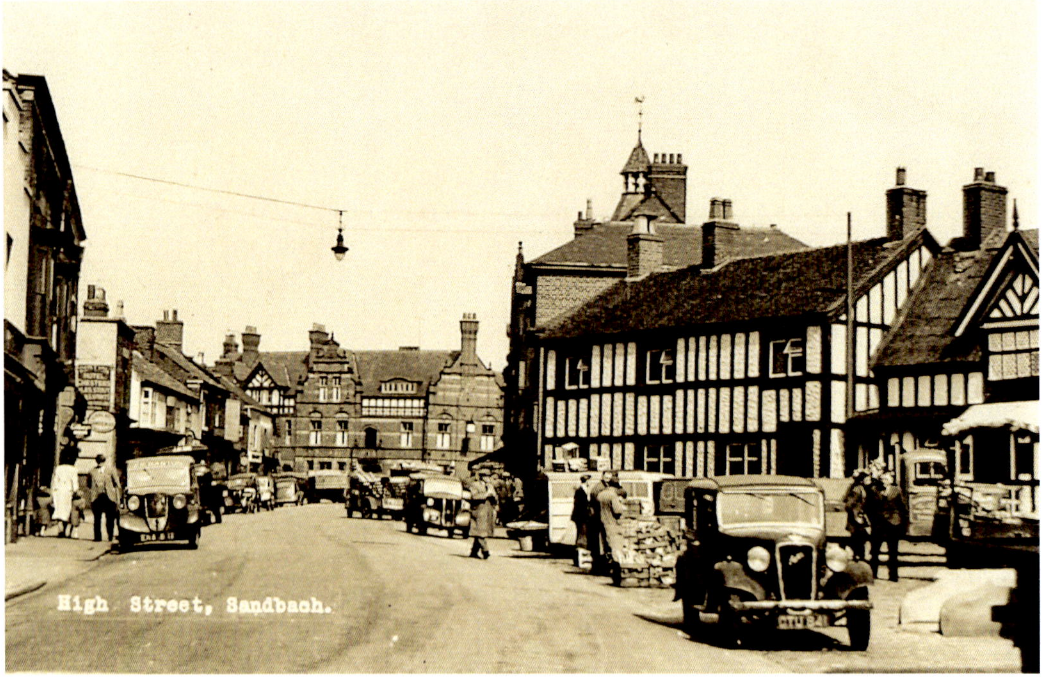

High Street, 1940s–50s and 2010

We move forward in time now to look at the top of the High Street in the years following the Second World War. With many period vehicles in view, in the older photograph we see that the pub on the left, now called The Lion, was then The Red Lion. We also get our first look at the ancient Black Bear.

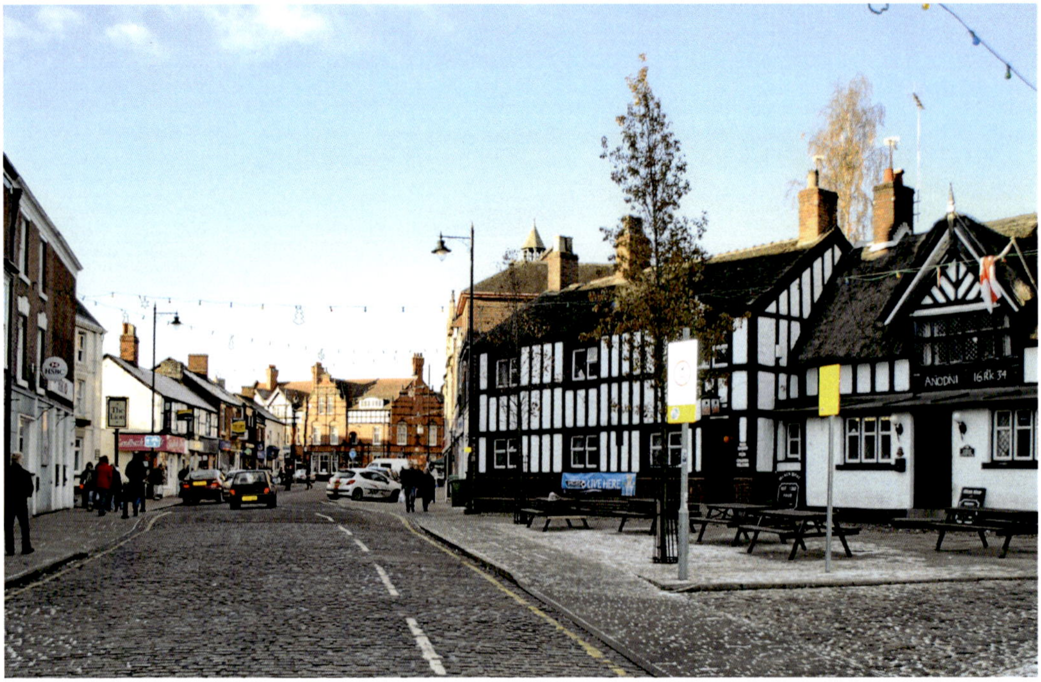

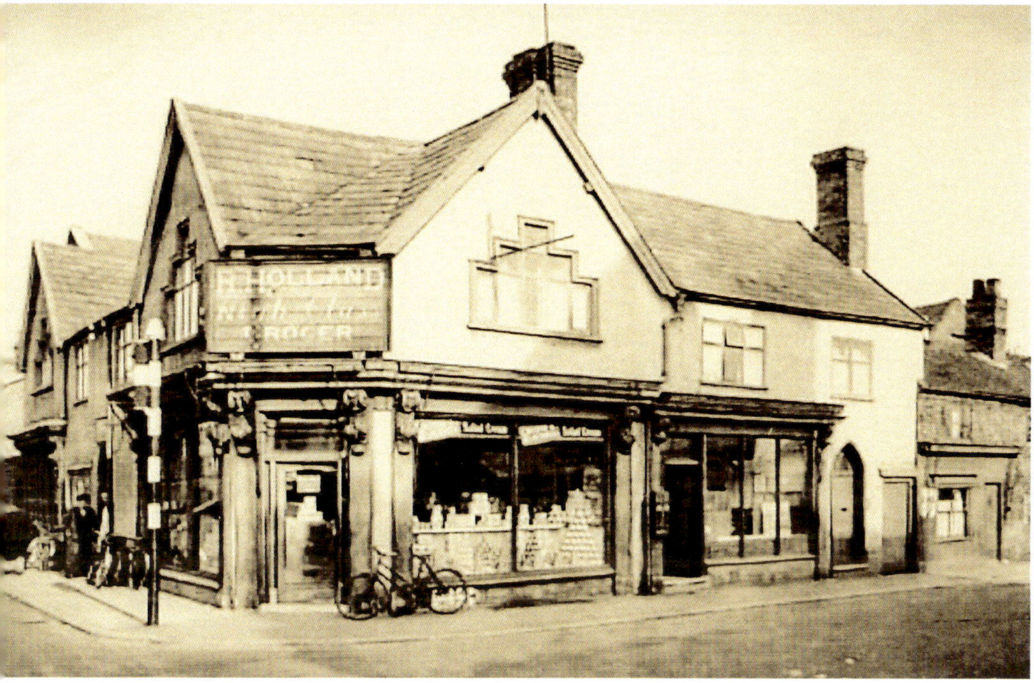

R. Holland's Store, 1930s and 2010

This attractive shop is on Congleton Road and was the premises of Robert Holland. It now houses the very attractive Burnell's shop selling cards, gifts and locally sourced items.

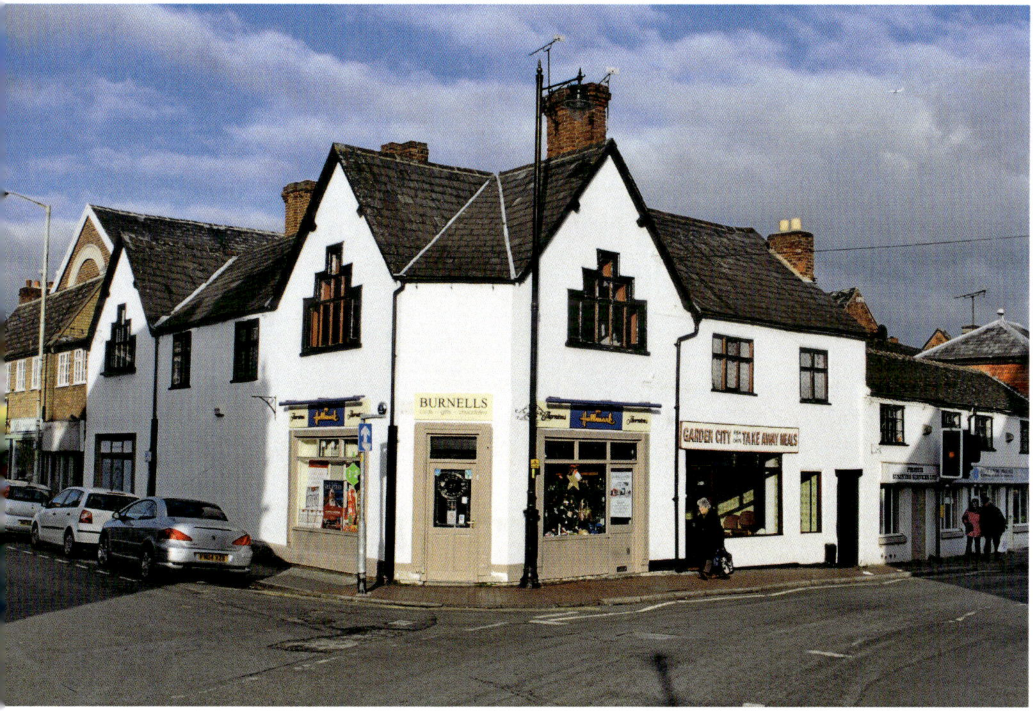

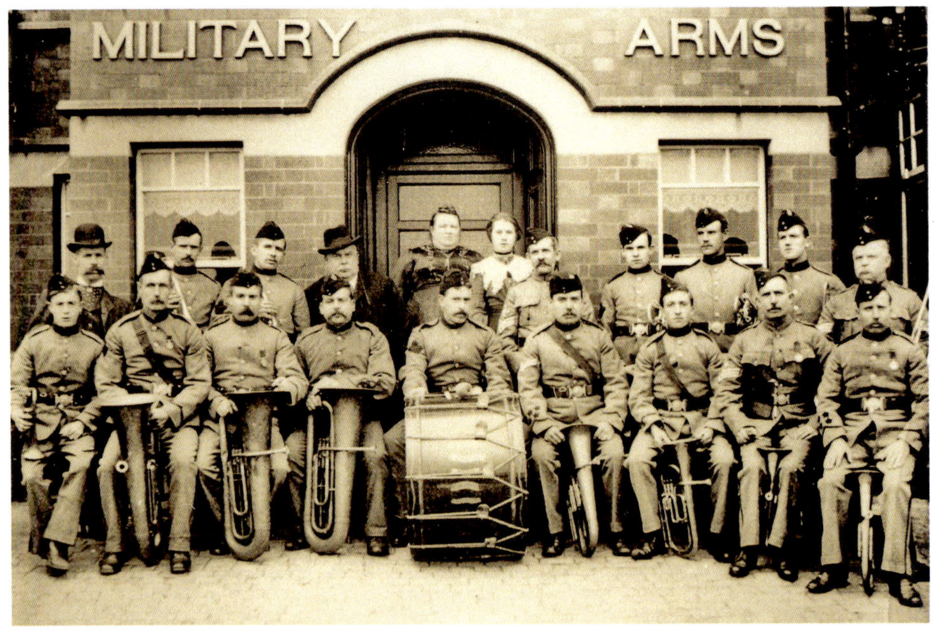

Military Arms, 1910 and 2010

This well-known local pub stands opposite Scotch Common and the open-air market. On the old photograph the original caption was 'William Bagnall's Band known as "Baggies Band"'. The landlord of this alehouse was, at the time, John Bagnall. On the common opposite, now called Scotch Common, a skirmish took place in 1651 – further details can be found in the Introduction to this book.

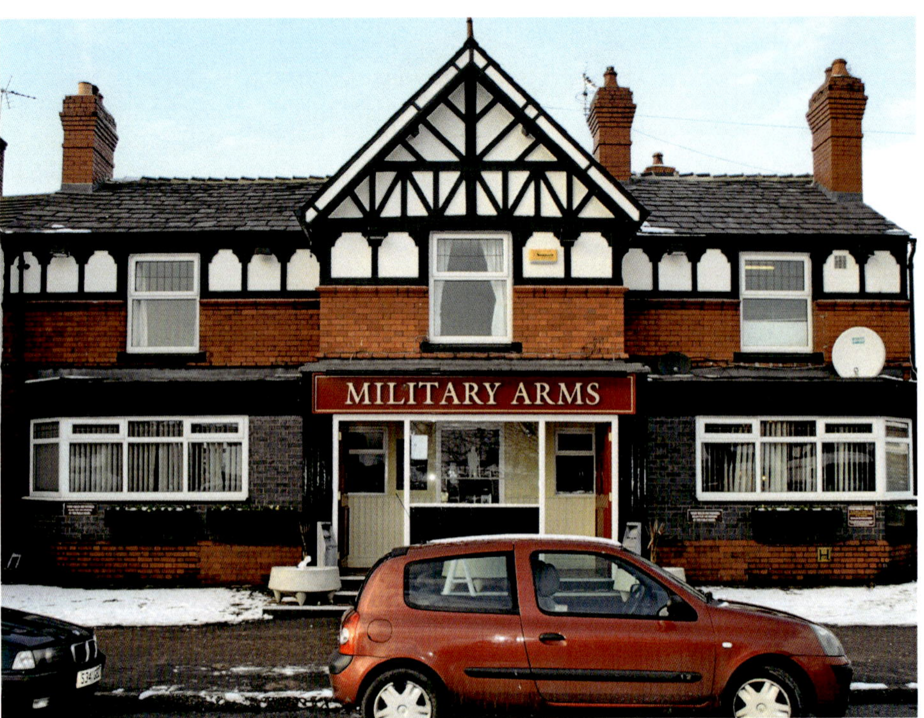

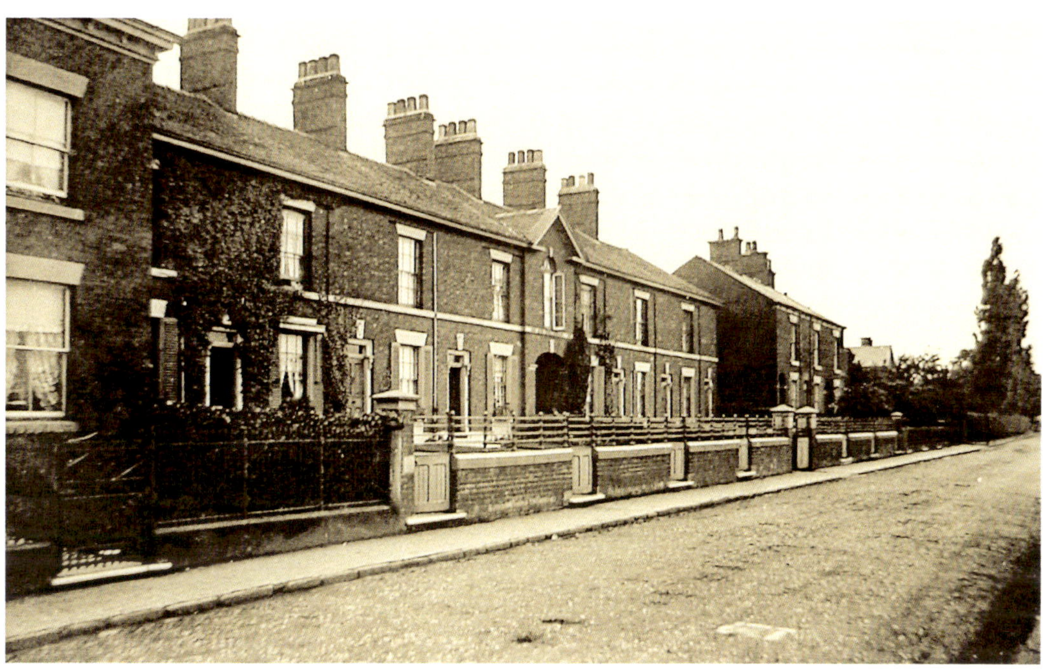

Newfield Terrace, early 1900s and 2010

Further along Congleton Road we come to this impressive terrace of houses that were built in 1850–51 and are now listed. The name above the main entrance is given as 'New Field Terrace'.

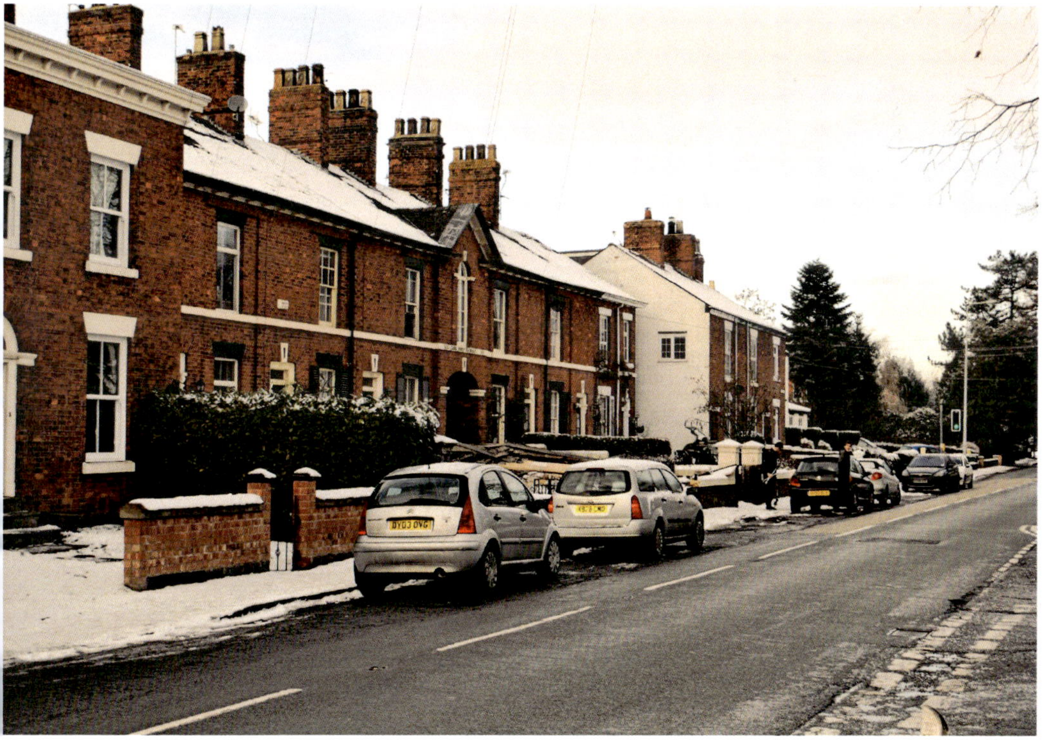

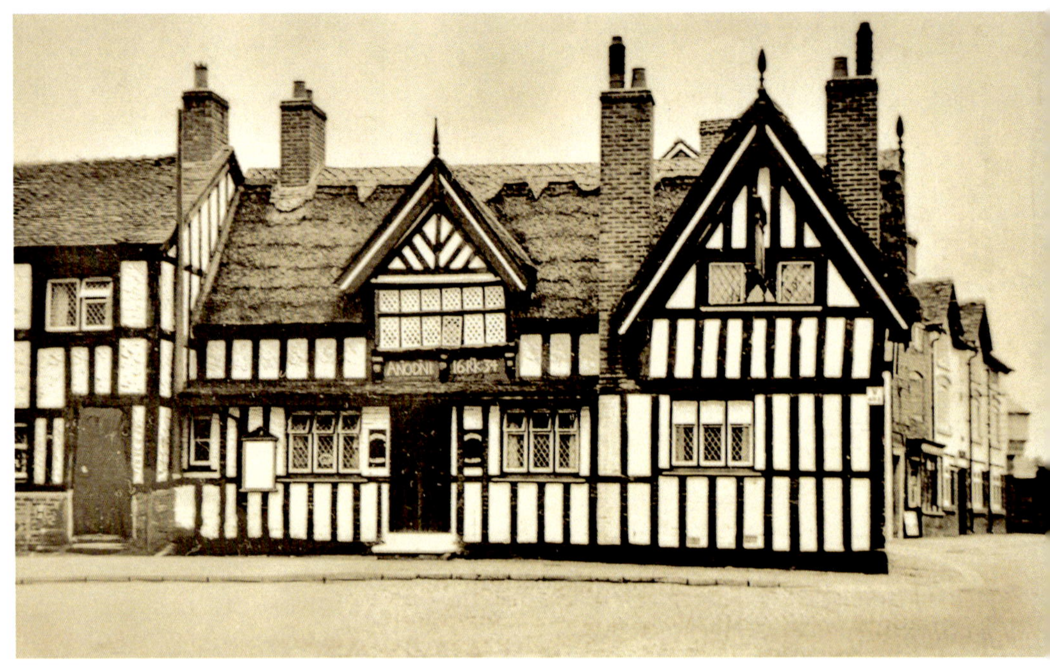

The Black Bear, 1950s and 2010

This ancient pub is one of the town's oldest inns, dating from 1634 as the sign above the door indicates. It is situated on the edge of the Market Square, a cobbled area famous for the Sandbach crosses that can be found there. As for the pub, when a building is beautifully constructed and not messed around with, it remains beautiful!

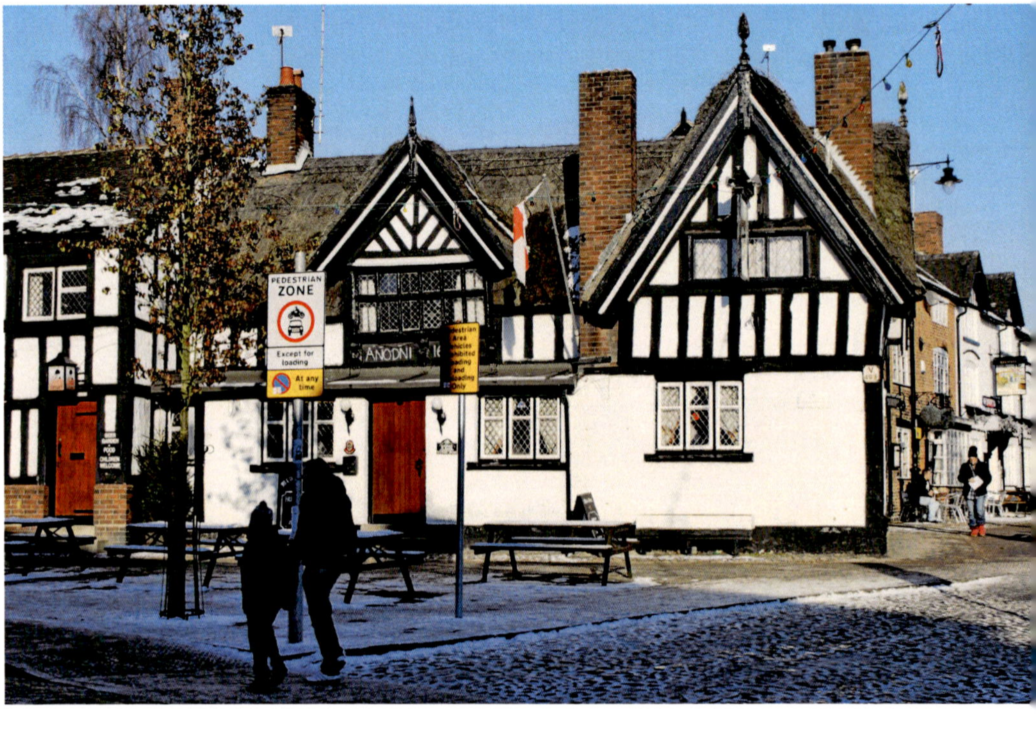

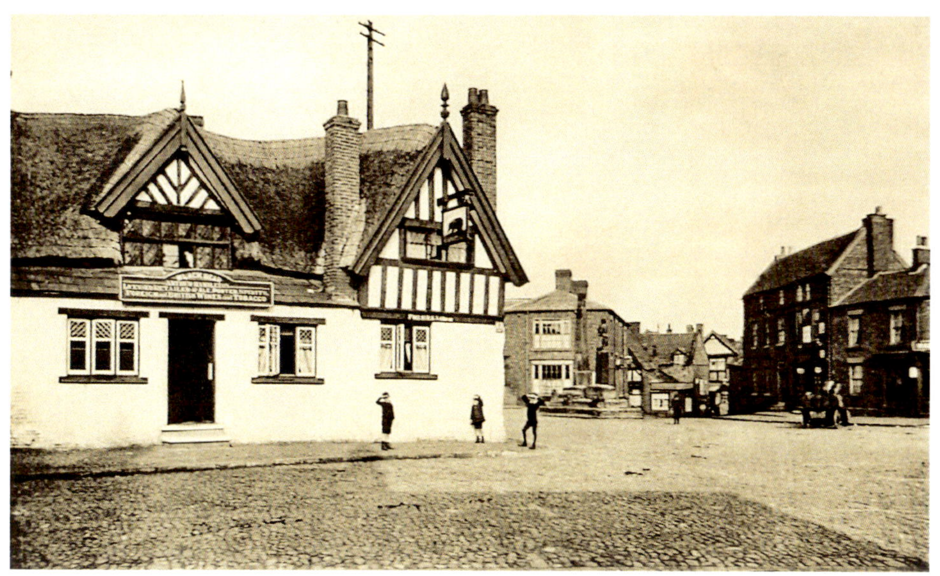

The Black Bear Pub, 1914 and 2010

We step back from the Black Bear here and look into Sandbach Square. For many years this held the regular Sandbach market. Several buildings surround and are off the cobbled marketplace. One of these was the national school built in 1841; in 1860, 120 boys and 270 girls and infants attended the school, whose teachers were Charles Goostry and Catherine Guinane. This school closed in 1961. There was a smaller national school built in 1848 at Elworth. The marketplace also boasted the town hall until 1889 and still has two more public houses.

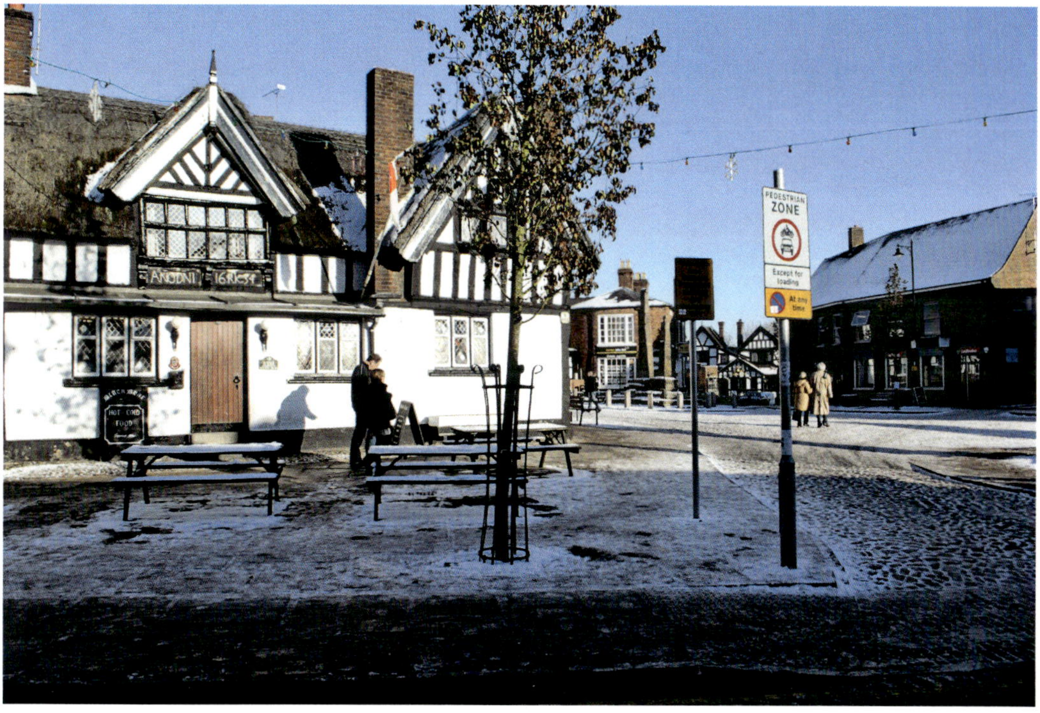

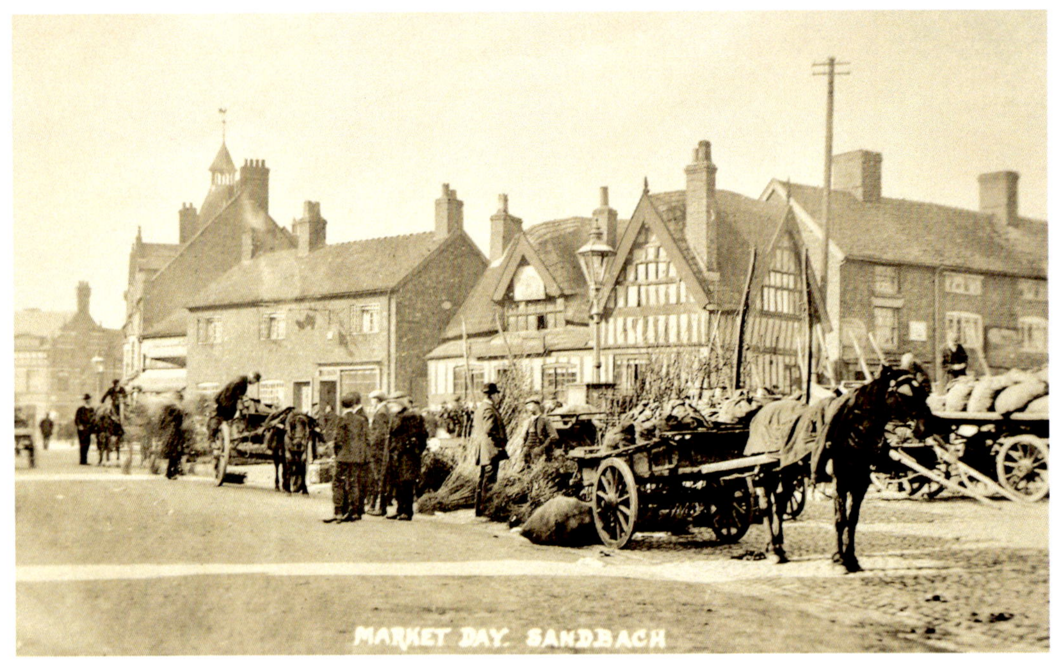

Market Day, Early 1900s and 2010

This is the first of a few photographs showing Sandbach wholesale market in the early 1900s. Sandbach has been a market town since 1579 under a charter granted by Queen Elizabeth I. Many years ago, a retail market opened on Scotch Common and in the market hall that was built for the purpose in 1889 and incorporated within the new town hall. The wholesale market on the square ceased many years ago. Last June, however, a farmers' market was introduced and is held on the second Saturday of each month.

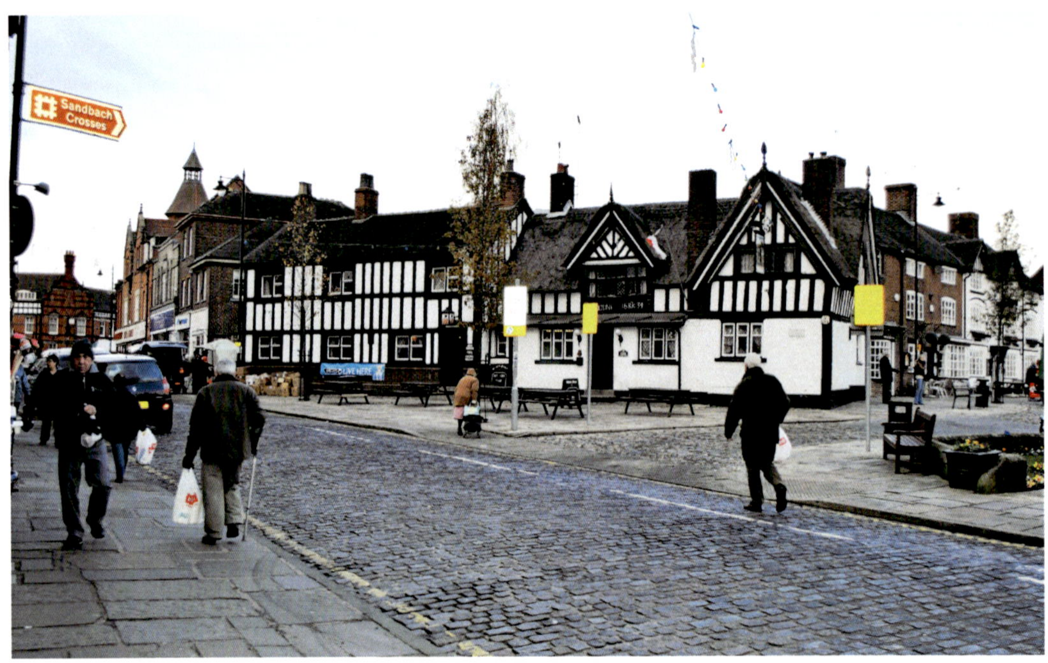

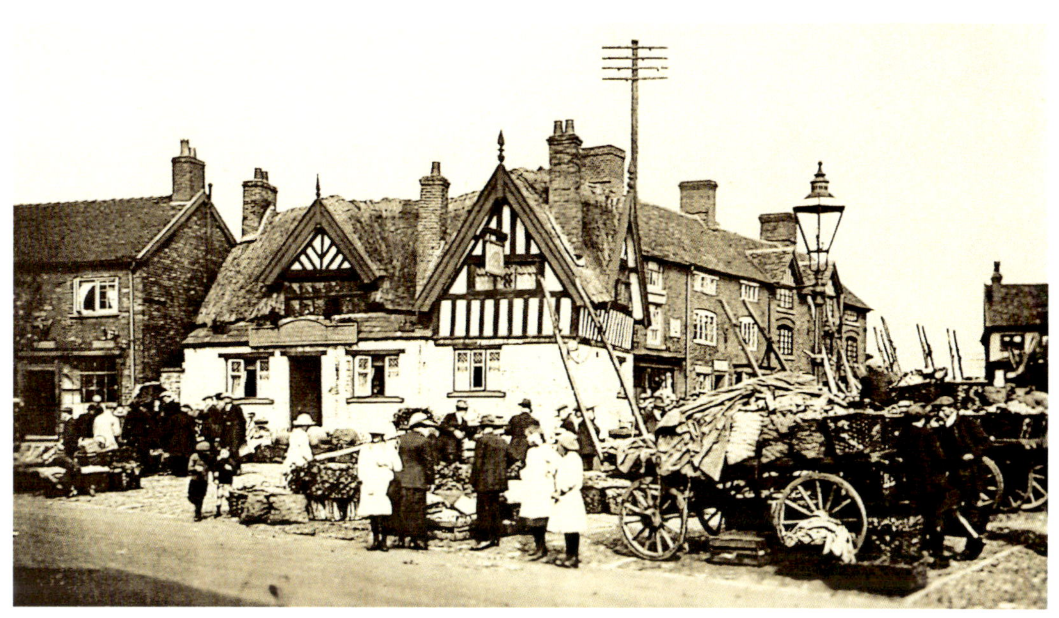

Market Day, Early 1900s and 2010

Another look across towards the Black Bear at the wholesale market that is in full swing with the farmers' carts loaded with produce. I have dated this shot at the turn of the last century, although it could very well be earlier.

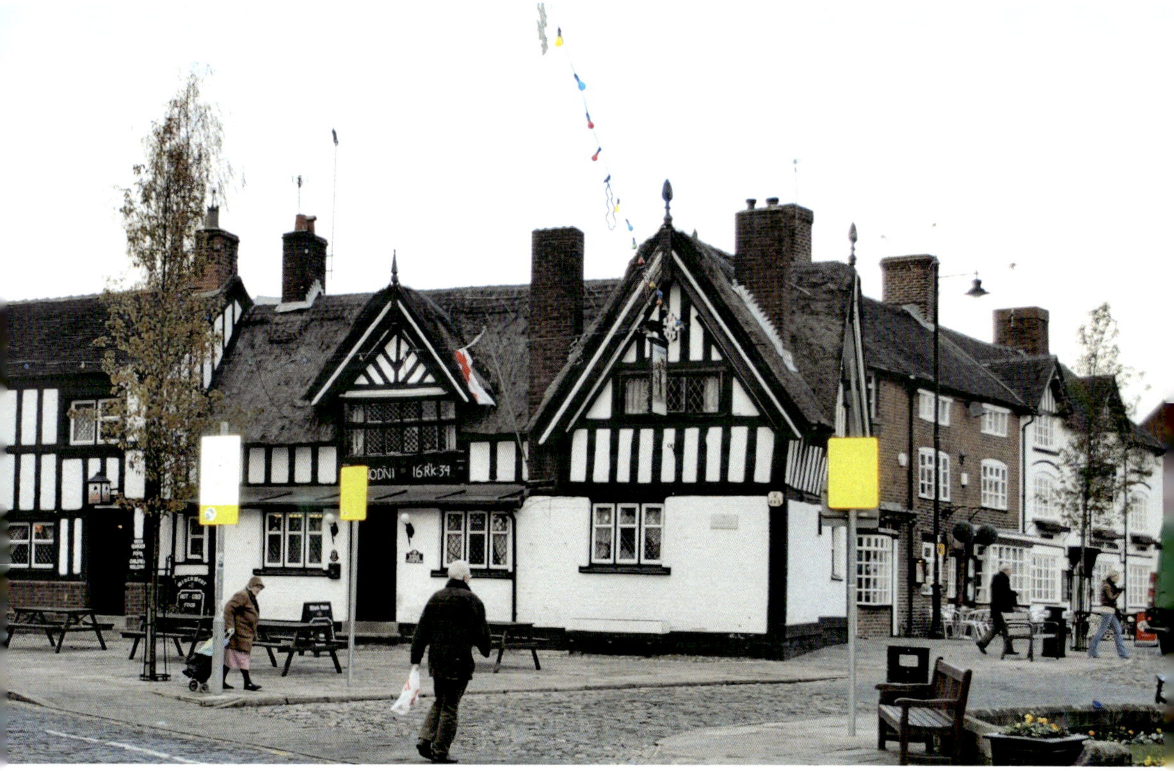

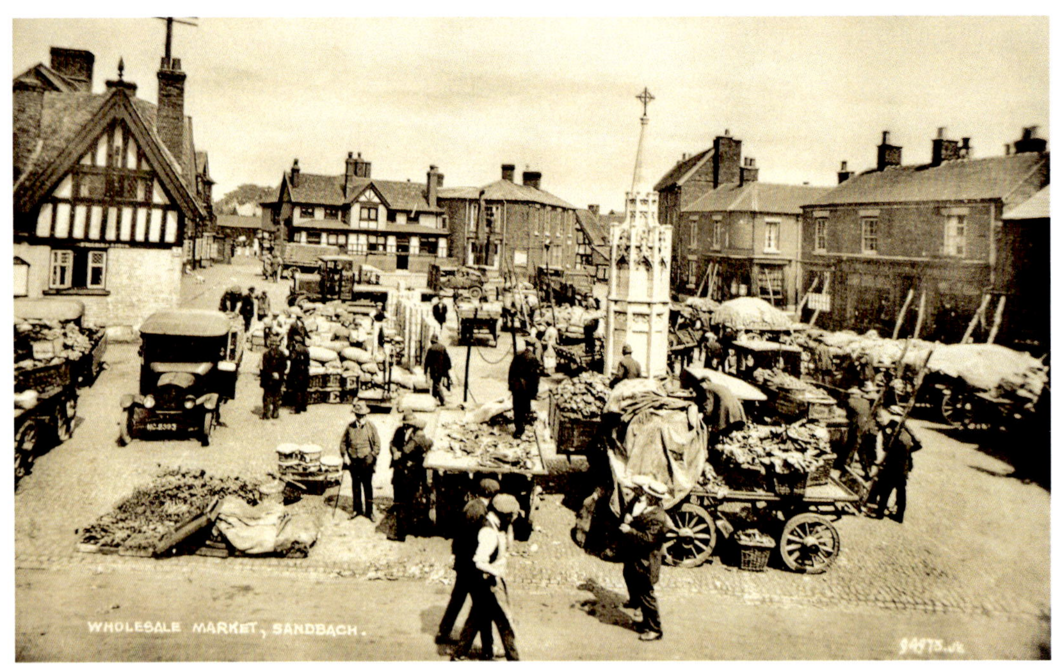

Wholesale Market, Early 1920s and 2010

A final look at the wholesale market during the early 1920s, when the war memorial would have been quite a new feature. Horse-drawn carts still predominate, but motor lorries have arrived on the scene. In the modern photograph, a garden of remembrance has been constructed around the memorial and many more names have been added following the Second World War. One hardy trader has set up his stall where many from outlying farms would once have been.

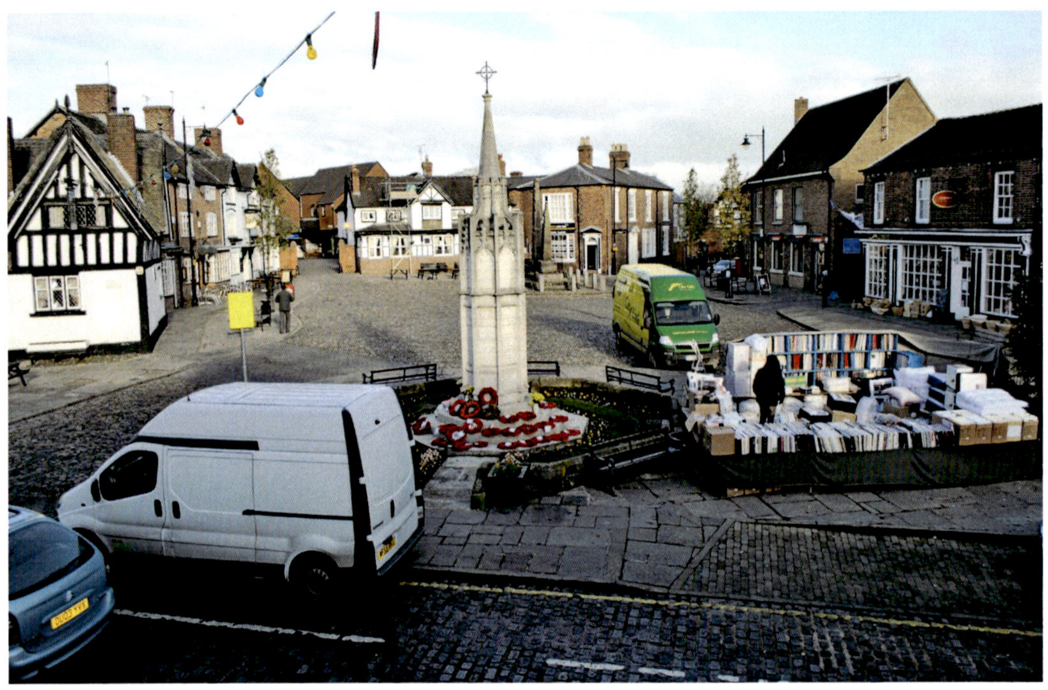

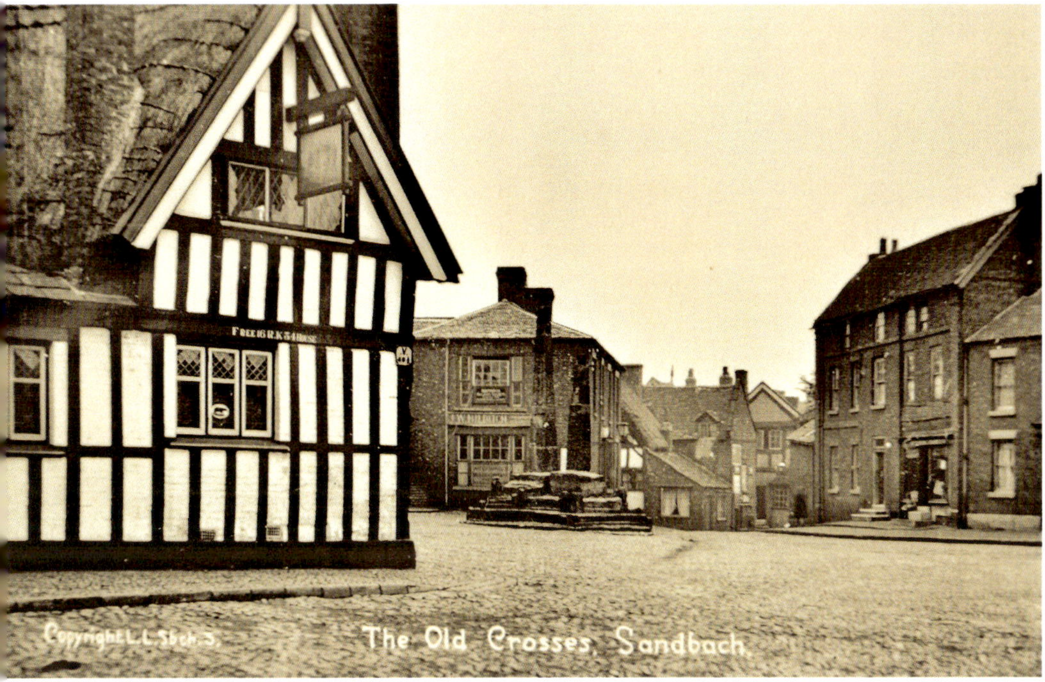

The Old Crosses, Sandbach.

The Black Bear and Old Crosses, 1930s and 2010

It is now a bit quieter in the Market Square, as shown in the old photograph dating to around 1930–40. The longstanding company of John W. Hilditch Auctioneers can be seen at No. 19. This company was taken over in 1969 and again in 1988. The auctioneers Andrew Hilditch & Son now work from Hanover House, 1A The Square. The owner, John Andrew, has worked on The Square since 1977, making him probably the longest-serving resident.

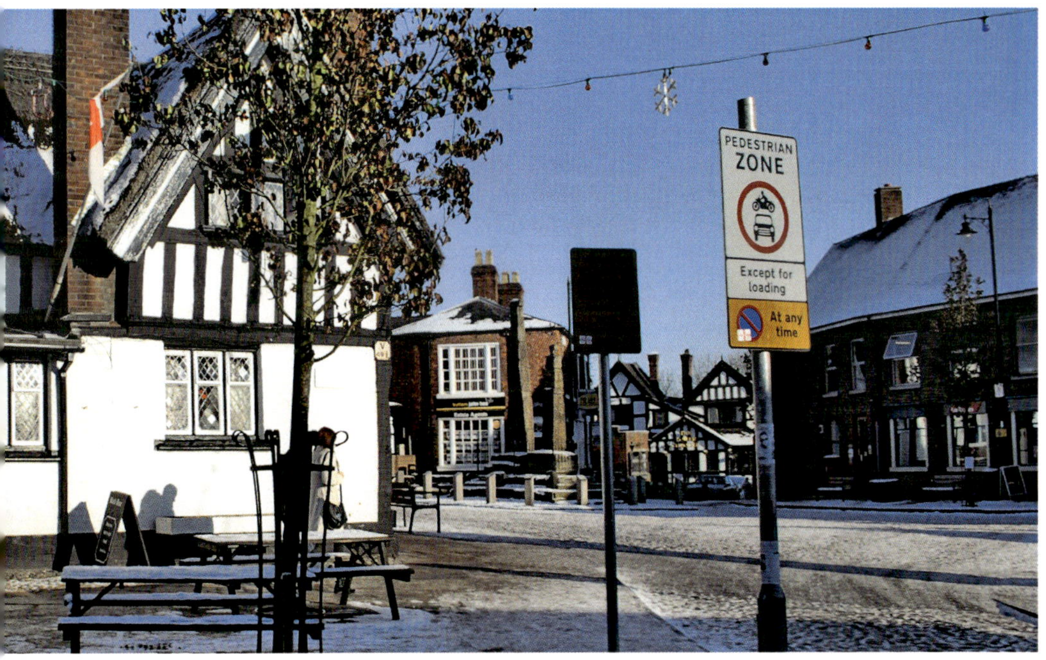

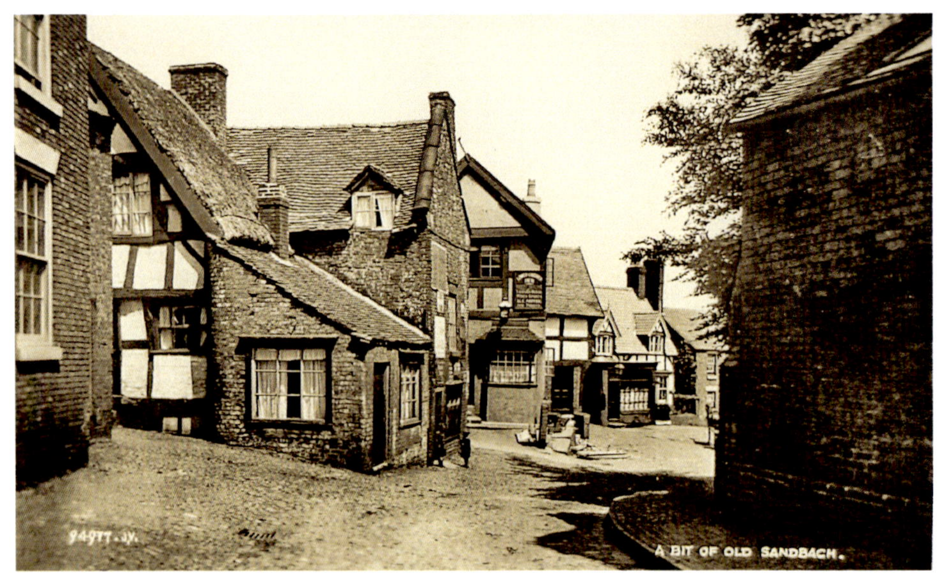

Lower Chequers, Early 1900s and 2010

We now look into Crown Bank and Hawk Street at the mixture of old, new and refurbished properties. Once a road out of the town, it is now a quiet thoroughfare leading down towards Dingle Lake past the churchyard, Church Street and Bath Street. The Lower Chequers Inn can be found here; it is said that in times past, given the great number of uneducated people, a chequer board was used to help them count their money. A cynic may say that the name and the chequer board will return to fashion soon! The inn is said to be the oldest building in Sandbach, dating from 1570.

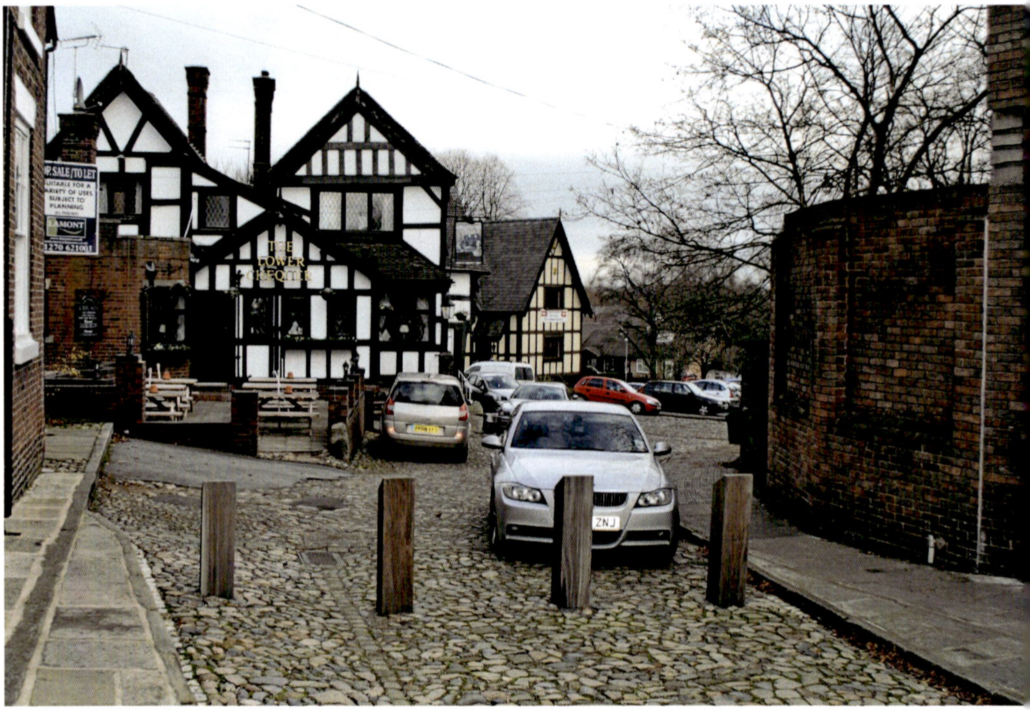

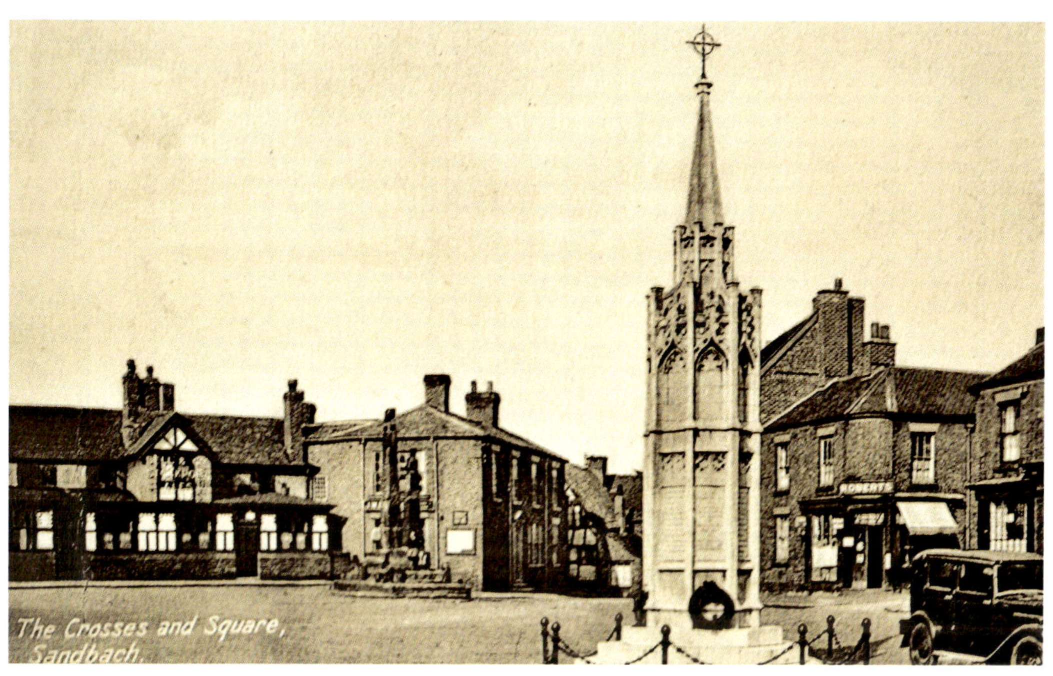

The War Memorial, 1930s and 2010

This is the Sandbach war memorial, which was unveiled on Sunday 16 April 1922 by Lt-Col. John Kennedy CMG, DSO of the Black Watch, whose family originated from Brookside, Arclid. Although many years have passed since the two world wars, the memorial bristles with wreaths placed there on the recent Remembrance Sunday. Unfortunately, even more names have been and are being added to the memorial as a result of the wars fought since the dark days of the 1940s.

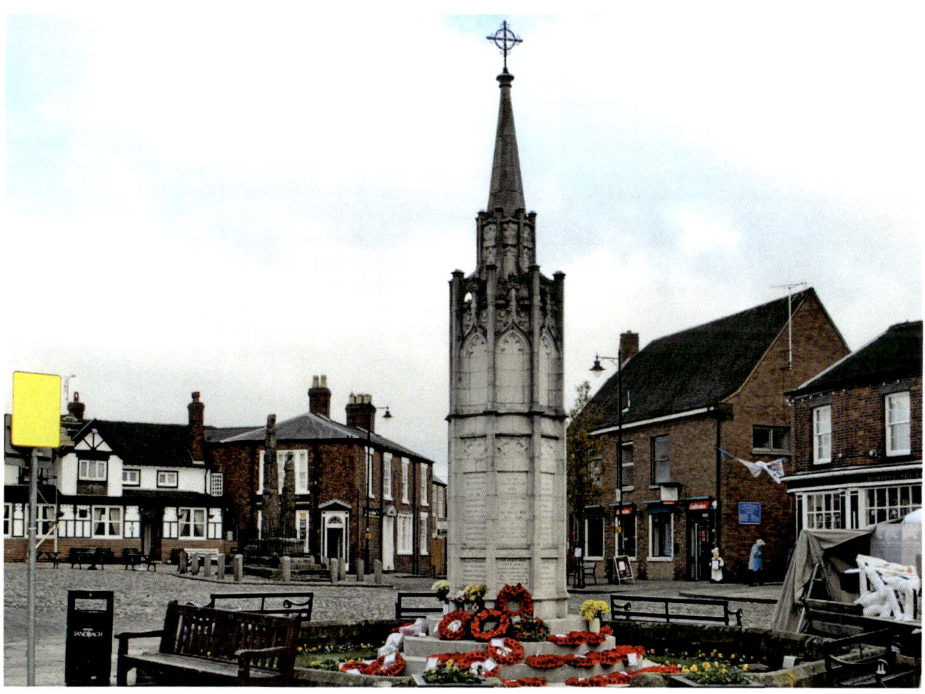

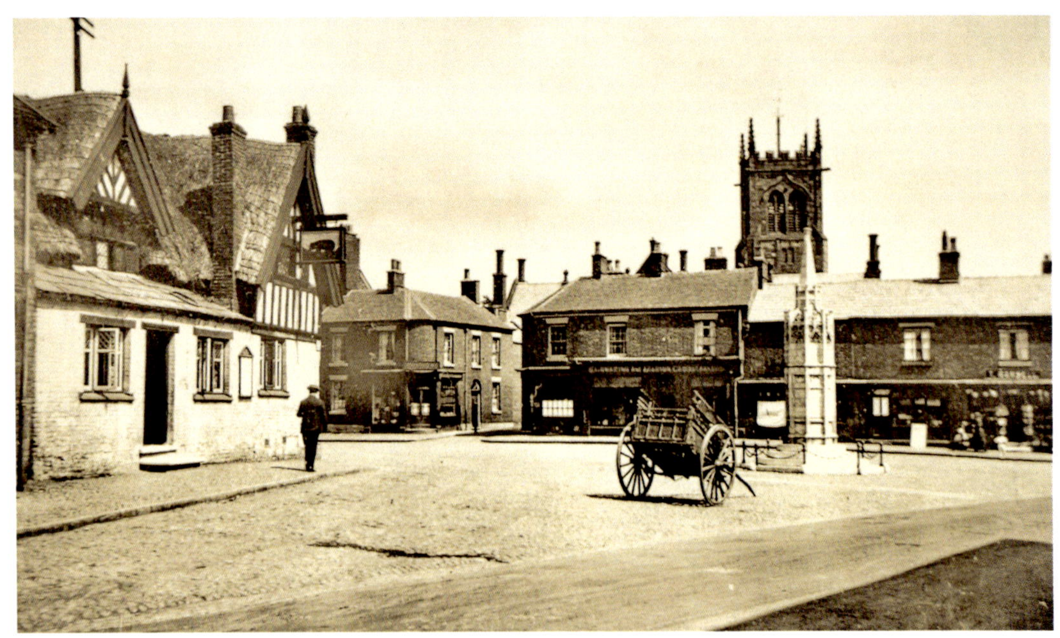

Market Square, 1910–20s and 2010

We look now across the front of the Black Bear to the then newly constructed war memorial and a quiet Market Square where a lonely cart stands upon the cobbles. On the far right can be seen the shop of Thomas Ramsell, glass and china dealer at No. 3, while the tower of the parish church stands serenely in the background. The gap in the buildings facing the camera leads to the church and the location of the national school.

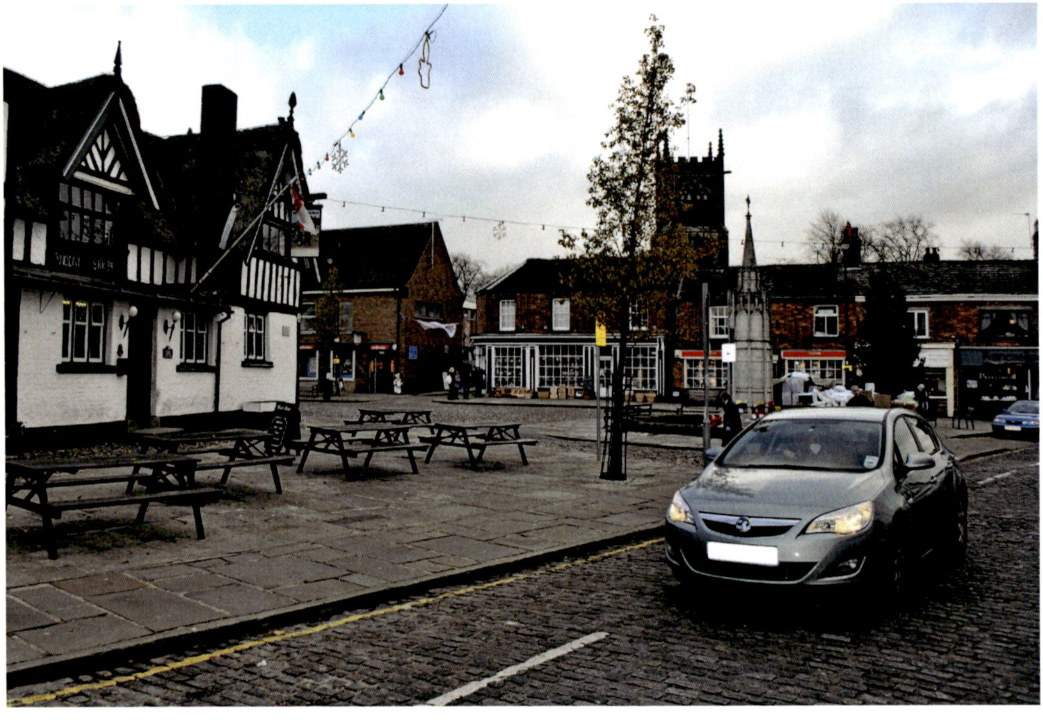

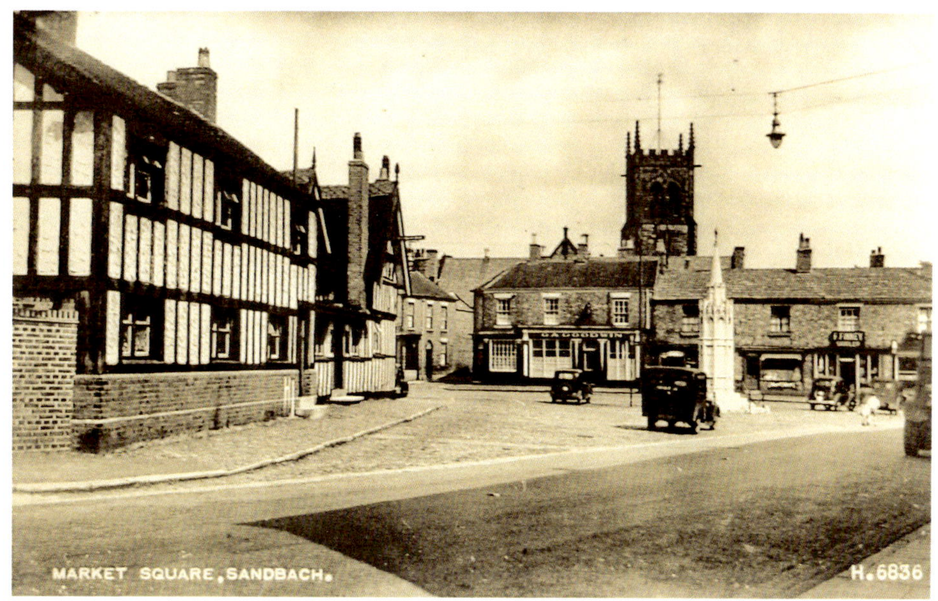

Town Square, 1940s and 2010

Here we have one last look across the Market Square with the period motor vehicles on show in the old photograph. It is possible that the Second War World is still being fought at this time and that the army lorry, which can just be seen on the far right, is being used for a military purpose. For some time after the last war, however, the surfeit of army lorries was bought by haulage companies and used privately. Either way, the lorry's presence adds to the period charm of the photograph.

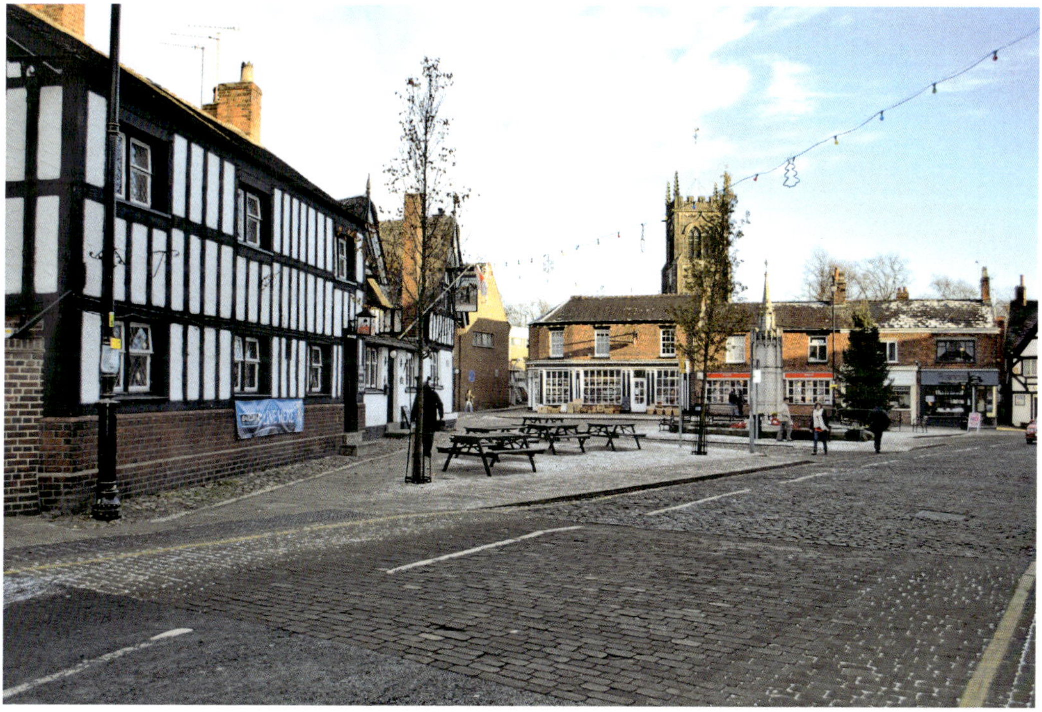

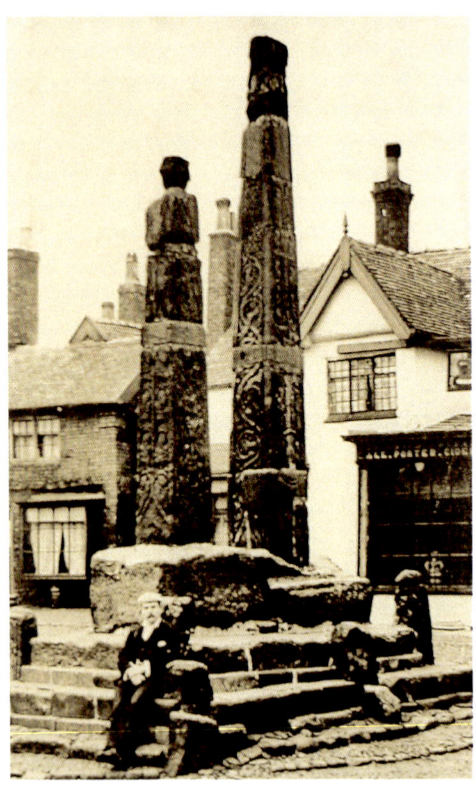

Old Crosses, 1920s and 2010

Let us now look at what Sandbach is really famous for: the ancient crosses on The Square. In the old photograph we see a man relaxing upon the steps with The Crown Inn in the background. In the modern photograph we see that little has changed over the years, save for the fact that the crosses have been fenced in for both aesthetic and security reasons.

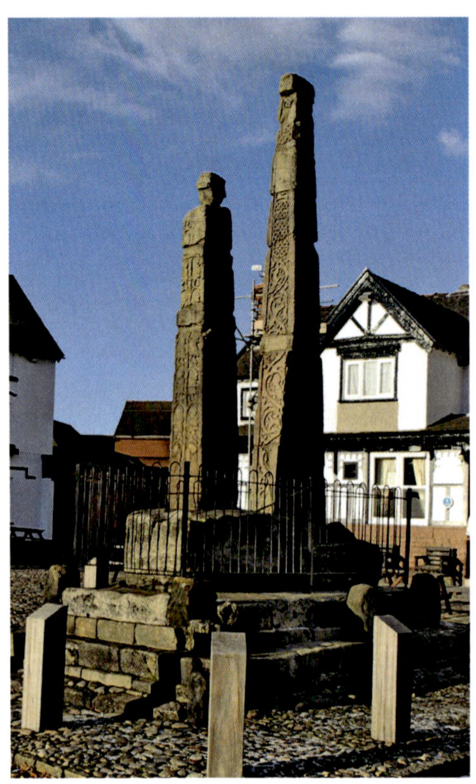

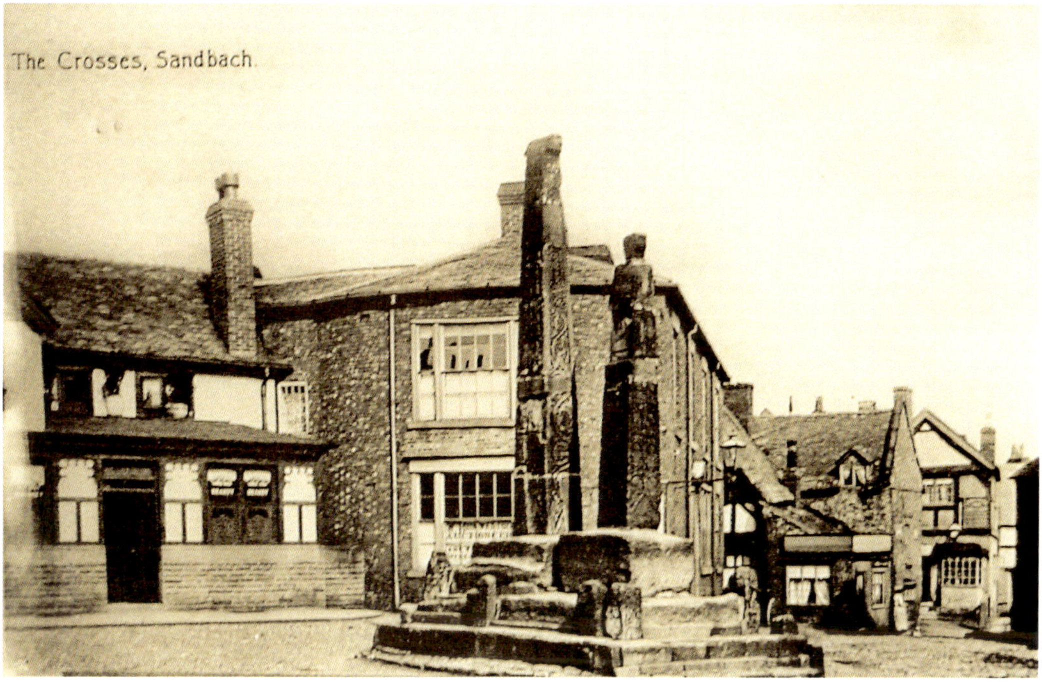

Old Crosses, Early 1900s and 2010

Now a look from a different angle into what was Hawk Street and what is now Crown Bank. Further details of the crosses can be found in the Introduction.

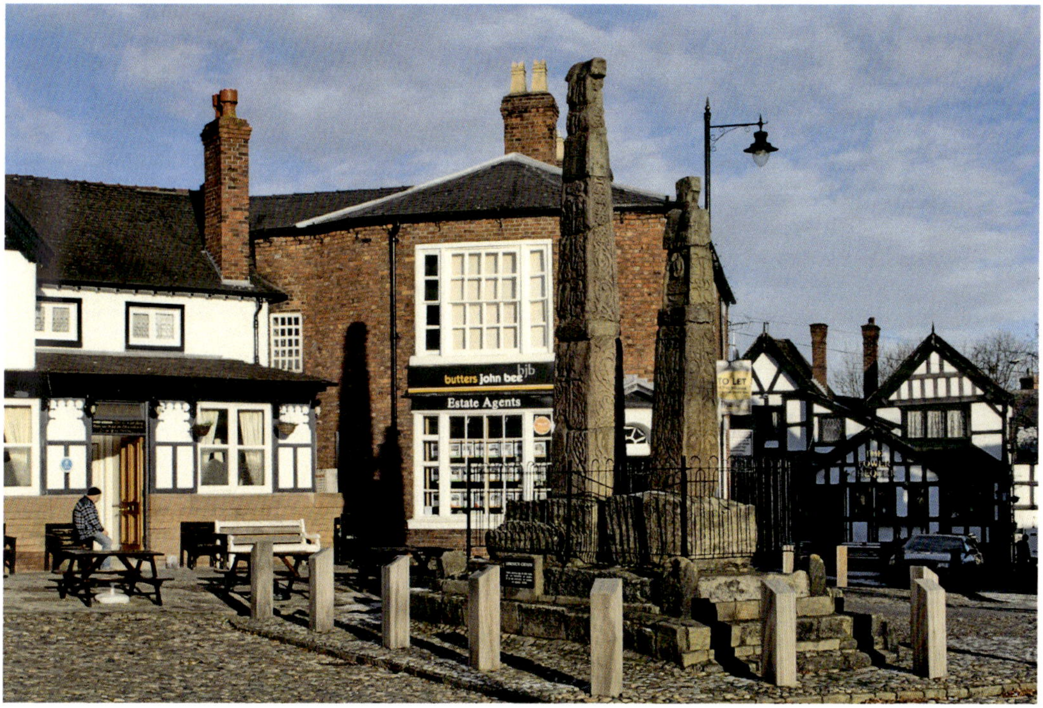

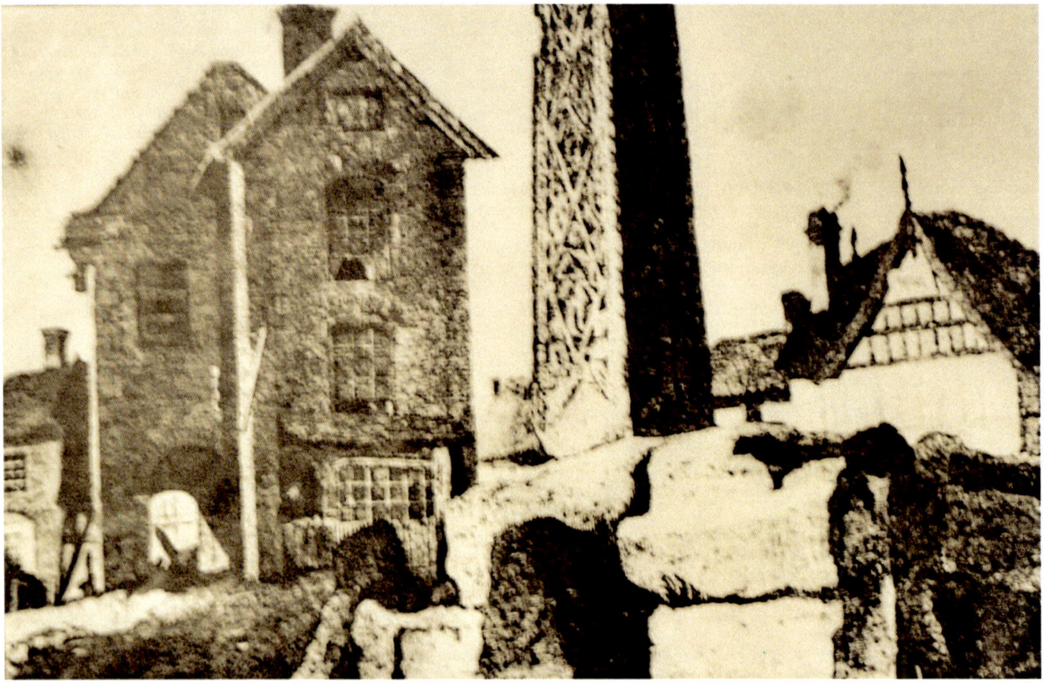

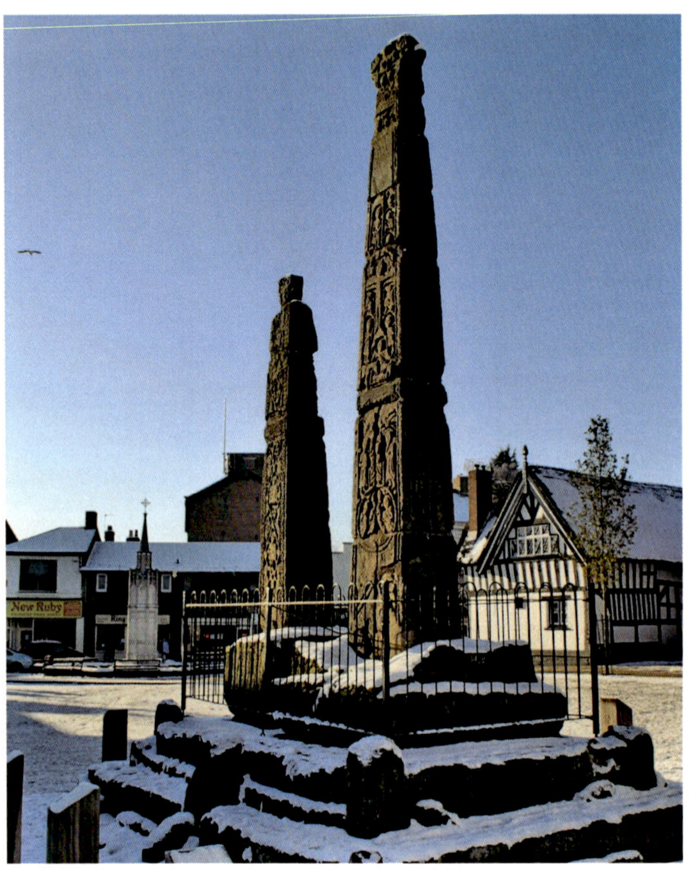

Ancient Crosses and Town Hall, 1800s and 2010

I have to apologise for the poor quality of the old photograph here, but it is the only one that I could find of the old town hall. This was the second town hall to have stood on this site and, as well as the usual purpose for which a town hall is used, it also contained two cells for prisoners awaiting their committal to the county gaol. The building was sited where the war memorial now stands and was demolished before the new town hall was built in 1889.

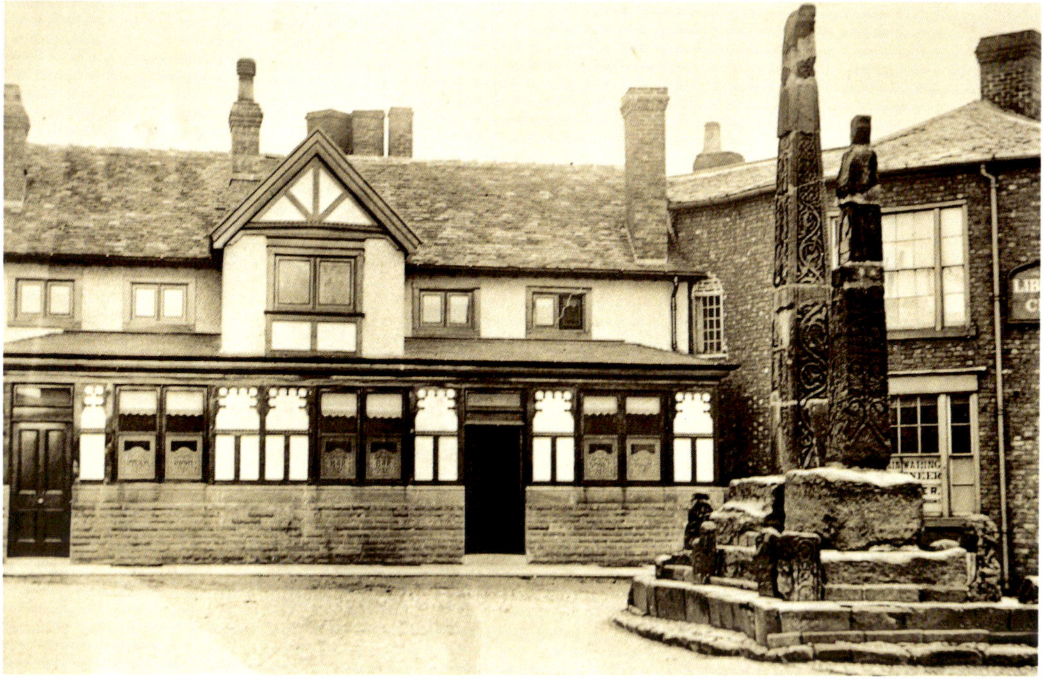

The Crown, Undated and 2010

In this penultimate old photograph of the crosses we see the Crown Hotel, which dates from the 1680s and still serves the community, as does the other pub on the square, The Market Tavern. The Liberal Club can be seen beyond the crosses; later it would be taken over by Hilditch Auctioneers.

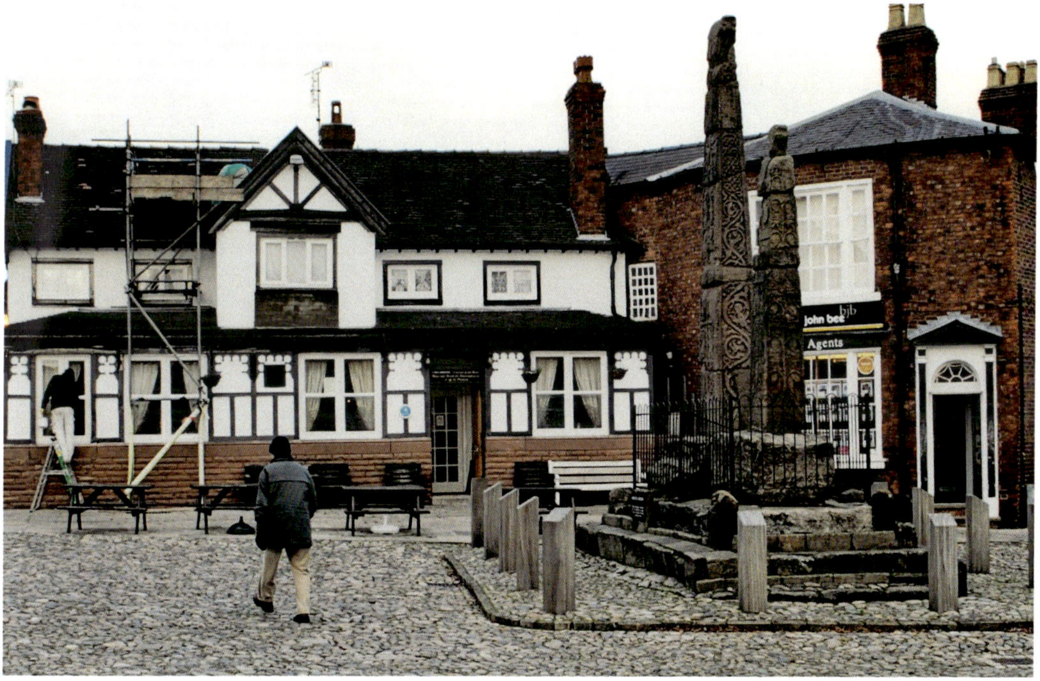

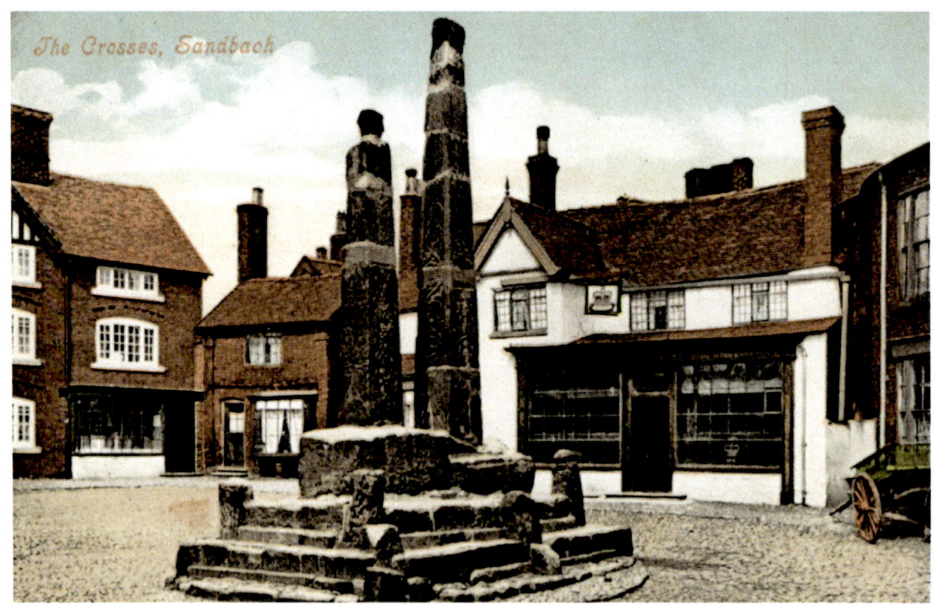

Crosses, 1900s and 2010

Finally, a hand-coloured postcard view of the crosses dated to around the turn of the last century. The Market Tavern, which dates from 1767, can be seen on the left. Originally it had small rooms for traders to conduct meetings, and it is still popular today, providing food and music – although the tiny rooms have been incorporated into a more usable facility. Another pub, called the Coach and Horses, also stood nearby. The house seen between the two pubs was later occupied by brother and sister Dicky and Betty, who were classed, in the politically incorrect terms of the time, as 'simpletons'.

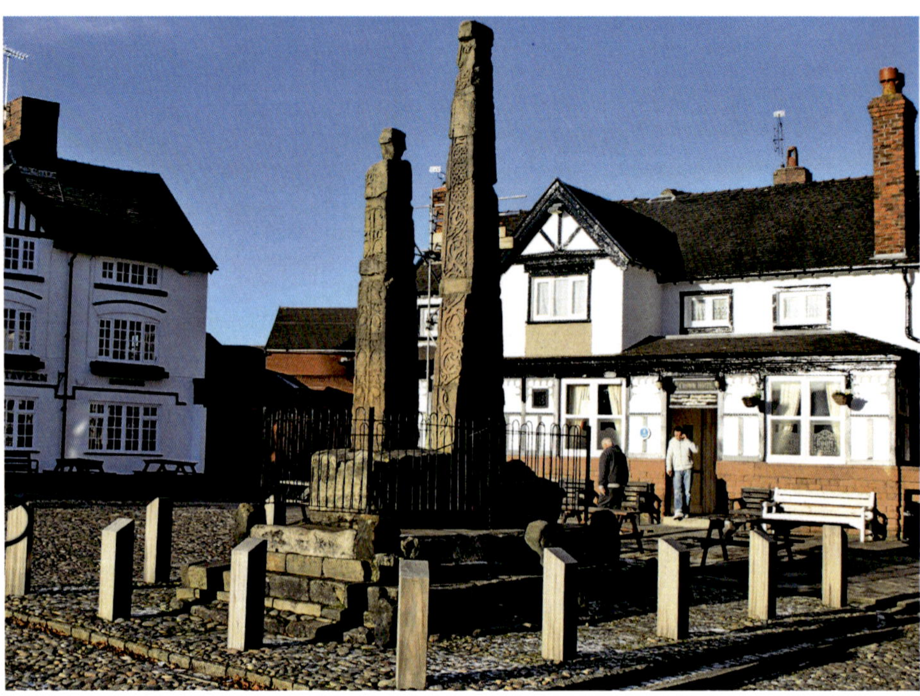

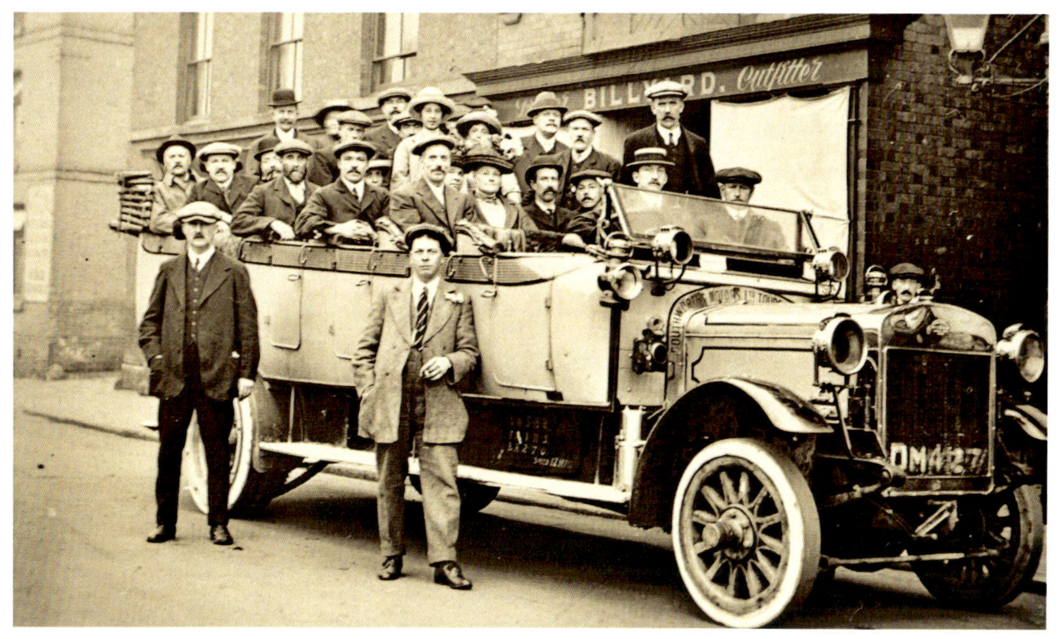

Outside Billyard's Shop, 1910–20 and 2010

This charabanc is all set to convey its well-dressed passengers on a bumpy ride to some holiday destination or day trip. It stands outside a draper's shop, the proprietor of which was Harry Billyard. The previous occupant of these premises was the draper's business of Galleys. Note that the rock at the bottom of the hotel wall to the left matches the one still there in the modern photograph. Also consider what has replaced this old shop: another piece of delightful twentieth-century architecture!

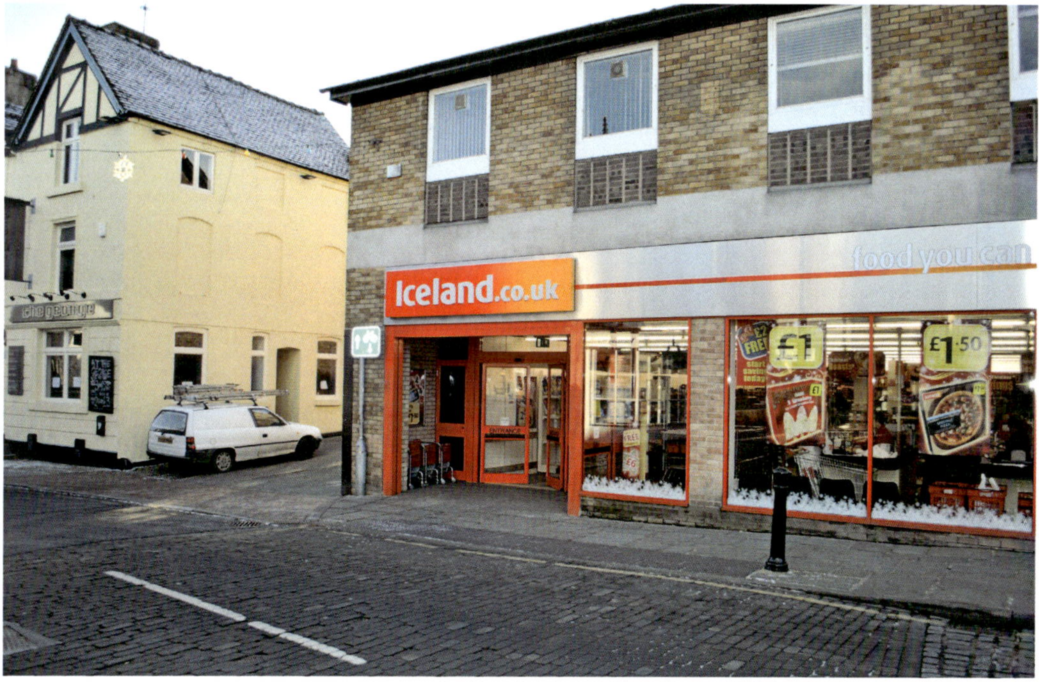

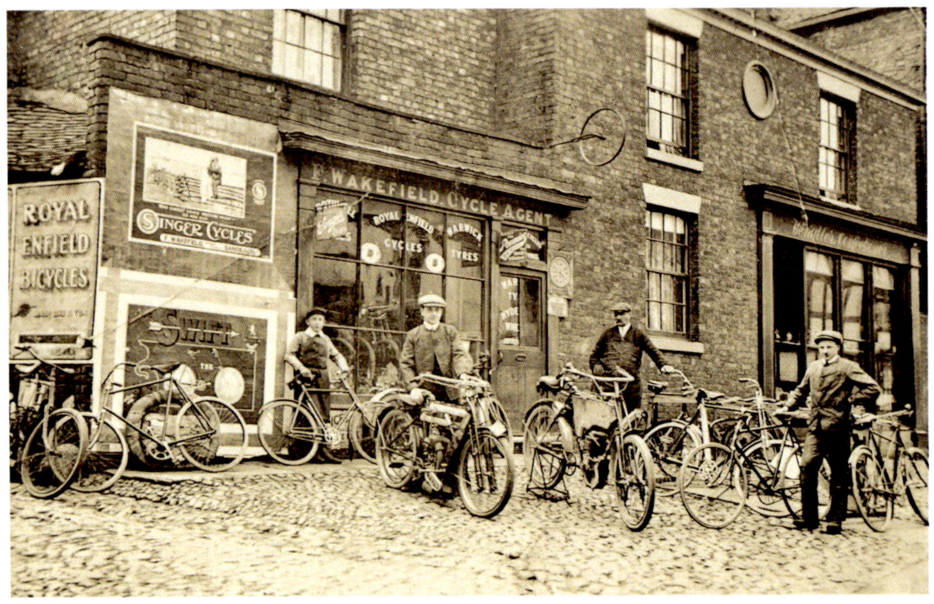

Wakefield's Cycles, 1910 and 2010

On the same side of the road as Billyard's, but a little further down, we find the shop premises of Frank Wakefield, a cycle agent. Eight years earlier the proprietor was Fred Wakefield. Next door is Thomas Venable's bakery and confectionery shop. In those long-gone days, cycling or bicycling (as it was correctly called) was very popular with both sexes. Ironmonger's and the like diversified into this new form of transport, adding motorcycles, as seen here, to their stock in trade. Some branched out even further to both car repairs and manufacture. By 1936 we find a George Wakefield, motor engineer, at 43 High Street.

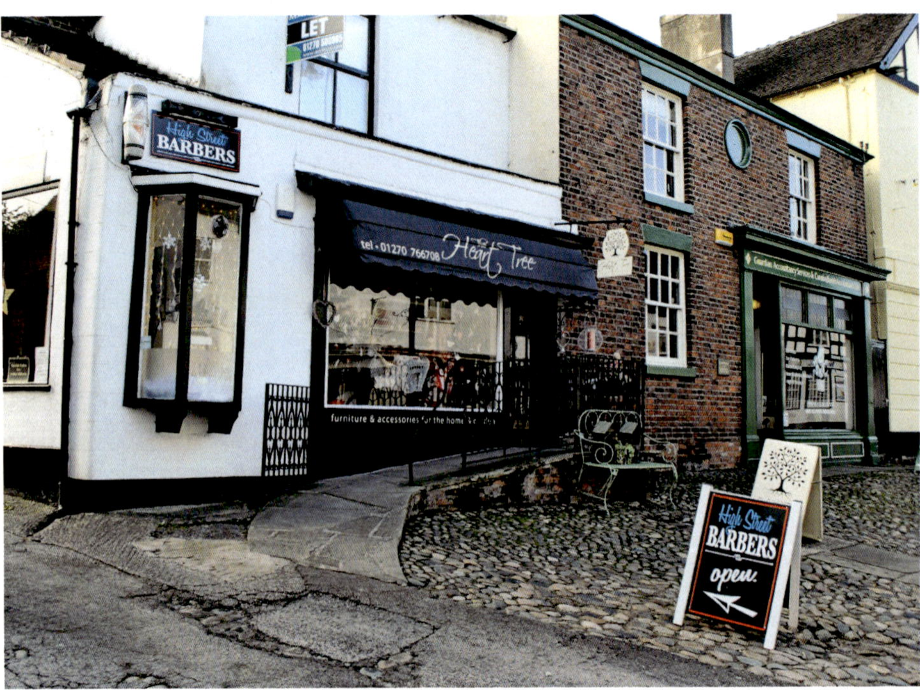

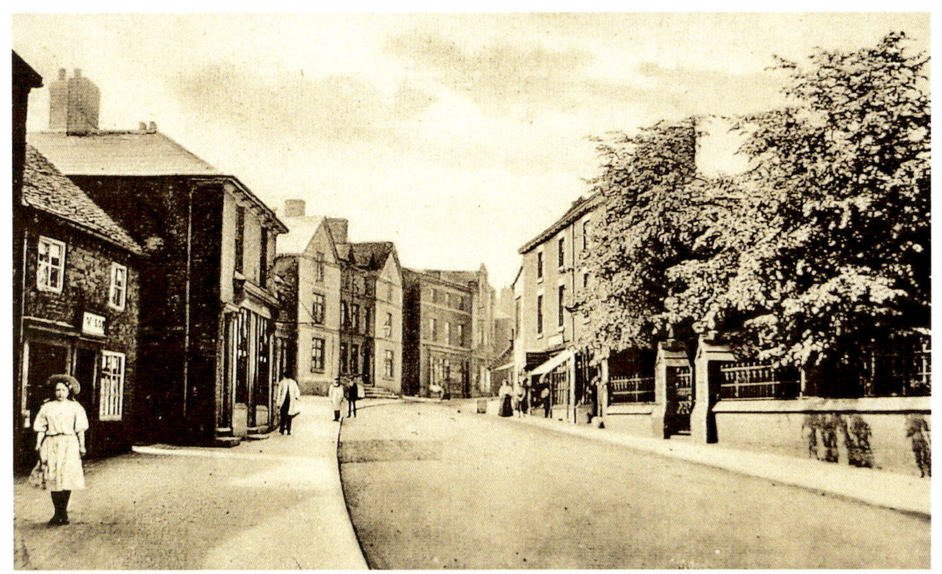

High Street Church Gates, 1910–20 and 2010

Facing up the High Street, we see the church gates on the right, while on the left in the distance is the large George Hotel that is about 300 years old and was once a coaching inn; it welcomed 'The Rocket' from Liverpool at 11 a.m., and the London coach called each day at 4 p.m. There is a little less foliage in the modern photograph, but other than that there is little change. The shop on the left, past the gates, is that of George Higgins, clog-maker and dealer of small and general ware.

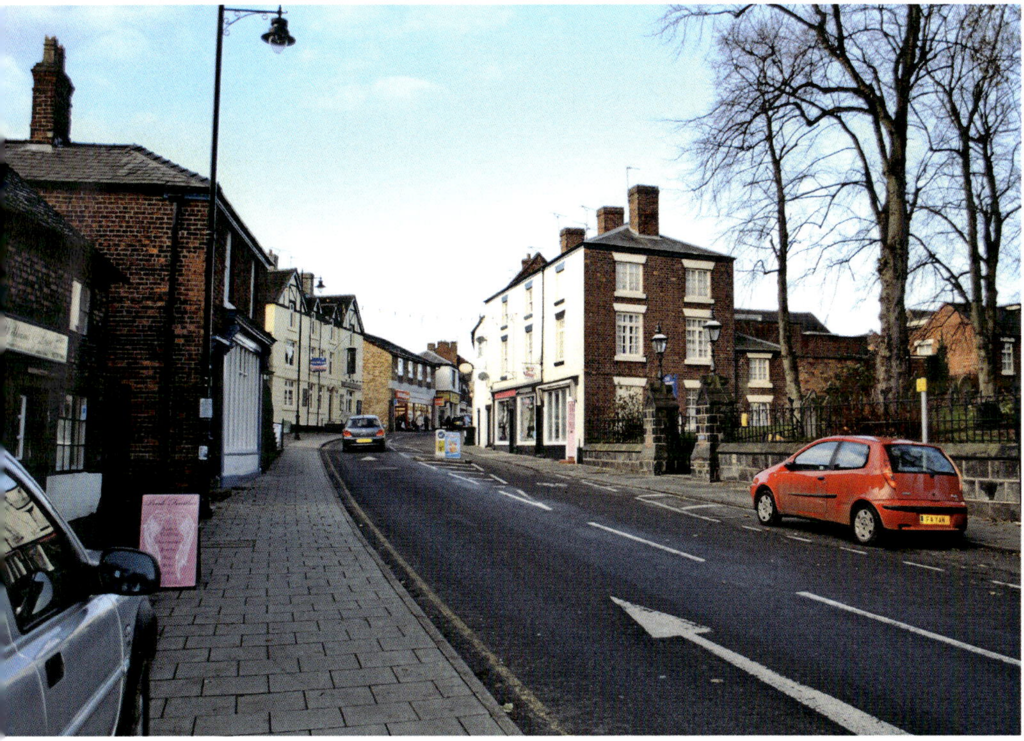

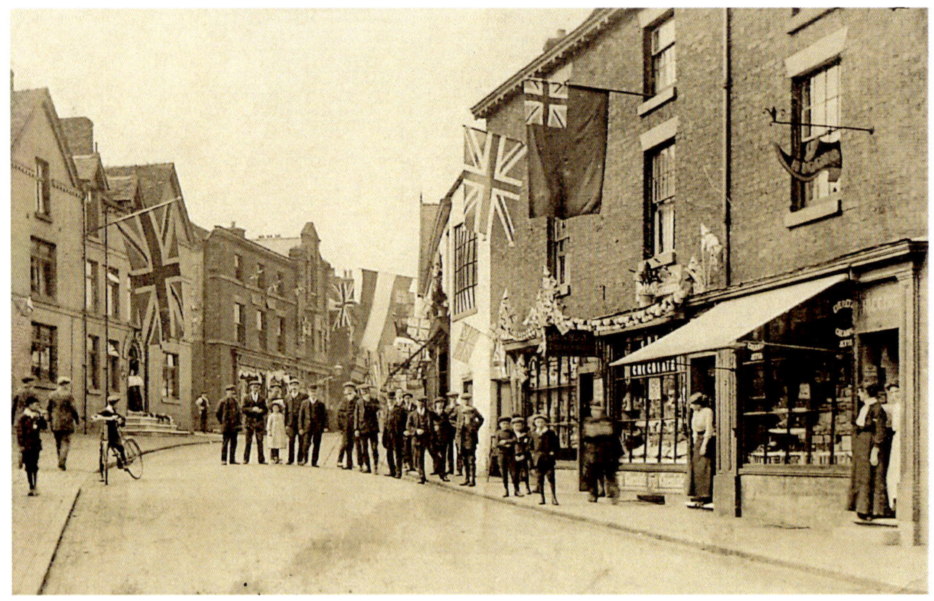

High Street Bend, 1911 and 2010

Still in the same location, but a bit closer, we see the bend in the High Street at this point with the George Hotel on the left. It is interesting to note that in one of the houses in this location in 1860 lived the Sibson sisters, two elderly maiden ladies who were very precise in their antiquated dress and manners and whose father was curate of the church for thirty-six years. Sara Sibson lived to be ninety and paid for the porch at the church. Her will provided for the building of the church on Sandbach Heath. The bunting would be for the celebration of King George V's coronation.

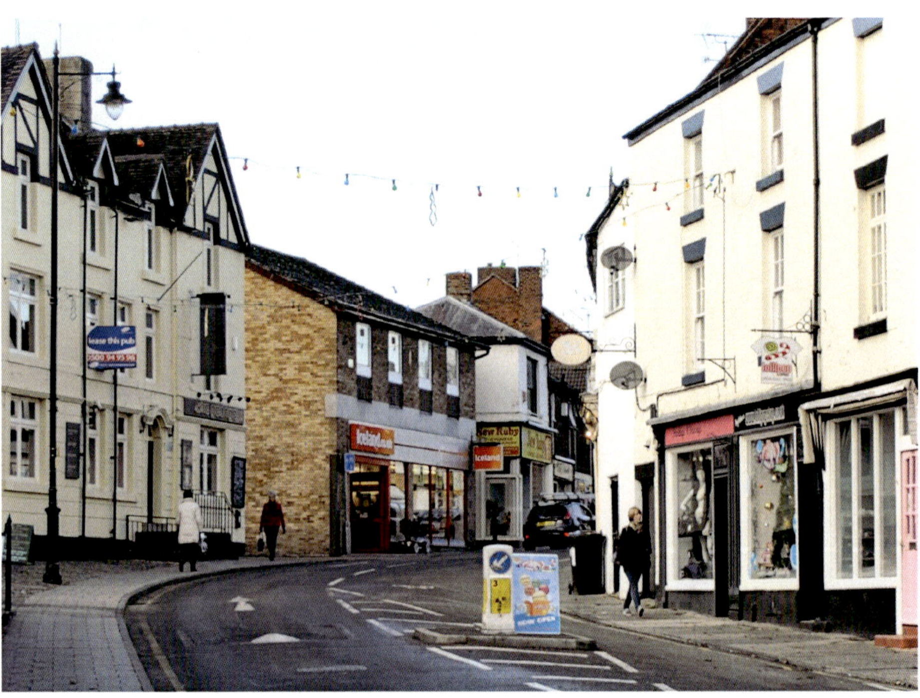

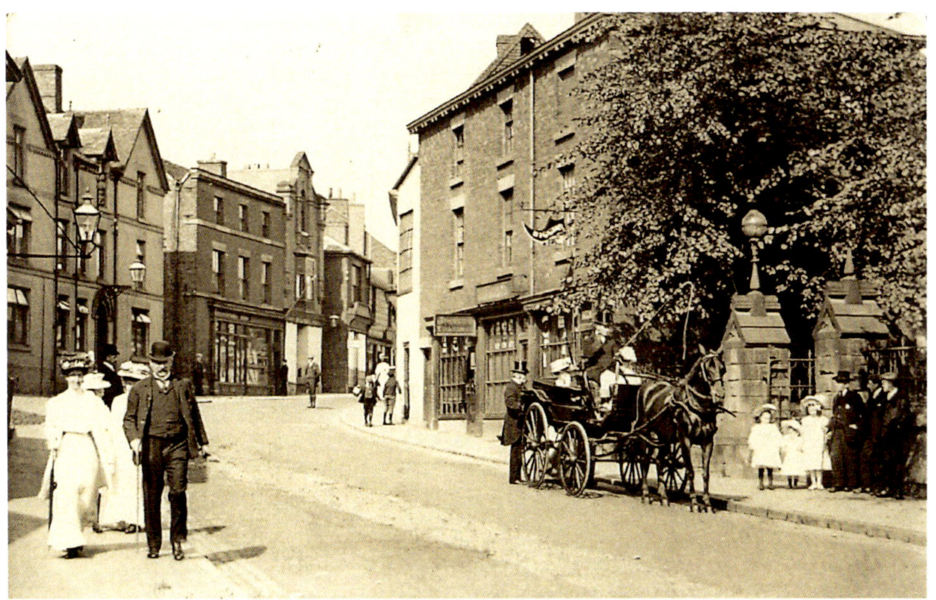

High Street with Carriage, Early 1900 and 2010

Here we have a last look at a High Street scene, around the turn of the twentieth century, with everyone in their finery. Outside the church gates is an expensive-looking coach whose occupants are important enough for passers-by to stop and stare – save for the important-looking gent who strides purposefully towards the camera. His wife walks beside him and presumably his daughters walk behind and try to keep up with papa and mama.

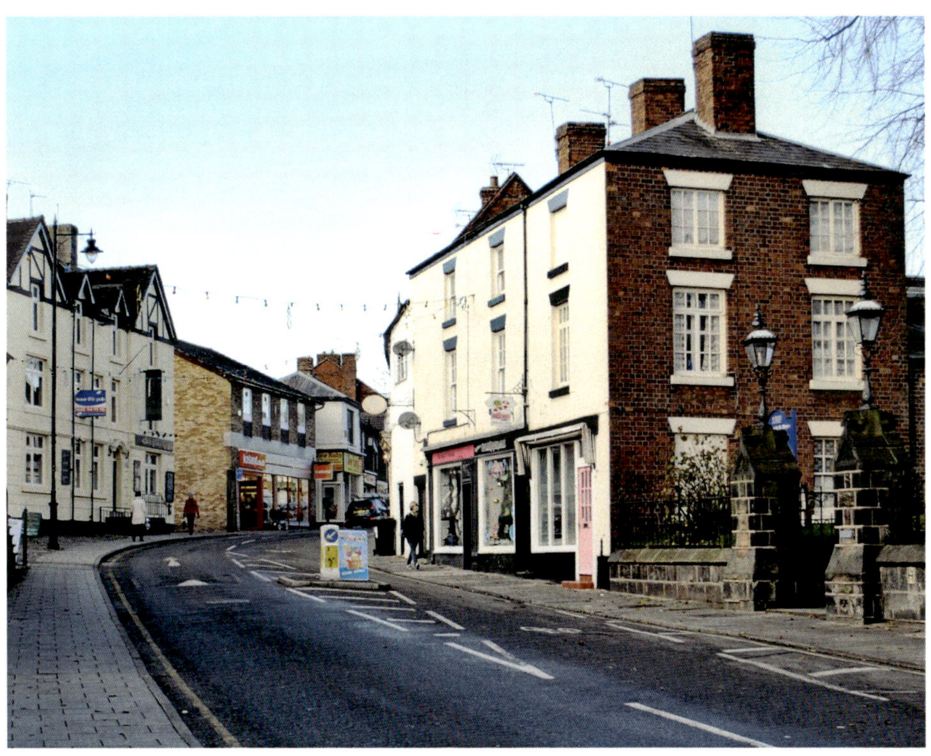

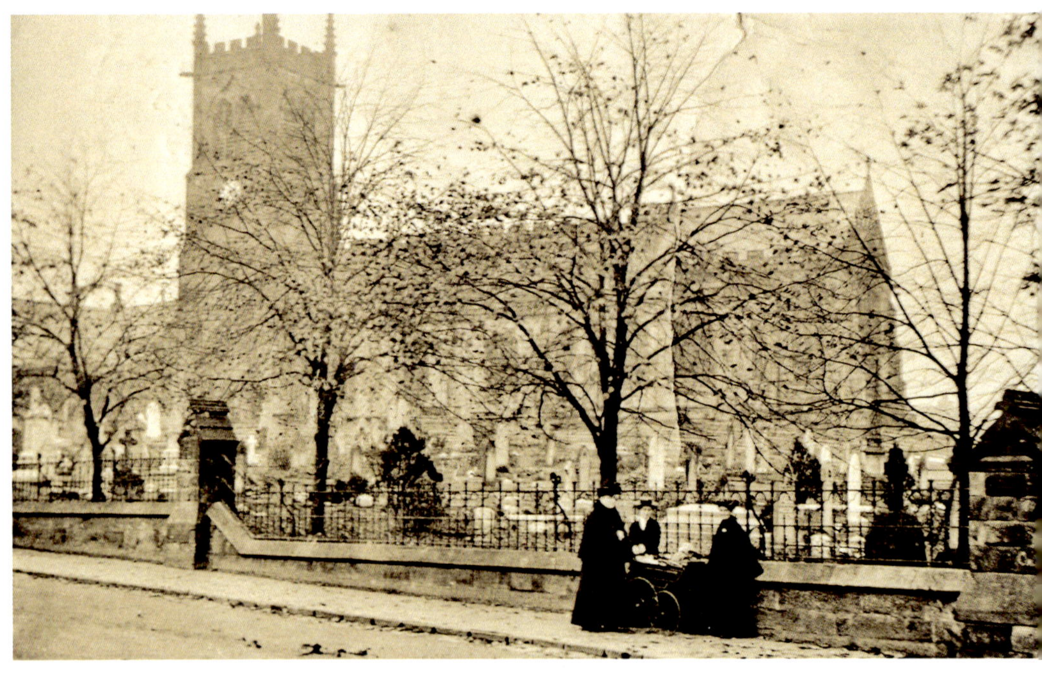

Sandbach Church, Early 1900s and 2010

These three ladies of the town have gathered with a pram by the church wall to have a 'clat' in Cheshire speak, or a chat for everyone else. They are dressed in the mourning attire popular at the time in view of either the recent death of Queen Victoria or, prior to that, in the fashion of the period. The perambulator appears to be one made in Warrington by the firm of Ashton Brothers & Phillips Ltd at their Osnath works.

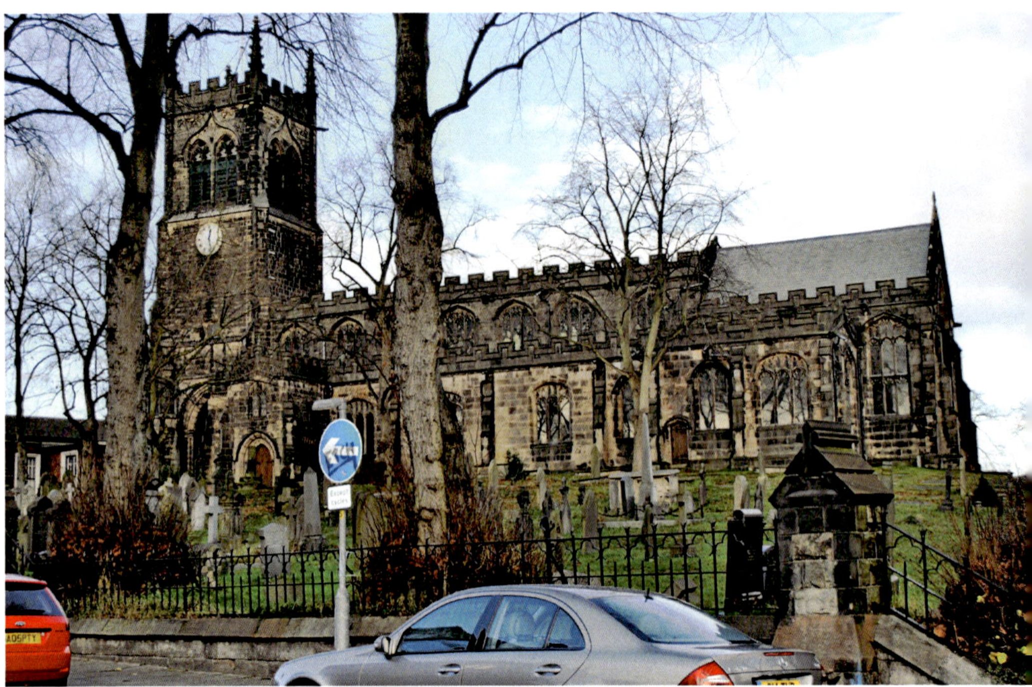

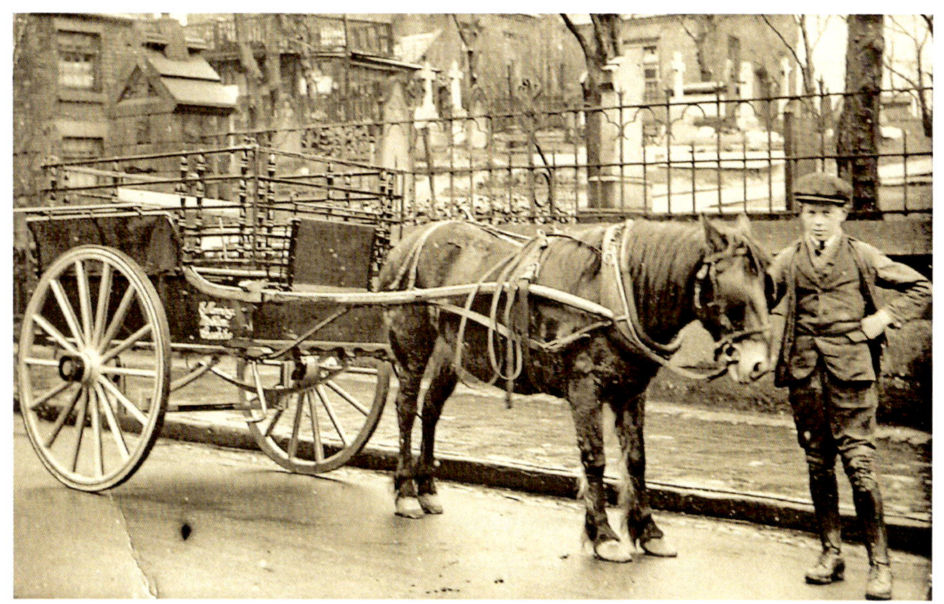

Pony and Trap, 1910–20 and 2010

Here we see a boy proudly holding the reins of his pony by the church wall. The trap that the pony is attached to seems to have railings around it – perhaps it has been converted to carry livestock. Either way, the boy is proud of his pony and trap and keen to show it off to the cameraman.

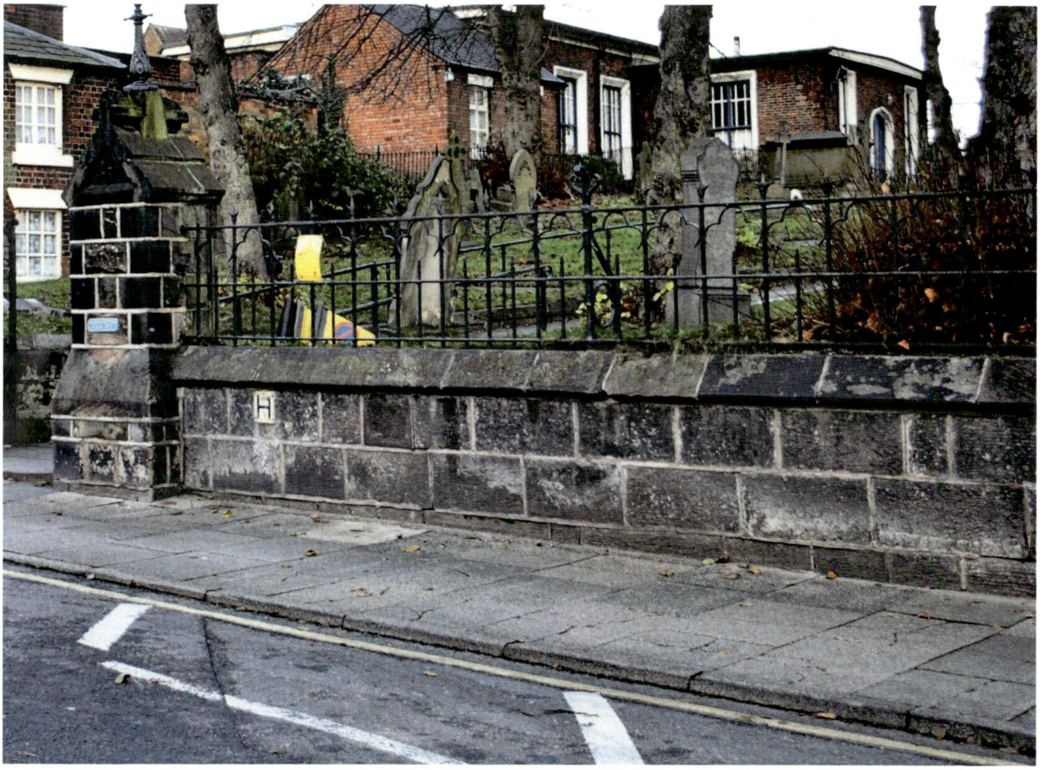

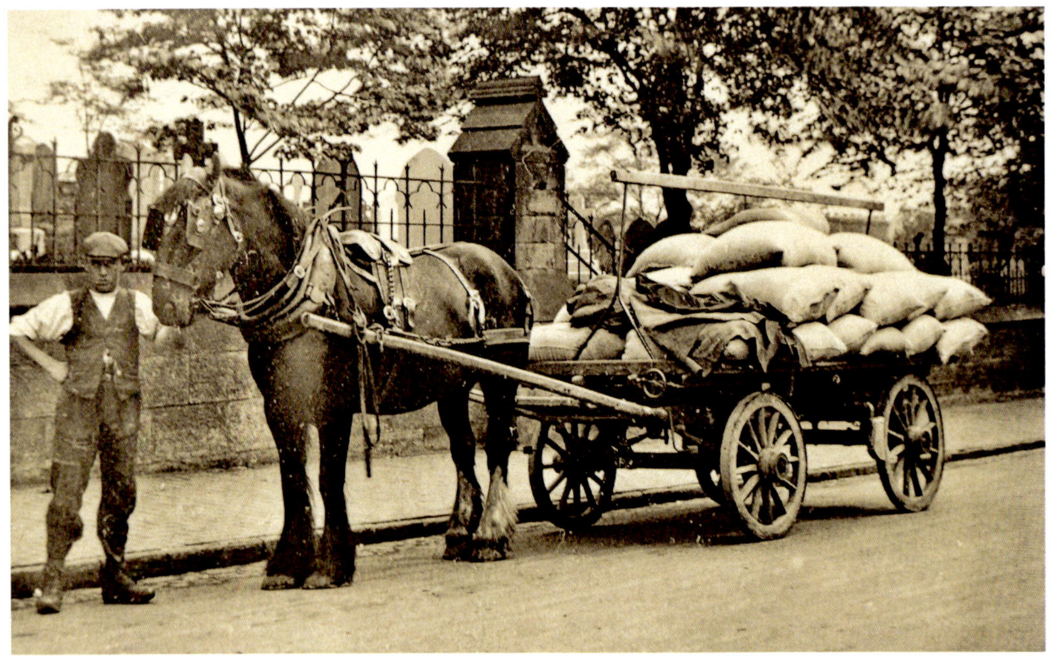

Horse and Lorry, 1920s–30s and 2010

Now we have an older man and his lorry and dray; this was the most common form of transport, even for some time after mechanically propelled transport arrived. It oozes historical charm, the man in his clogs with his jacket resting upon the sacks of corn as he stops for the convenience of the cameraman. The circular control wheel for the brake, which can be seen at the front, has probably been locked on due to the hill – a true snapshot in time.

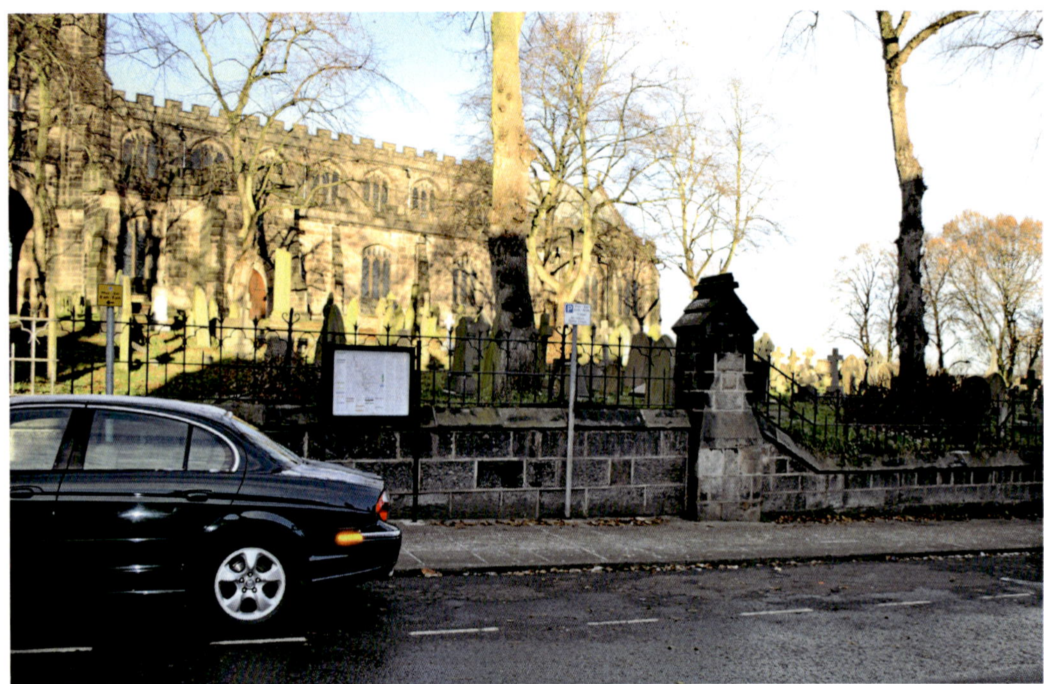

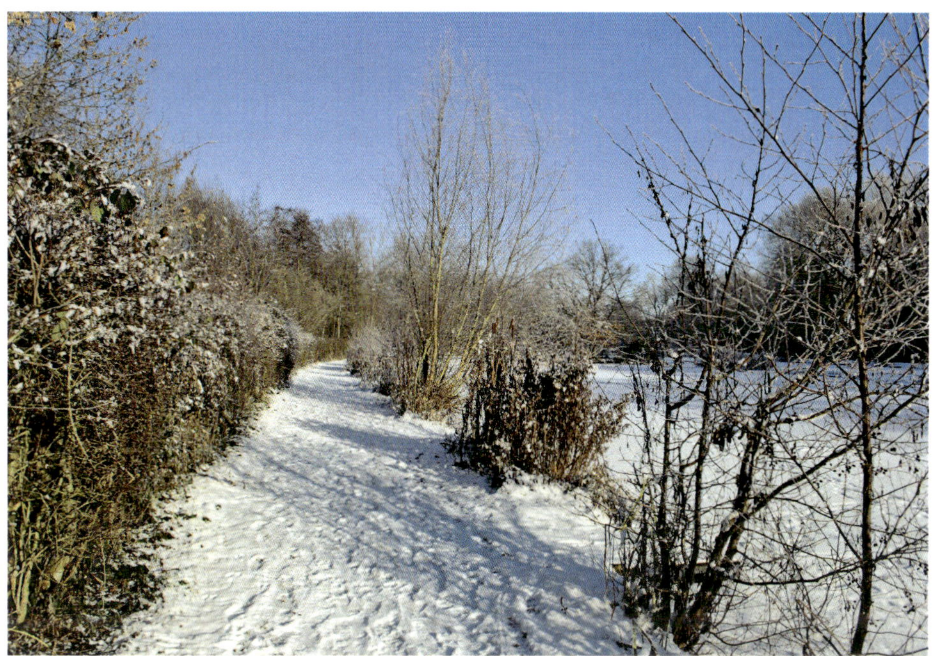

Dingle Lake, 2010 and Undated

Continuing on down the High Street and the steps near the end, we come to Bath Street and then Dingle Lake. Now used by fishermen, this lake and the area around it was once a hive of activity and fun, known as Happy Valley and Dingle Lake. It was a low field until Mr Walter Lea constructed an artificial lake with an island in the centre in about 1903. Around it stood an open-air swimming pool and a dance hall. In 1906 this was in full swing and remained so for thirty years. Mr Lea lived at the nearby villa named The Dingle. Bath Street is named for the public baths that were there for many years before the lake.

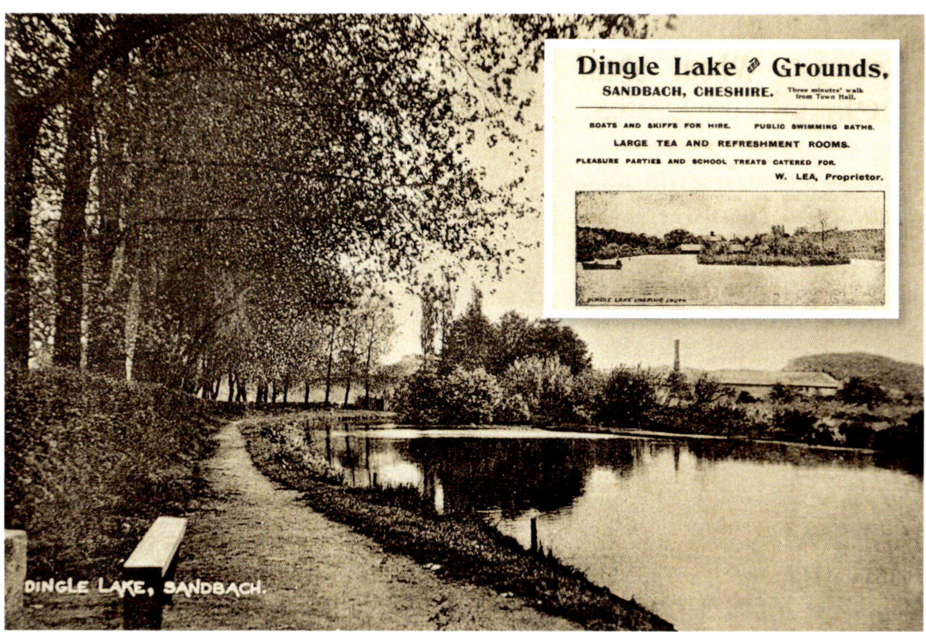

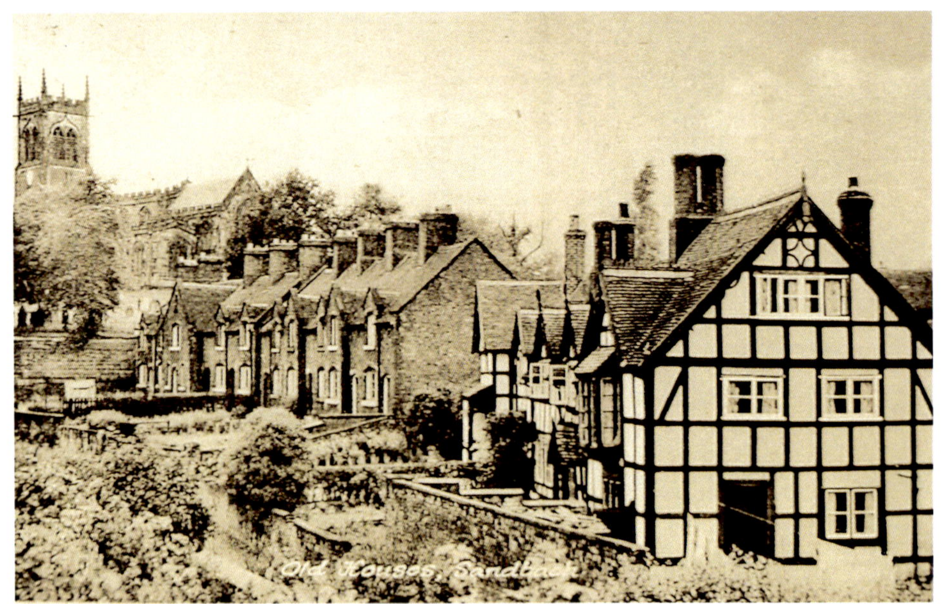

Front Street, Undated and 2010

Walking back now to the steps, we find Front Street, which runs parallel with the High Street back towards the churchyard where it ends. This street was once the main road in and out of the town from the south, but in 1875/7 it was closed off to enlarge the churchyard and became a cul-de-sac. At the same time the town spout, at which the town obtained its water supplies, was also redirected. This was originally at the foot of the steps. Some of the houses nearest the camera date from 1639.

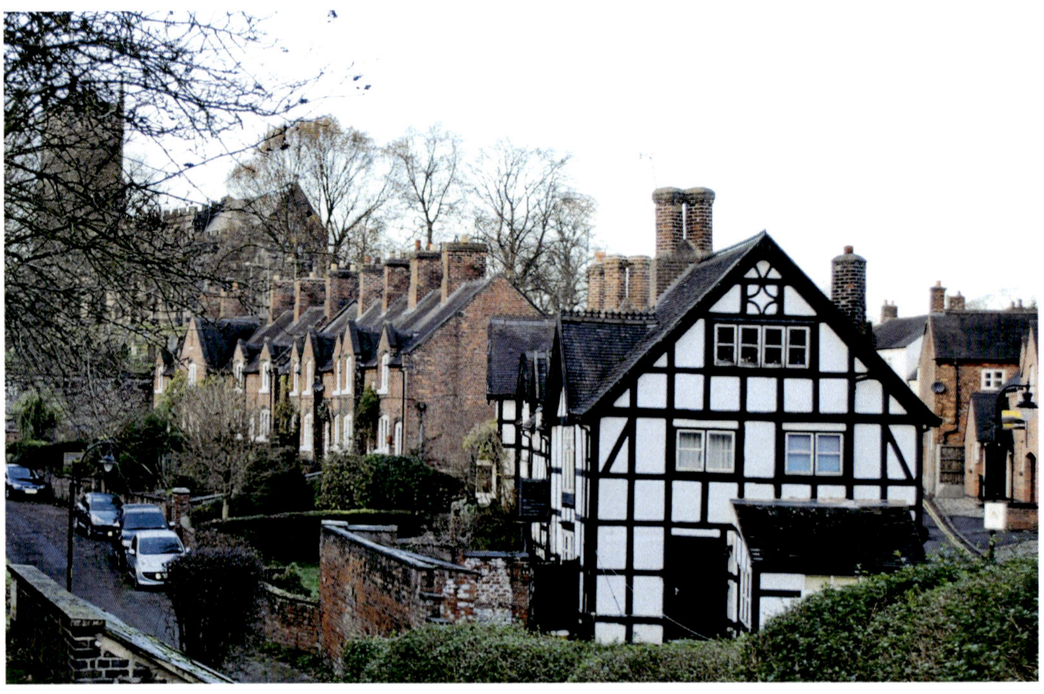

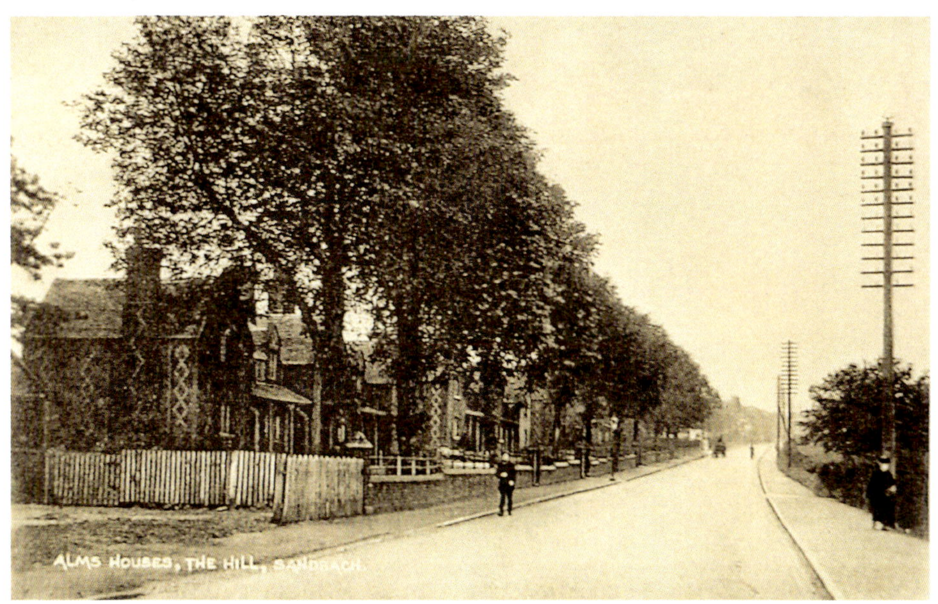

Almshouses, The Hill, 1900–15 and 2010

The Hill leads out of Sandbach to Newcastle-under-Lyne and on the left can be found this row of almshouses. They were built in 1865/7 at a cost of about £2,600 and were designed by a local architect, Thomas Stringer (although perhaps to the design of Sir George Gilbert Scott R.A.). In 1892 they were described as 'arranged for 20 inmates (either men or women)' that were elected by the governors of Sandbach Consolidated Charities and granted an allowance of six shillings per week.

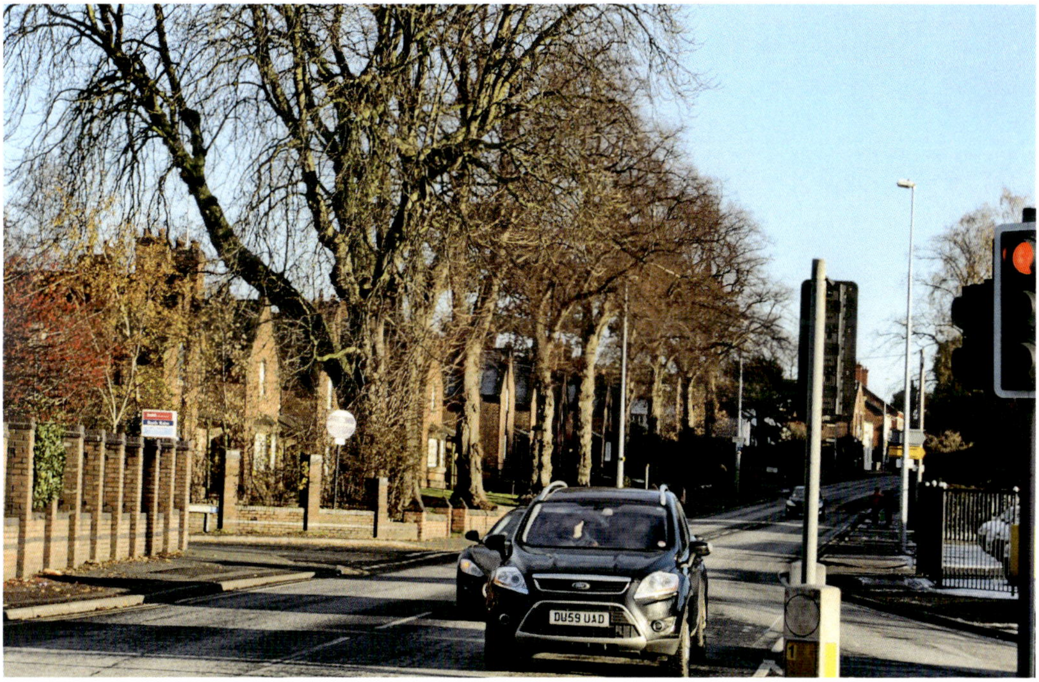

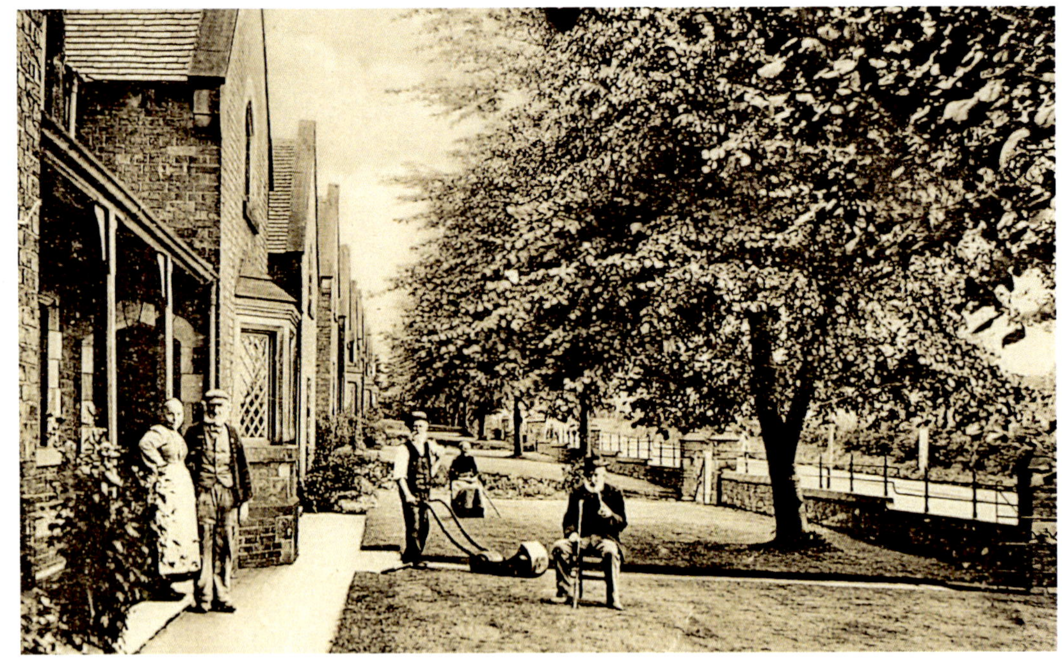

Almshouses, 1900–10 and 2010

Here we have closer look at some of the residents of the almshouses both relaxing and gardening at the turn of the last century. The grass is well cropped and the whole area is well kept. In the modern photograph little has changed and the gardens are still well tended. Now David and Christine Barnes live in one of the houses and they say that their house is comfortable and cosy.

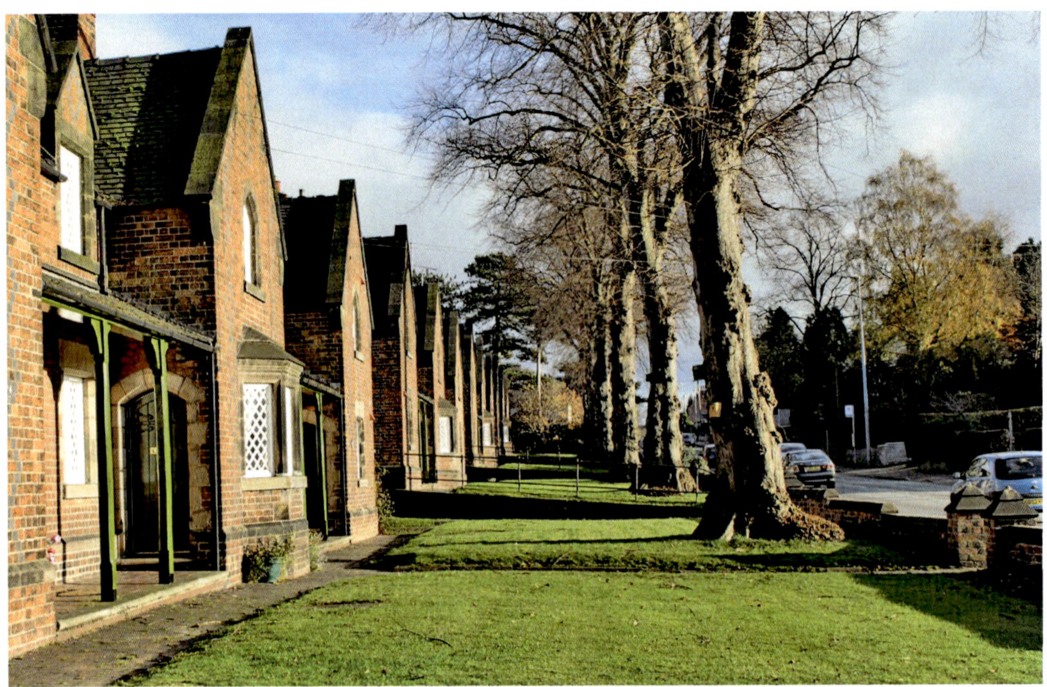

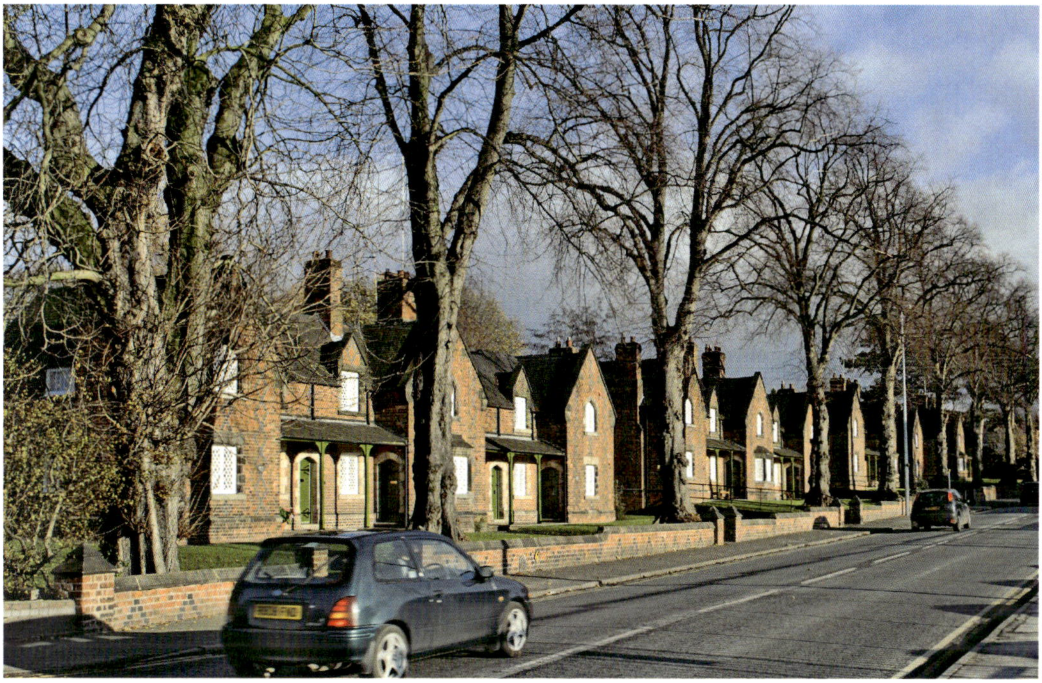

Almshouses, 2010 and Undated

A last look at the almshouses and we see that the trees have noticeably grown between the old and the new views. There is also a good view of the houses themselves and their excellent build-quality. The perimeter wall has also been lowered together with the gate posts: the ironwork went to help with the war effort. Before the almshouses, two poorhouses stood on the site.

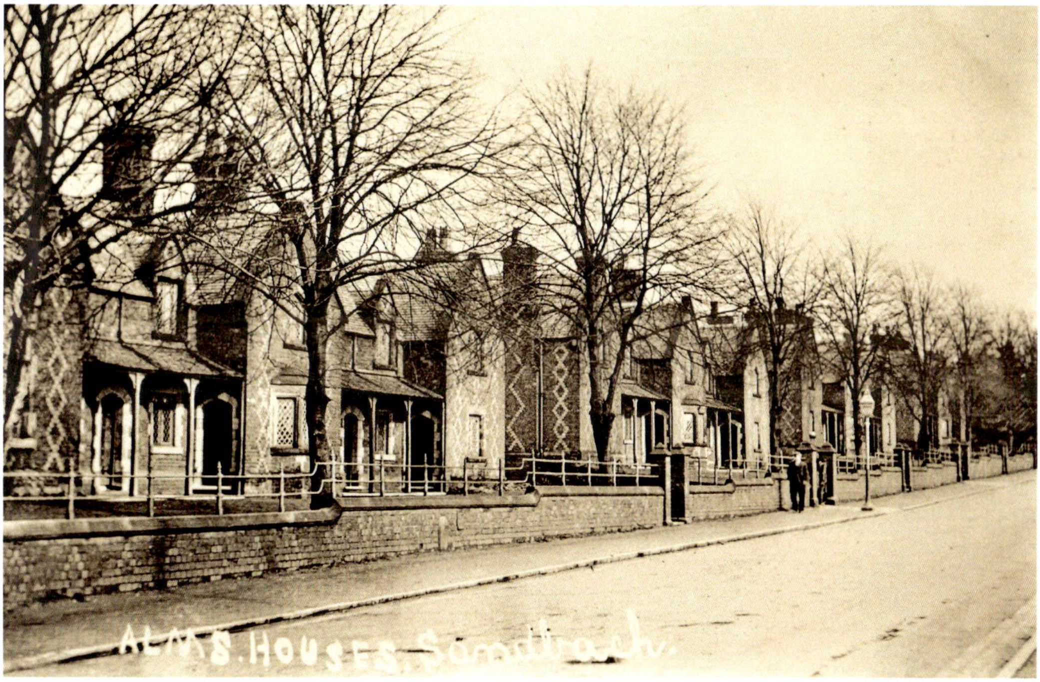

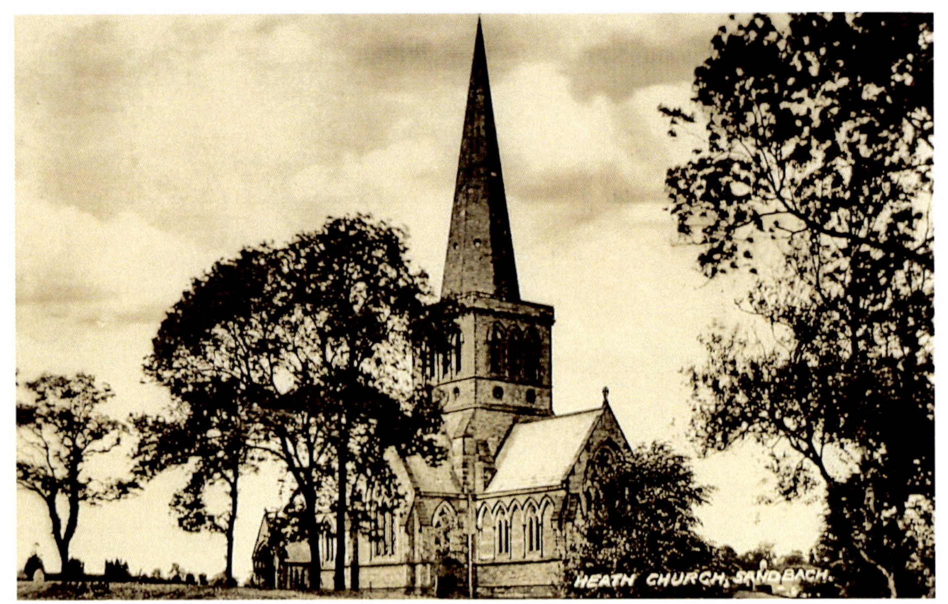

Sandbach Heath Church, Undated and 2010

The church of St John the Evangelist on Sandbach Heath was built and endowed in 1861 at the sole cost and in the will of Miss Sarah Sibson, daughter of the Revd John Sibson, curate of Sandbach for thirty-six years. He died in 1796, aged sixty. Miss Sibson died on 11 July 1857, aged ninety (her sister, as mentioned above, died aged sixty). The architect of the church was the late Sir Gilbert Scott R.A. and it cost £5,000. The Revd Sydney Henry Armitstead M.A. was the first vicar.

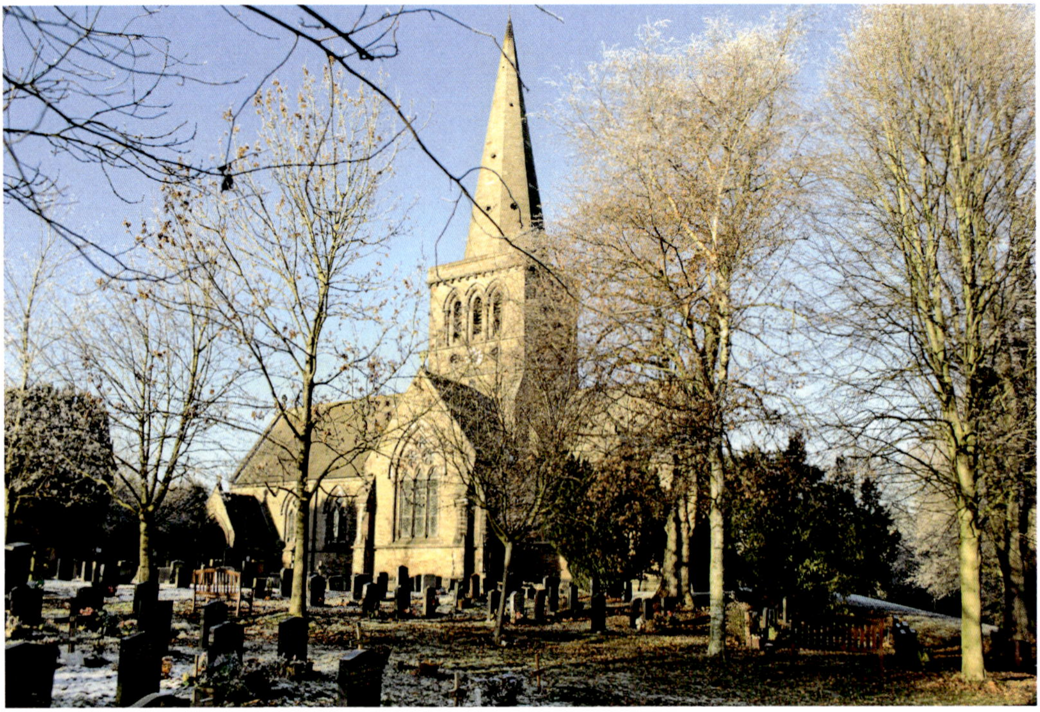

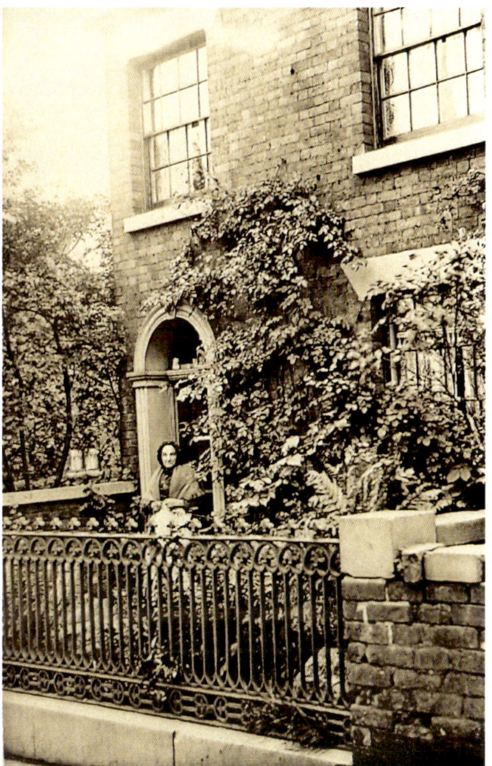

11 Bell View Terrace, Early 1900s and 2010
On the corner of Belle View Terrace and Crewe Road, Dr Charles Latham, 'old Dr Latham', had his medical practice. After his death on 6 July 1907, Latham Memorial was set up by the townspeople in his honour. This is mentioned earlier in the book. These photographs are of No. 11 Belle View Terrace. In the old photograph, the aged resident stands in the doorway, while foliage bedecks the front of the house.

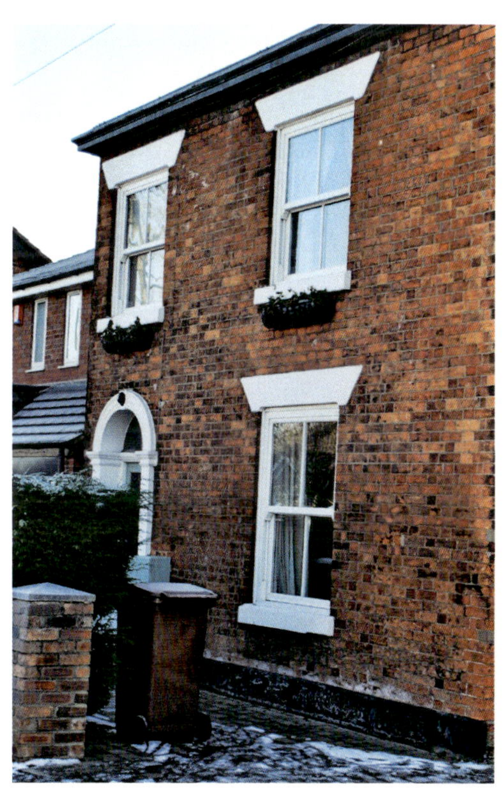

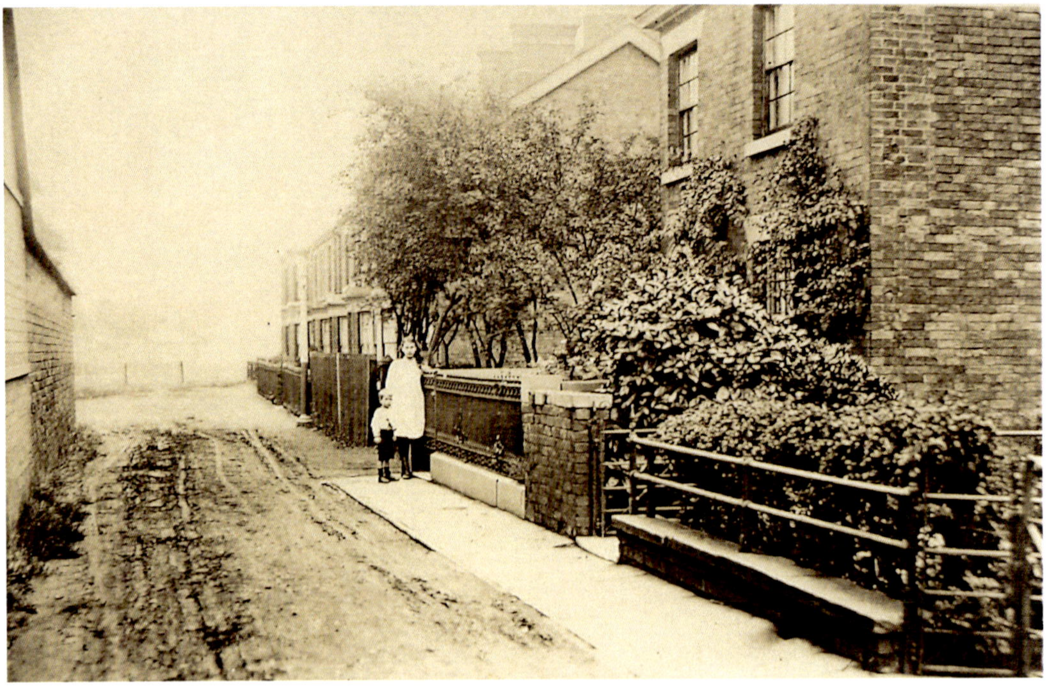

Belle View Terrace, Undated and 2010

Still in the road made famous in days past by Dr Latham, we see a young girl and small boy standing outside one of the houses. The new photograph was taken in the freezing winter of 2010. This terrace is just out of the town on Crewe Road on the way to Wheelock.

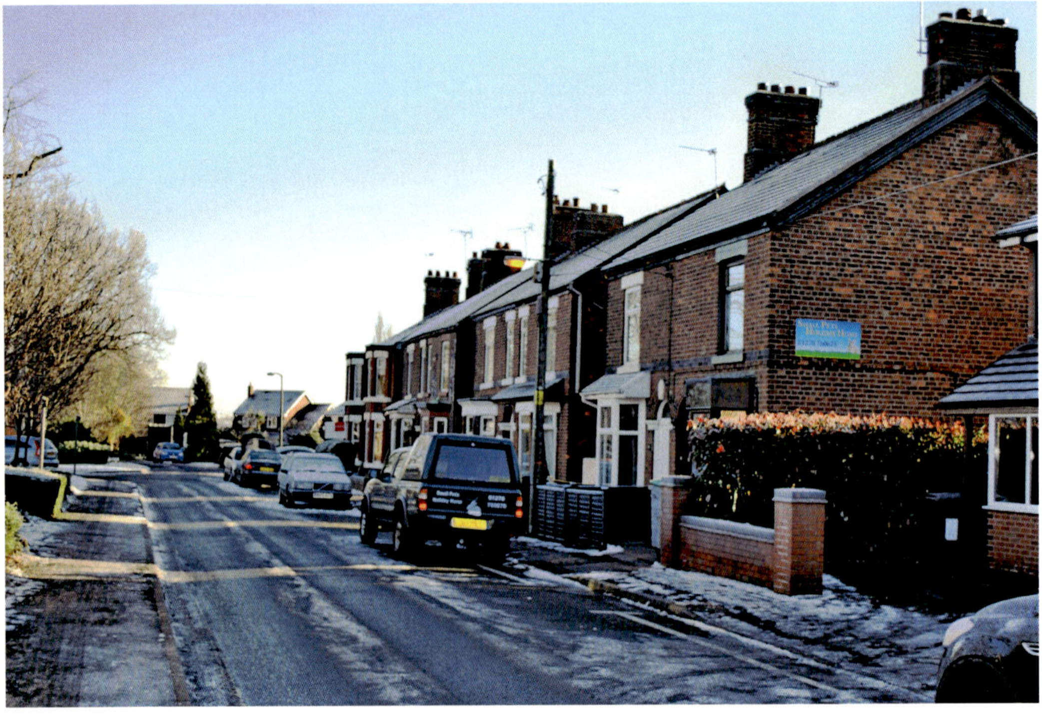

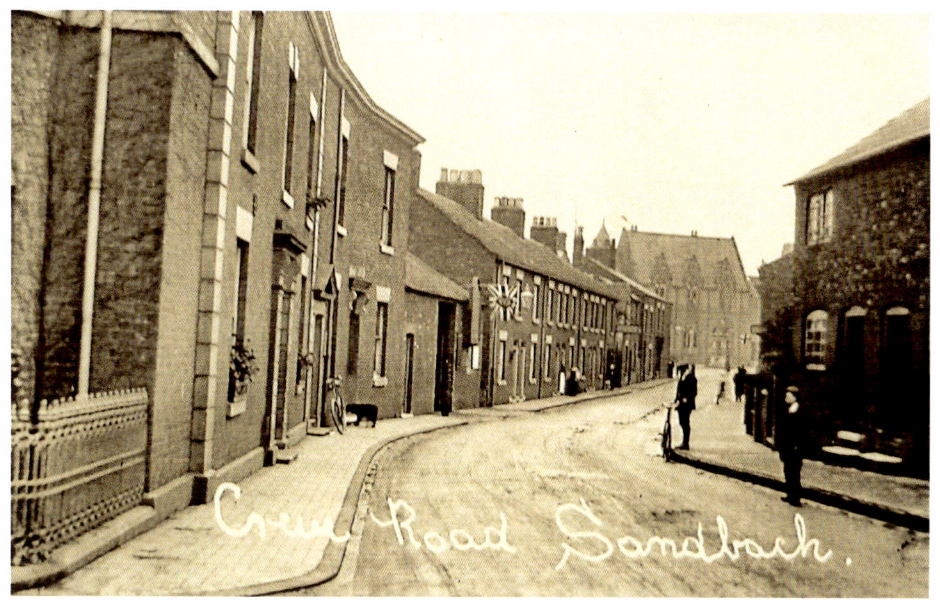

Crewe Road Into Town, 1919–20 and 2010

Just before we continue on our journey to Wheelock, we turn and look back into town to see what changes have been made over the years. The most obvious is the roundabout which the row of terraced houses has been demolished to make way for. Buildings on the right have gone as well, and the iron railings on the immediate left no longer brighten the view. The Literary Institute can be seen in the far distance; it was erected in 1857 from plans drawn up by Sir George Gilbert Scott R.A. and it housed a reading room, billiard hall, county court and library.

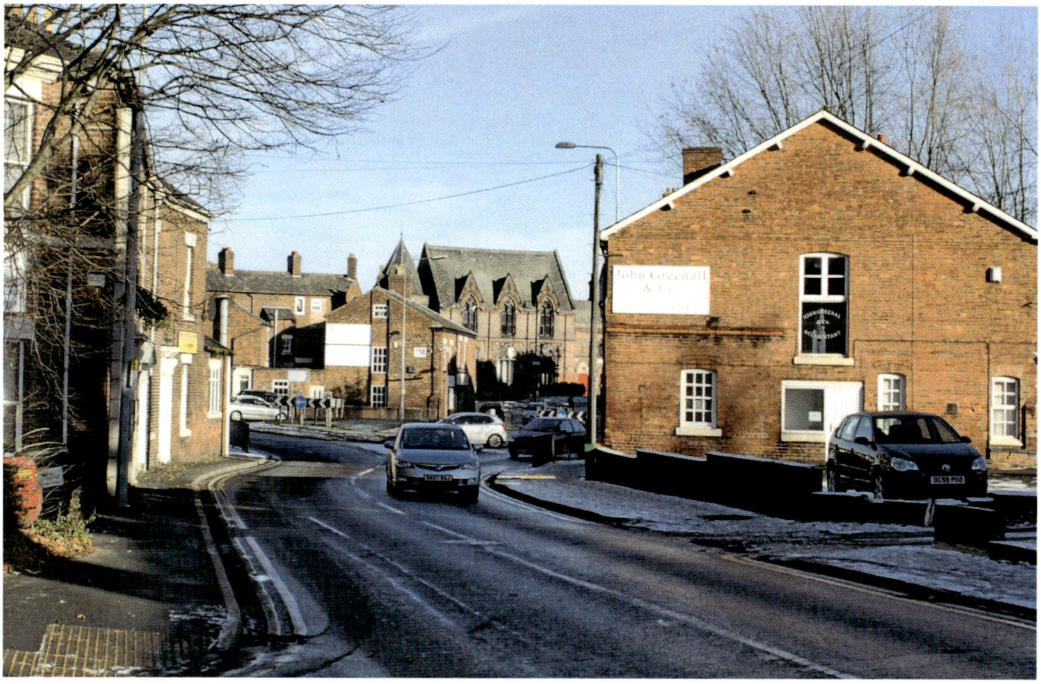

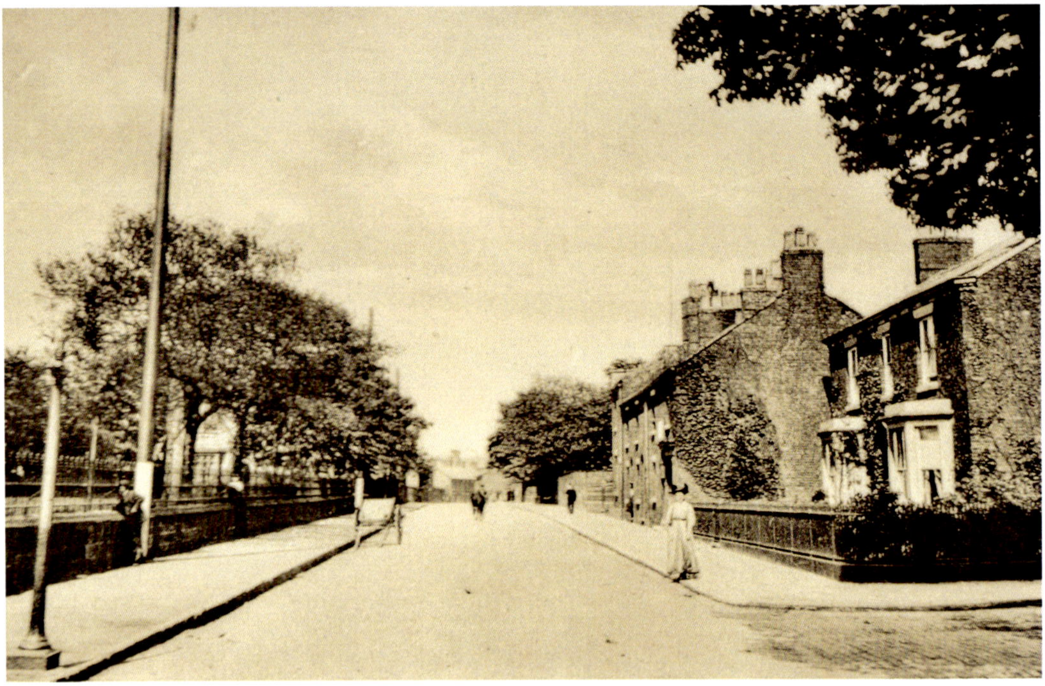

Cricketers Arms, Early 1900s and 2010

A little further along Crewe Road, we come to the grammar school on the right, but opposite the grounds is this double-fronted house, set back from the road, as well as the Cricketers Arms public house. When the old photograph was taken this was classed as a beerhouse and Edward Butler was the licensee.

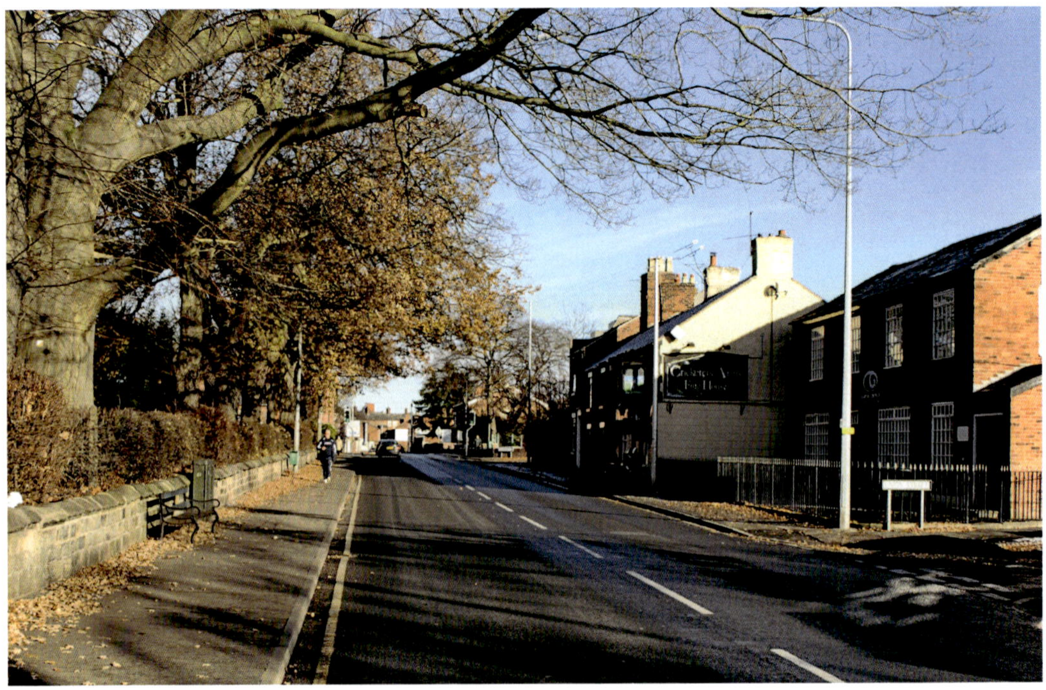

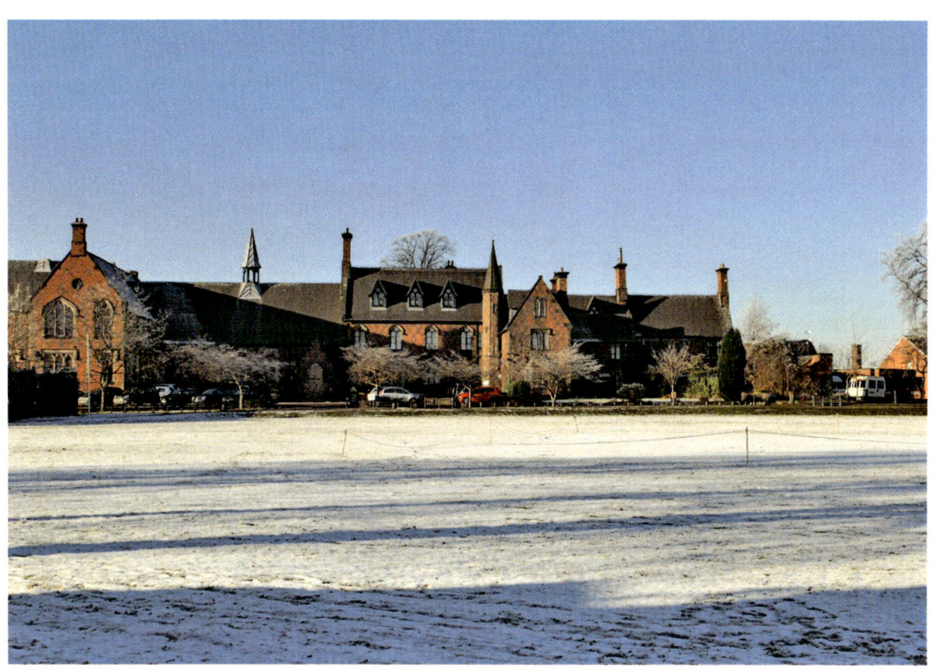

Sandbach School, 2010 and Early 1900s

Now we turn and look across the road at the prestigious school building and grounds of Sandbach School. Sandbach has had a school from around 1606 and it was funded by the gentry of the town. In 1848 an Act of Parliament was passed to provide for better administration. Some very wise investments had been made and land was sold at a vast profit in Burslem and Cobridge for mining and pottery works. The money rolled in and in 1849–50 the school seen in the photographs was built, the architect once again being Sir George Gilbert Scott R.A. The school has always been one of the top schools in Cheshire and continues to serve the town well.

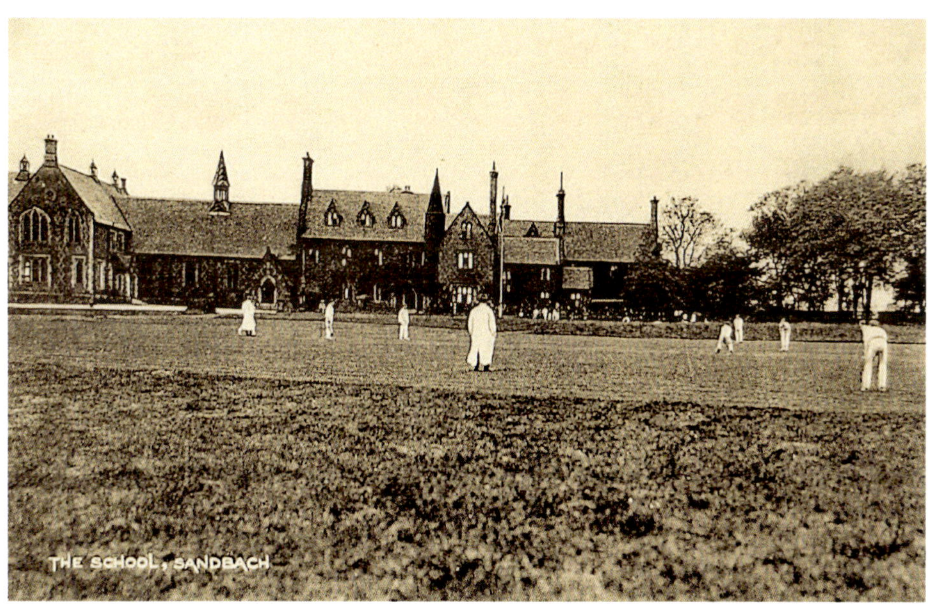

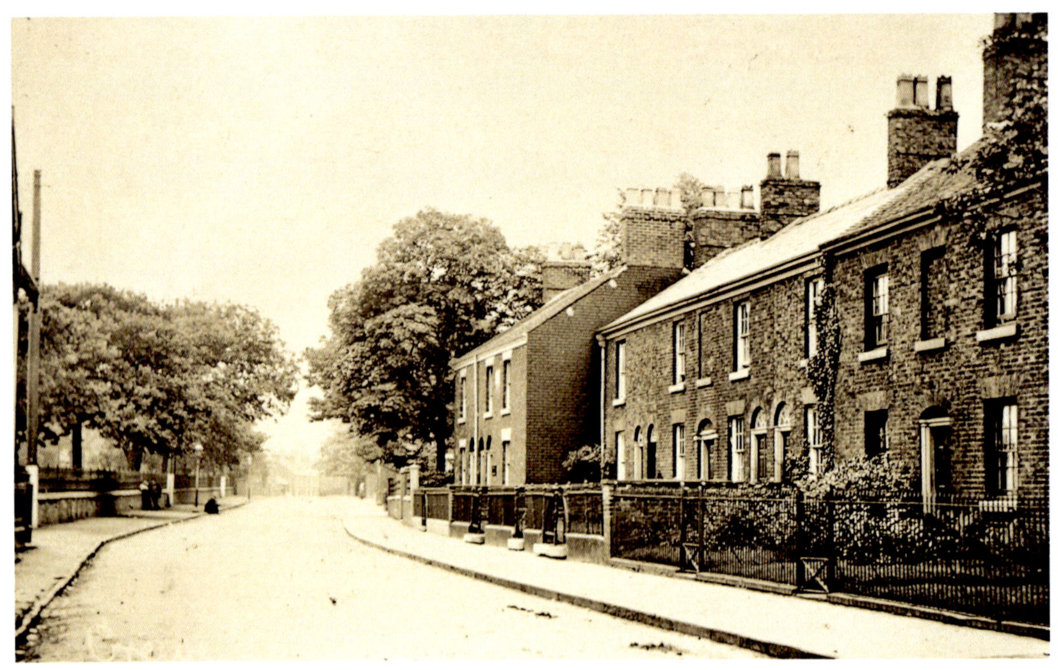

Crewe Road, Early 1900s and 2010

These houses are situated almost opposite the school gates as we look back towards Sandbach. The old photograph, taken around the turn of the last century, depicts a quiet road with a covering of horse manure. There are also attractive and sturdy iron railings and a few pedestrians, possibly waiting for transport into town at what in the new photograph is a better signposted bus stop.

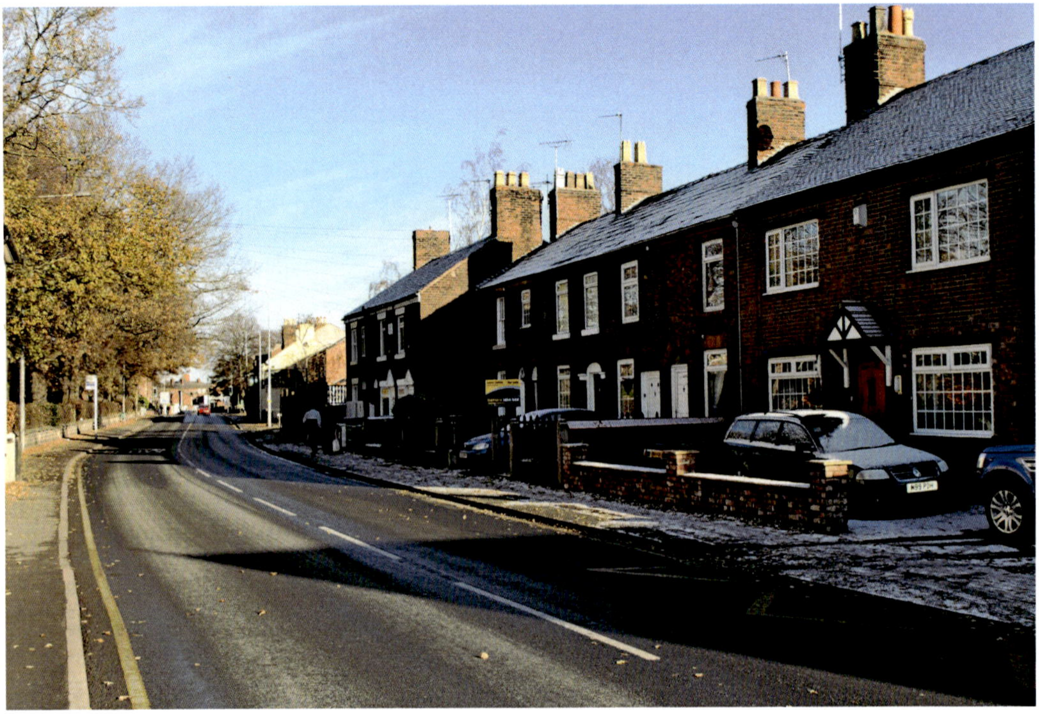

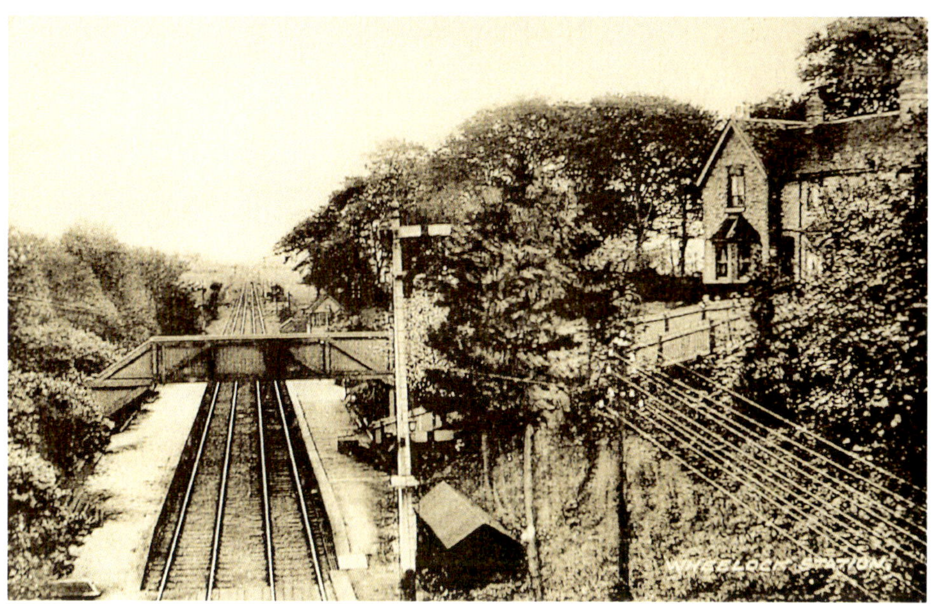

Wheelock & Sandbach Station, Early 1900s and 2010

We continue our journey towards Wheelock and arrive at FastFit tyres on the left (see inset below). This business occupies the buildings of Wheelock & Sandbach railway station which, along with this short line, was built by the North Staffordshire Railway Company in 1852. The line ran between the Harecastle–Crewe line and Sandbach with an intermediate station at Lawton and later Hassall Green and a goods yard at Ettiley Heath. It was known as The Salt Line as one of its initial jobs was to convey salt from Northwich and Middlewich to the Potteries and to serve the salt works in the area.

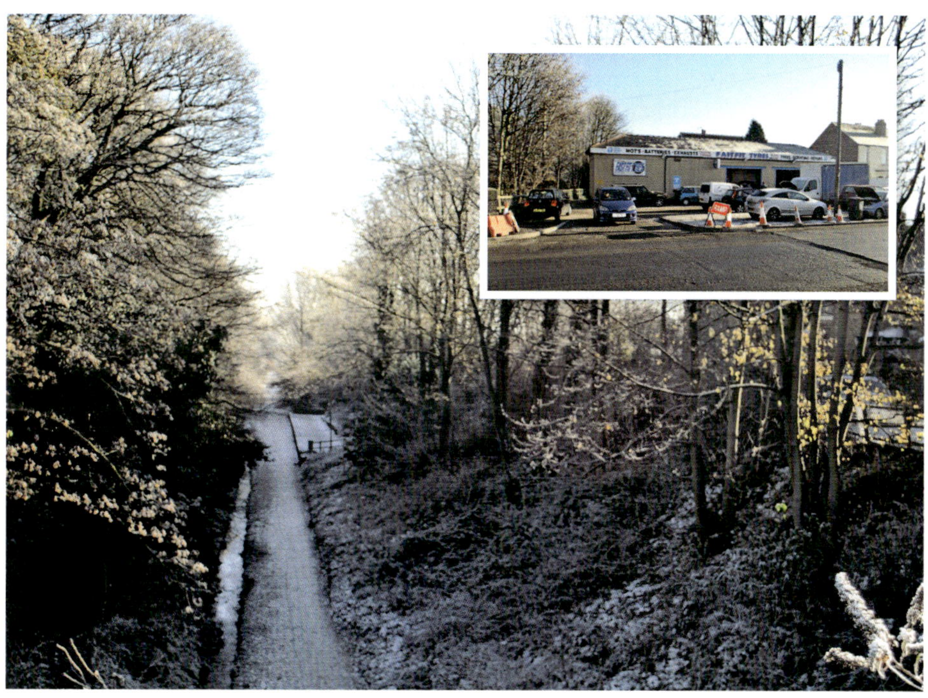

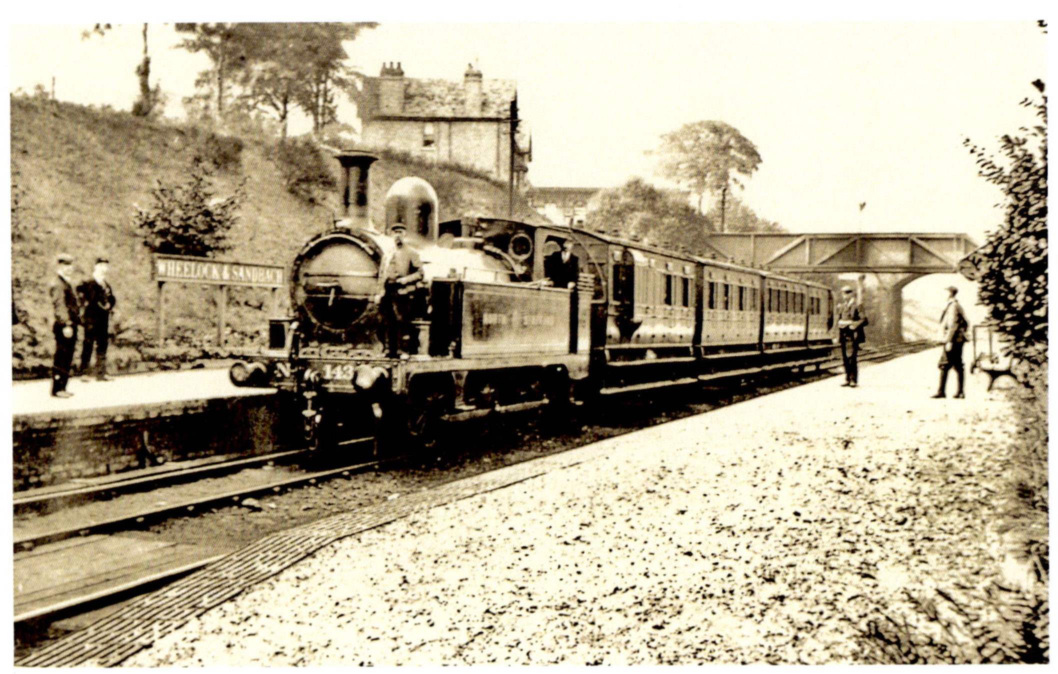

Platform at Wheelock & Sandbach Station, Early 1900s and 2010

Down the steep path now to the platform and in the old photograph one of the North Staffordshire engines has arrived with a short train to Sandbach. Passenger services were not introduced until 1893 and lasted through to 1930. The line now forms a pleasant walk and the platform has been tidied up, with the opposite platform removed.

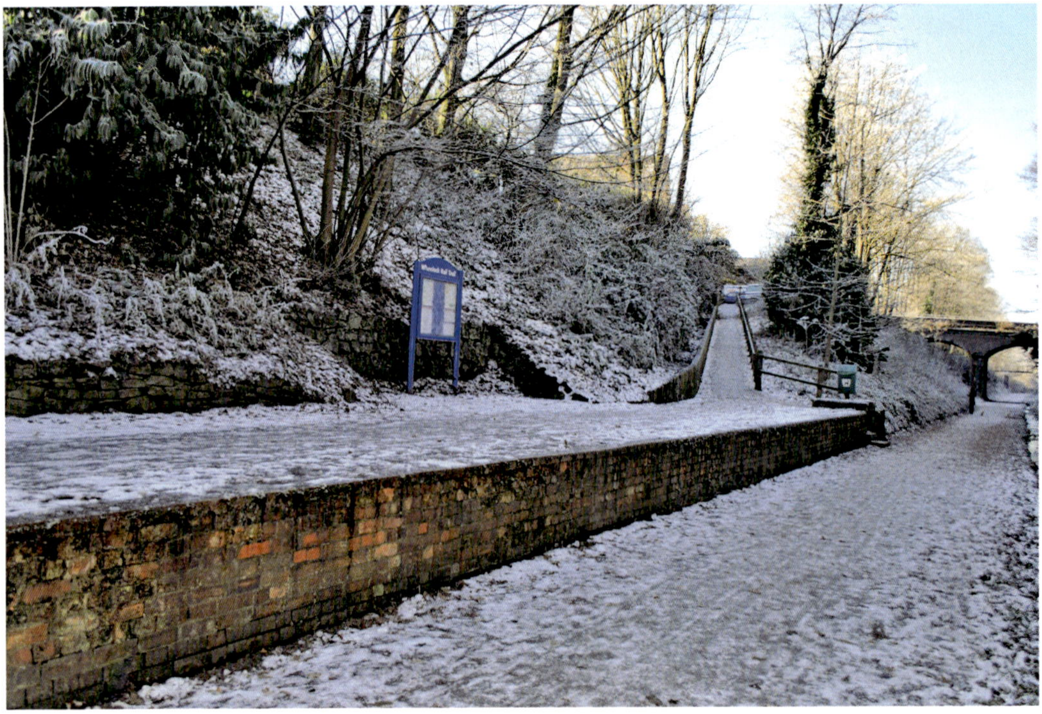

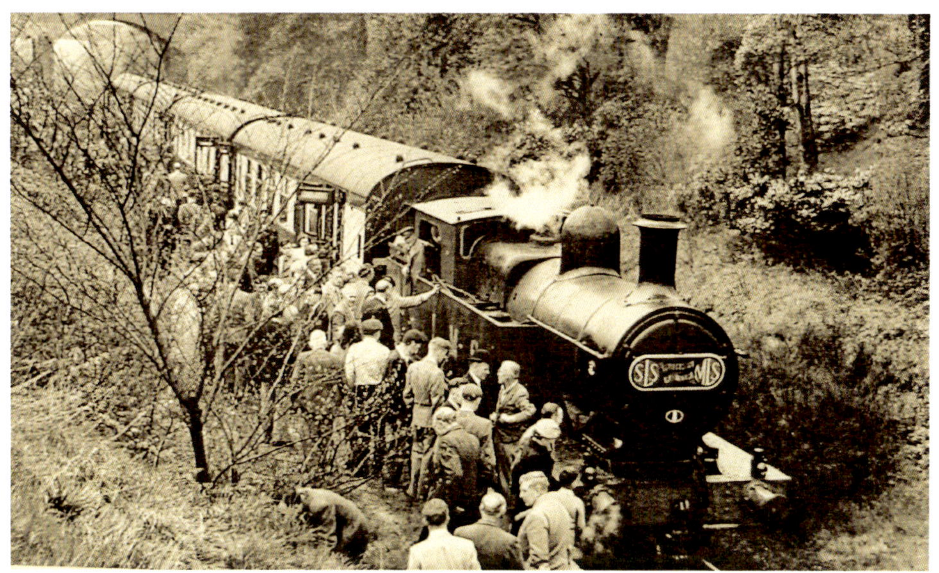

Rail Tour at Wheelock & Sandbach, 1952 and 2010

This photograph can be a quiz question for our rail experts out there. The photograph shows a train at the platform surrounded by enthusiasts. The photograph is thought to be of the last passenger train on the line: a rail special of 1953. Here is the evidence: the carriages and clothing is correct for the period. The opposite platform has gone and is overgrown. We know that passenger working ended on 28 July 1930 and the line occasionally carried freight until the early 1970s. The SLS/MLS were enthusiasts' organisations. The engine is from Warrington Dallam (8B), but why does it have LMS on the side and not a British Railways logo, since that is what the LMS became part of in 1949? It's over to you.

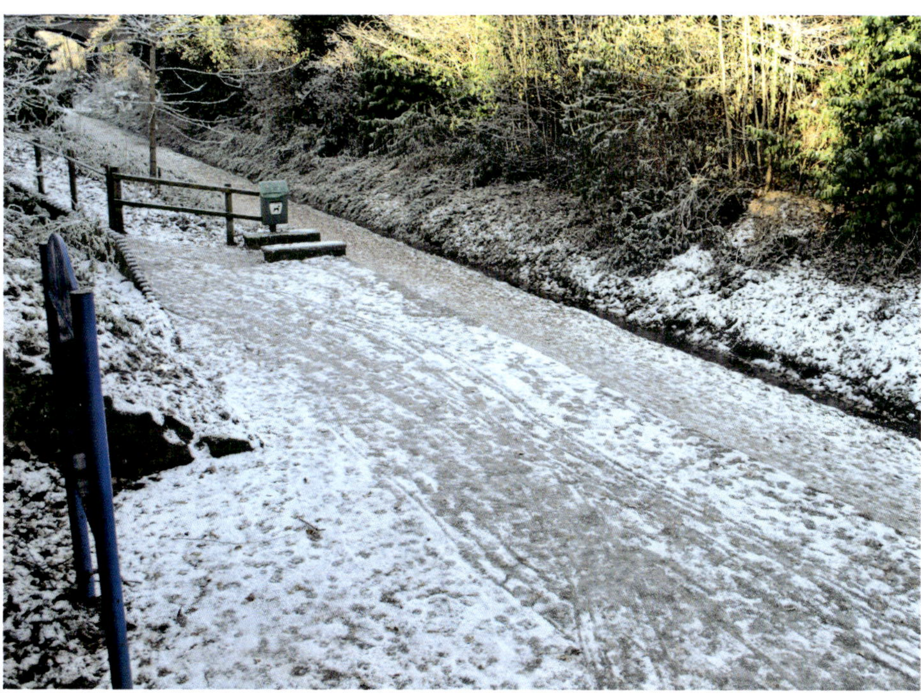

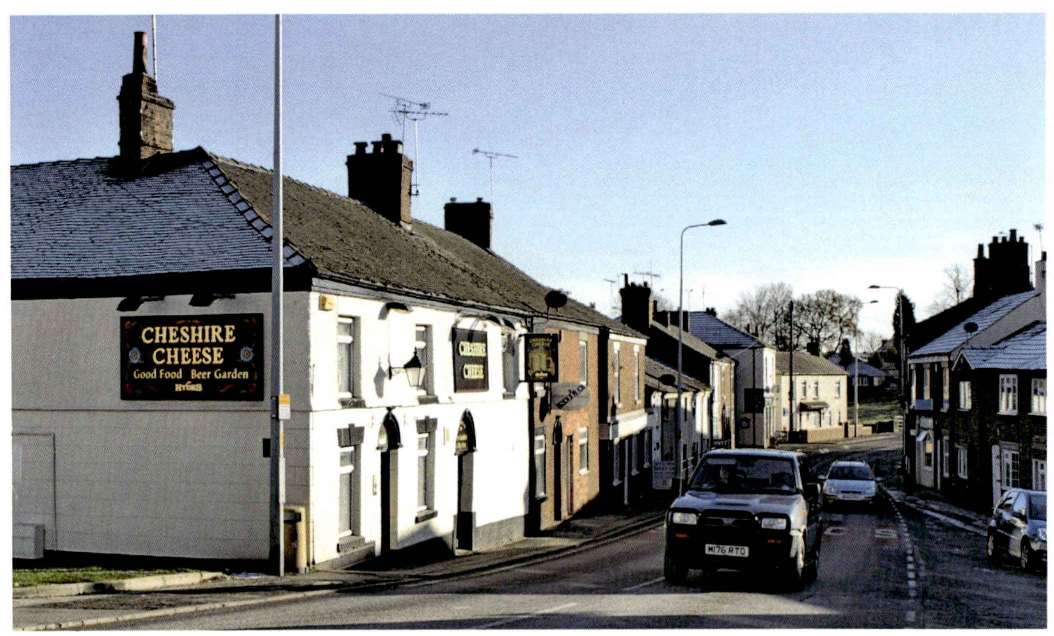

Cheshire Cheese, Wheelock, 2010 and Early 1900s

Arriving now in Wheelock, we stop on the canal bridge and look down into the village. The Cheshire Cheese pub on the left has been altered somewhat over the intervening hundred or more years. The licensee at the time of the old photograph was Fred Thomas and the road has become less busy in terms of pedestrians but more busy as regards traffic. The photographer of old is able to stand in the centre of the road and attract the attention of the many children in their smart clothes.

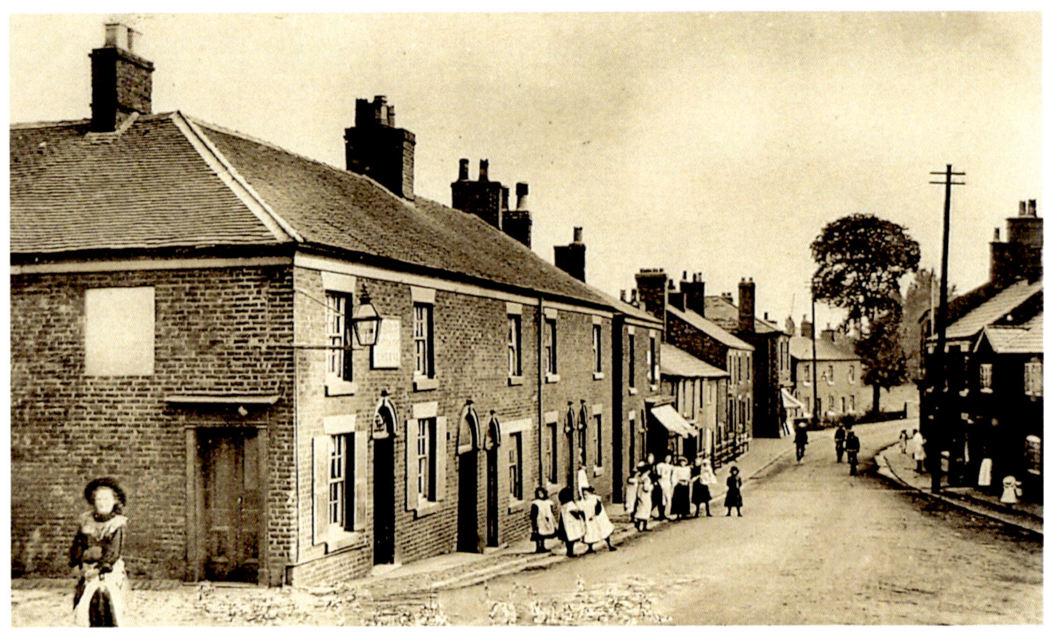

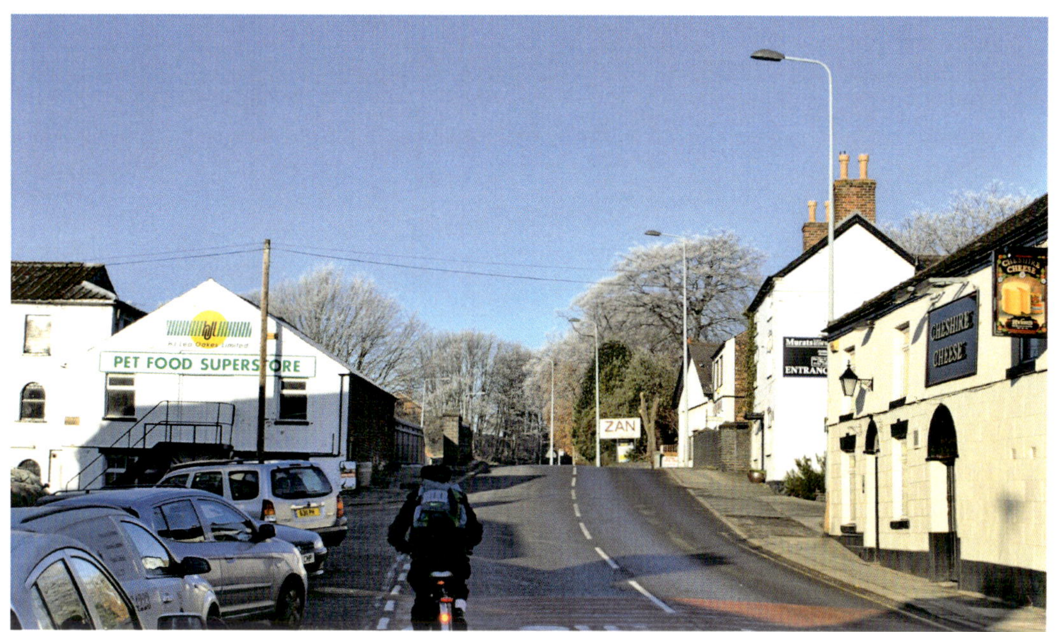

Wheelock Canal Bridge, 2010 and Early 1900s

Now we pass the Cheshire Cheese and turn to look back towards Sandbach. In the old photograph we see the tall chimney that served the mill that was here. Over the road the area still goes by the name of the Zan Industrial Park. For over ninety years, products were made here under the Zan and Hopol brand names, including all forms of household cleaners and cleaning equipment, together with requisites for farmers and gardeners. These products were exported worldwide, many starting their journey on the adjoining canal.

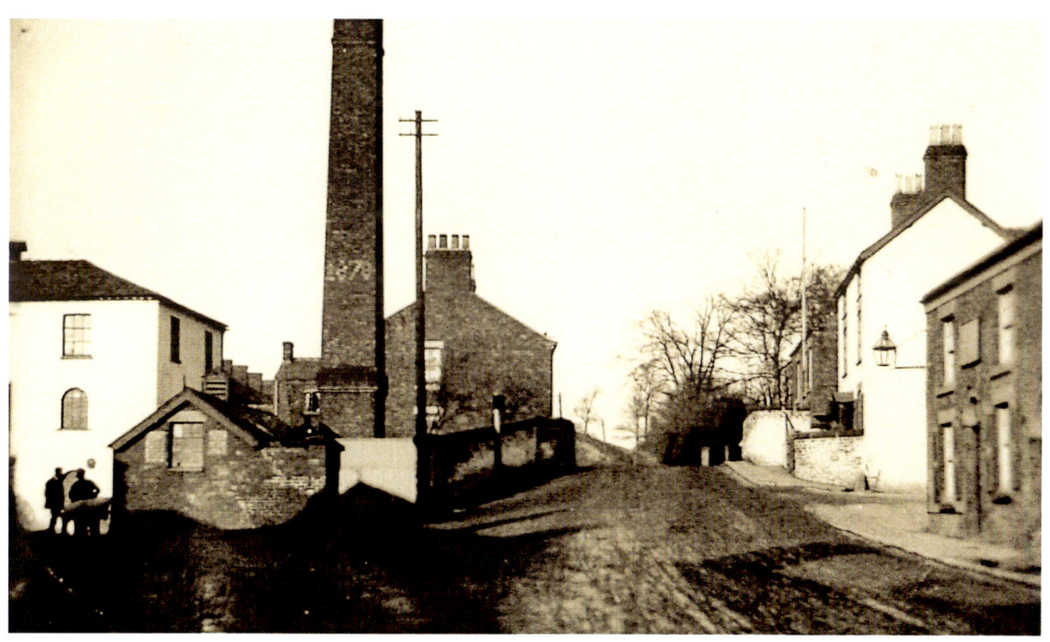

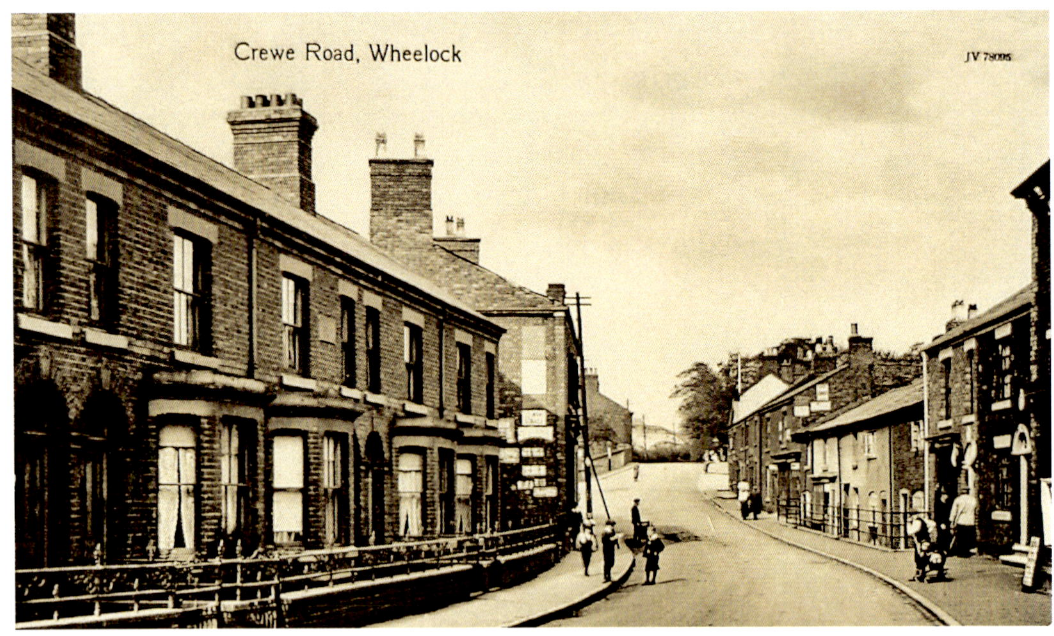

Crewe Road, Wheelock, Early 1900s and 1910

Having continued down the hill, we look back towards the canal and perhaps wonder if it would be nice to twin this Wheelock with the one in the United States. But perhaps not: it's a ghost town in North Dakota!

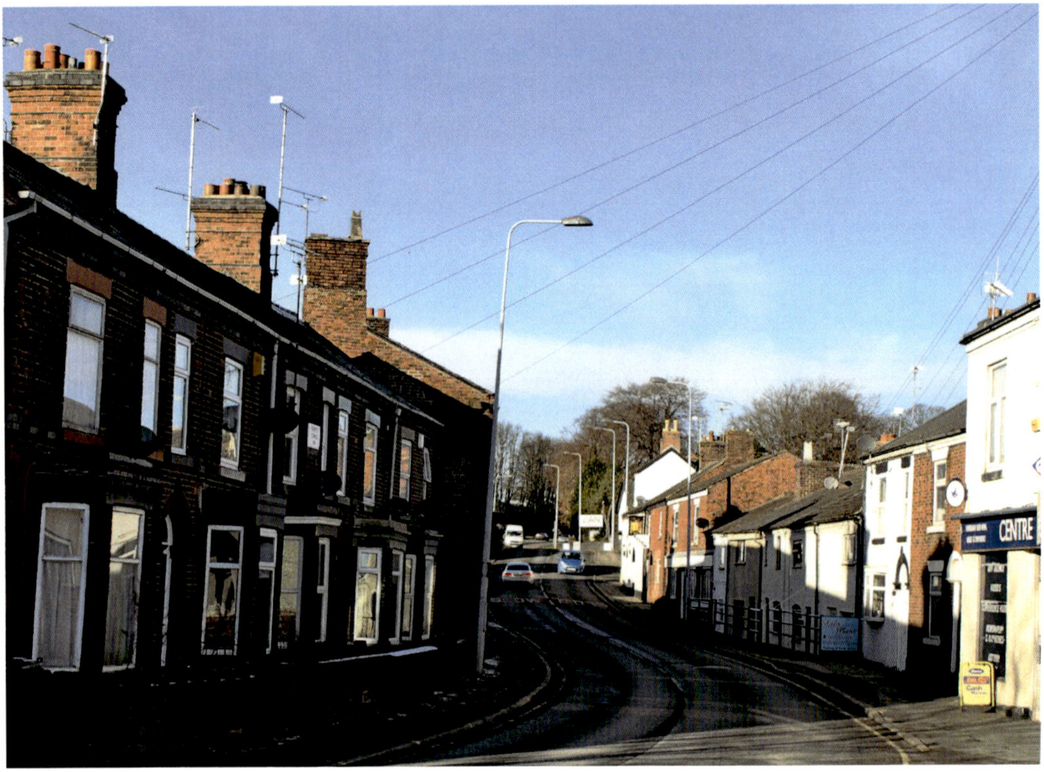

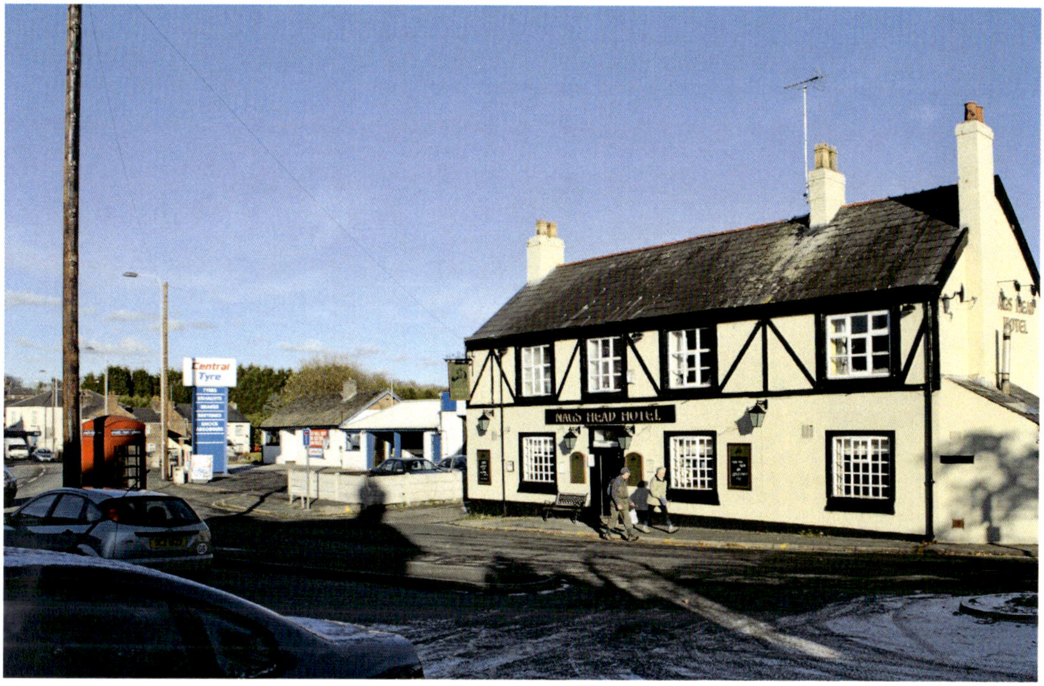

Nag's Head, Wheelock, 2010 and Early 1900s

Onward now and we cross over the river that gives the village its name. There has been a lot of development here over the years, but the pub has remained. The changes, to the pub at least, have been beneficial. The Germans dropped a landmine near here during the last war, causing a considerable amount of damage.

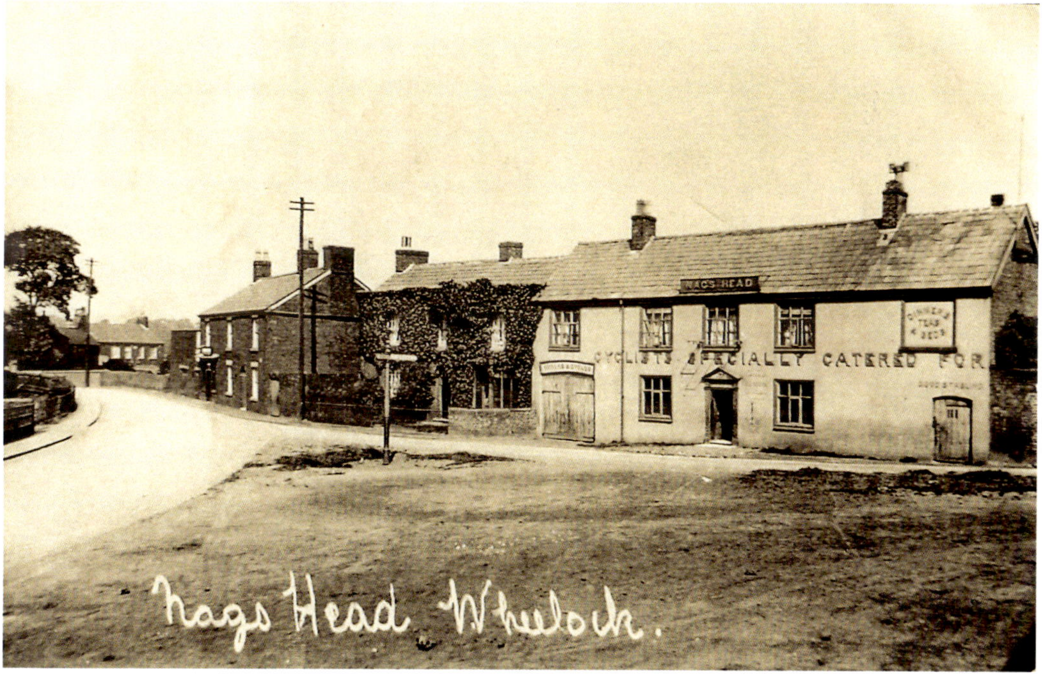

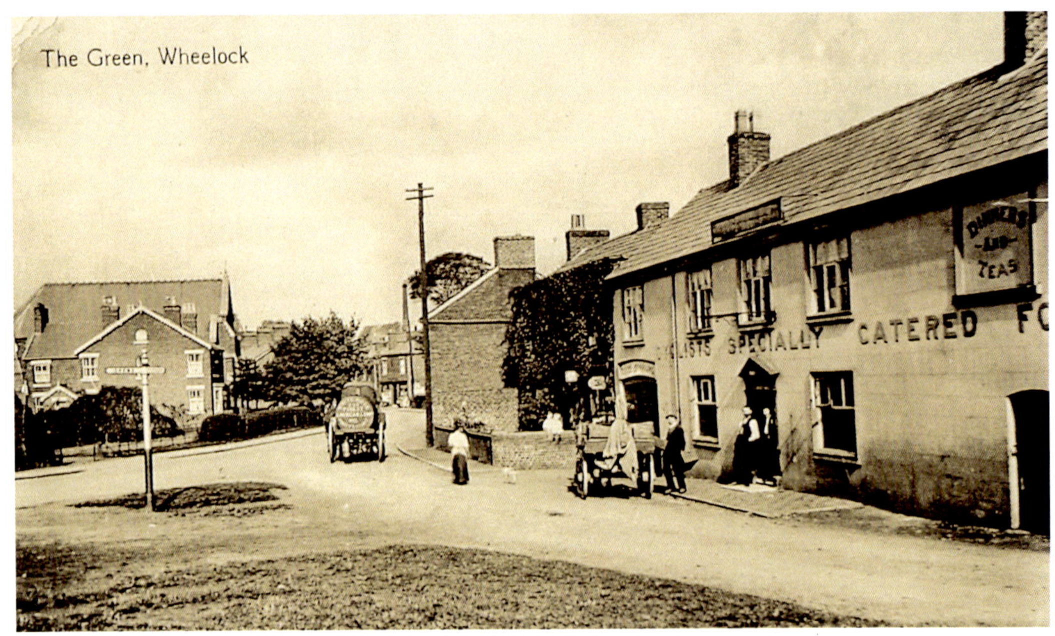

The Green, Wheelock, Early 1900s and 2010

A final look at this old public house. At the time the old photograph was taken, Sarah Bamber was the licensee. We can see from this photograph that she had ordered a delivery of lamp oil for the lighting. The White Rose lamp oil tanker has just made a delivery and is setting off back towards Sandbach.

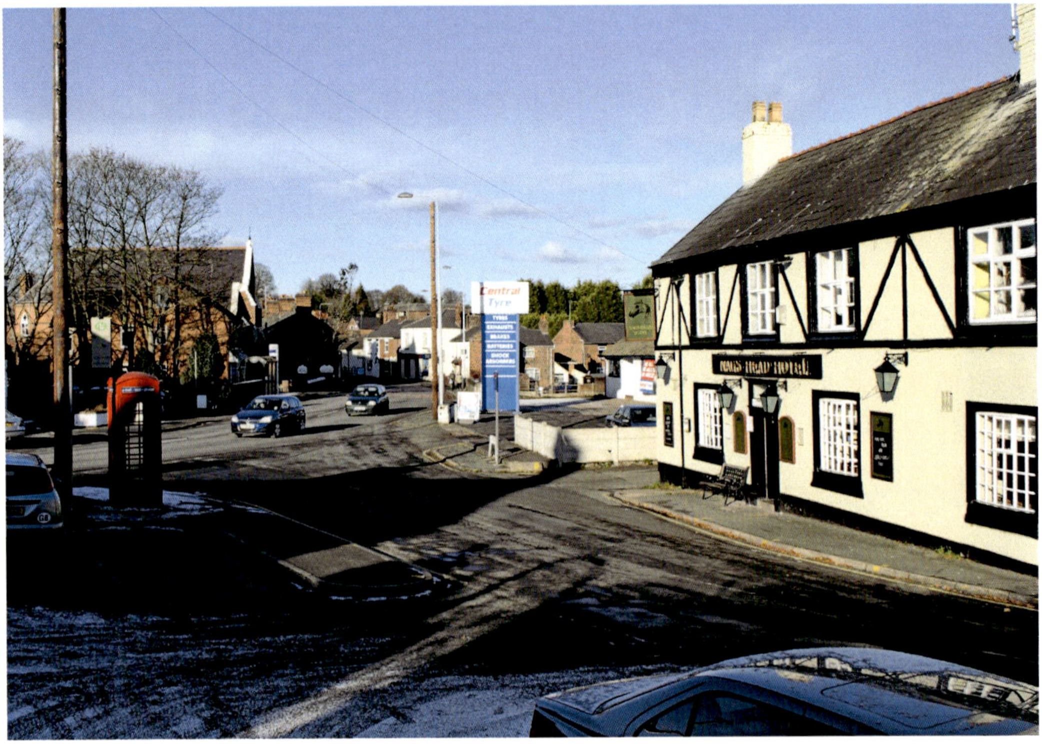

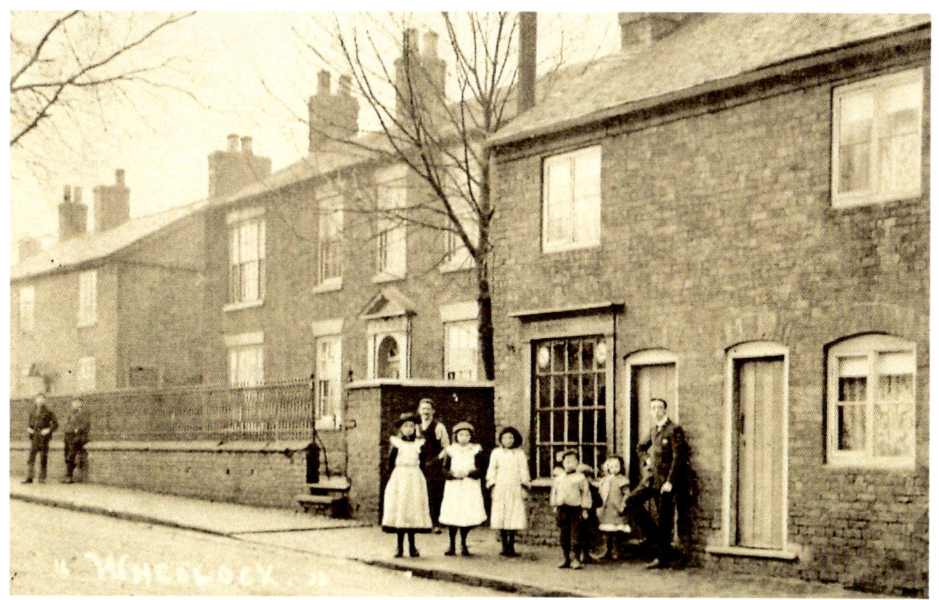

Brook Terrace, Early 1900s and 2010

We round the bend now on Crewe Road and on the right we find Brook Terrace. Here is an example of dwelling houses that have received many alterations over the years. The large house past the entry has been converted from one large dwelling to two with a second front door placed between the windows. The house nearest the camera, however, has gone the other way: it was a house and a shop and now one of the doors has been blocked up to make a larger dwelling house.

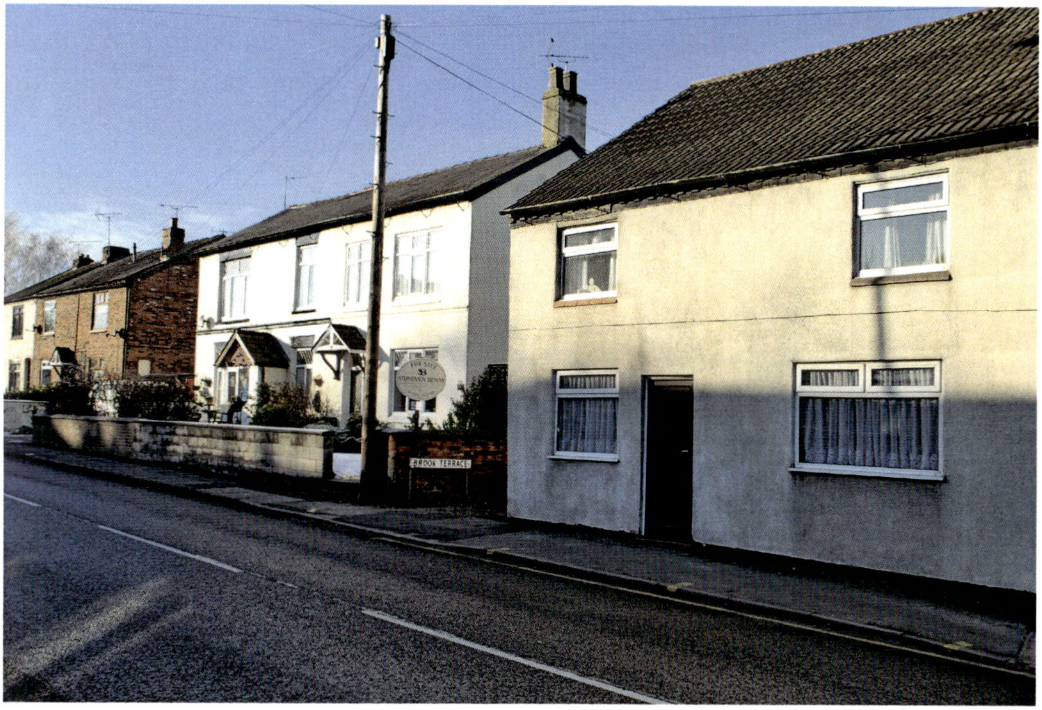

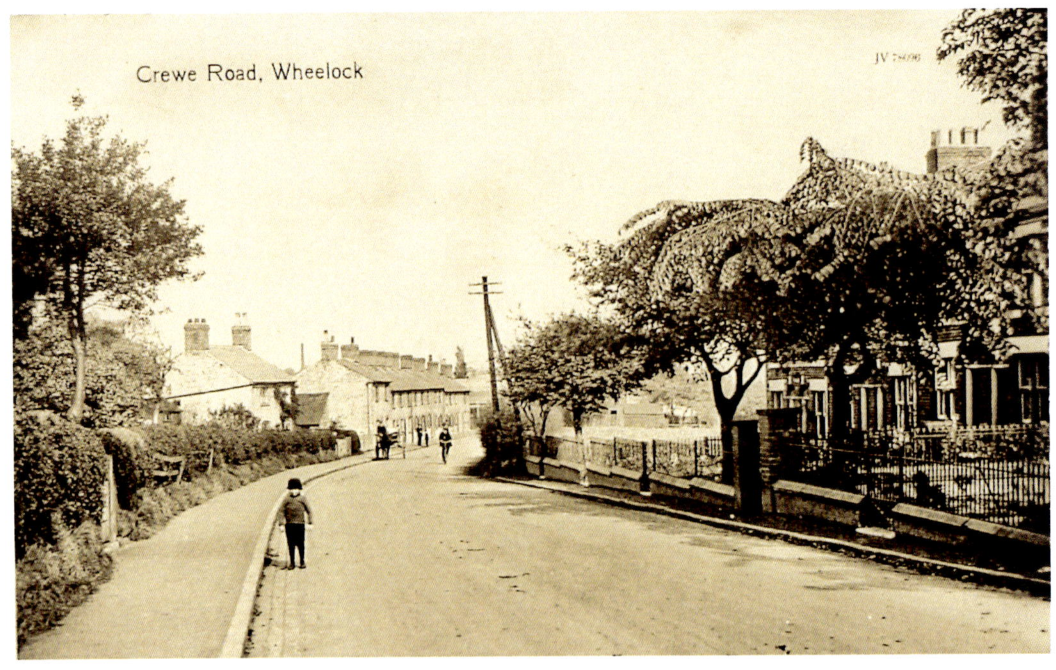

Crewe Road, Wheelock, Early 1900s and 2010

Passing Brook Terrace, we continue towards Crewe and from the top of the bank turn around to look back down towards the Nag's Head. The photograph speaks for itself, although it is interesting to see how the tree on the right has grown.

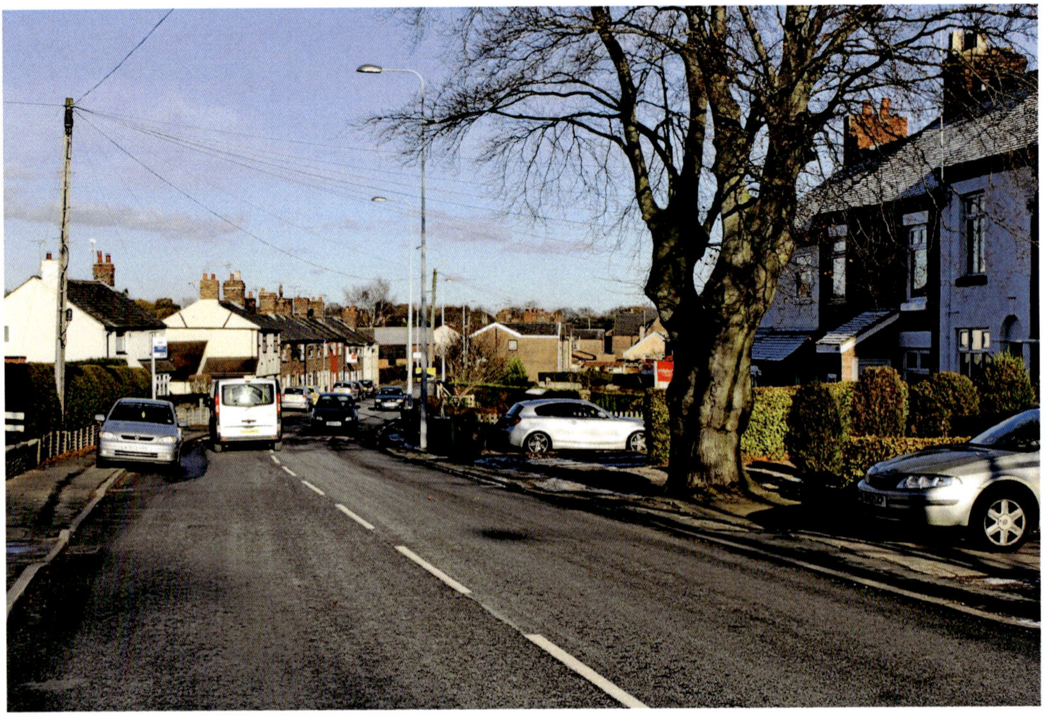

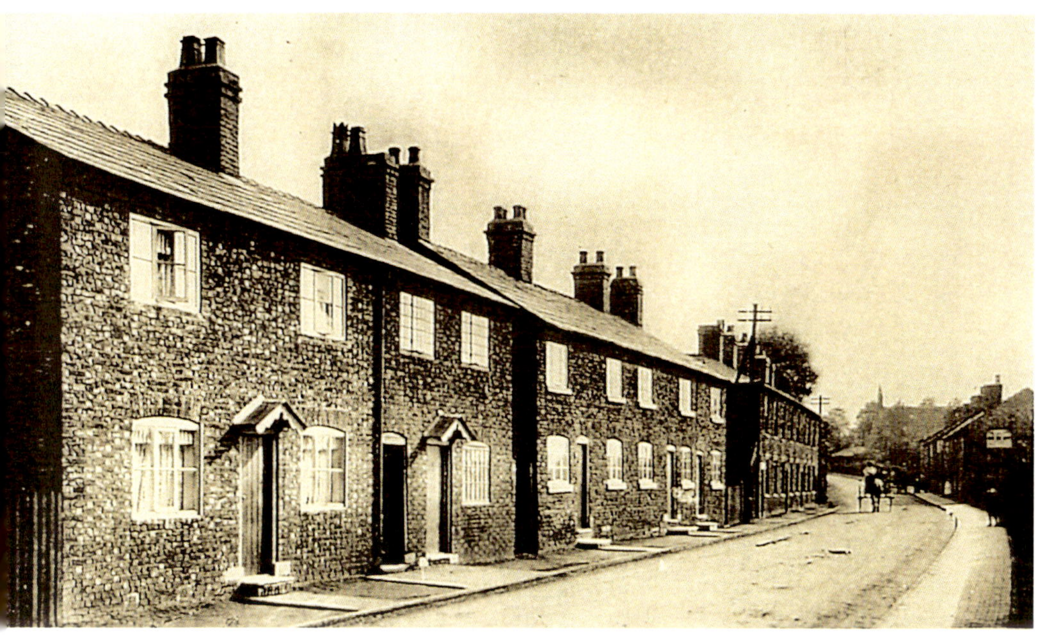

Cottages, Wheelock, 1900 to 1910 and 2010
These rows of cottages are between the last two sets of photographs; they are on Crewe Road and have changed little over the years. I tried many times to improve the modern shot but without success, the sky is grey and will have to stay that way at this location! It was either grey or dazzlingly bright.

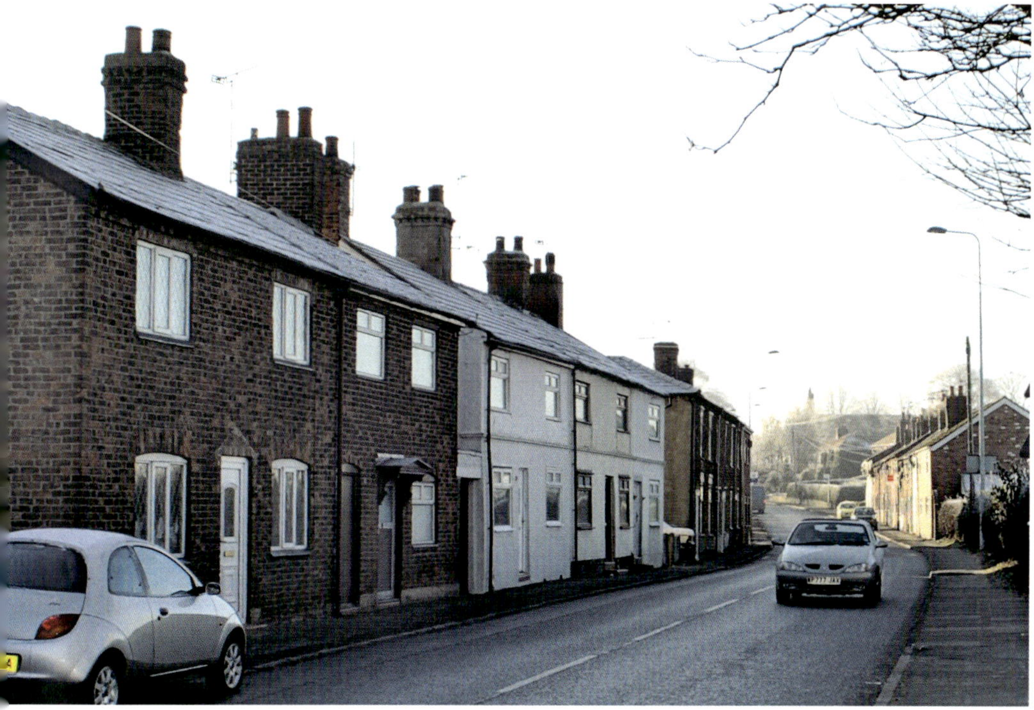

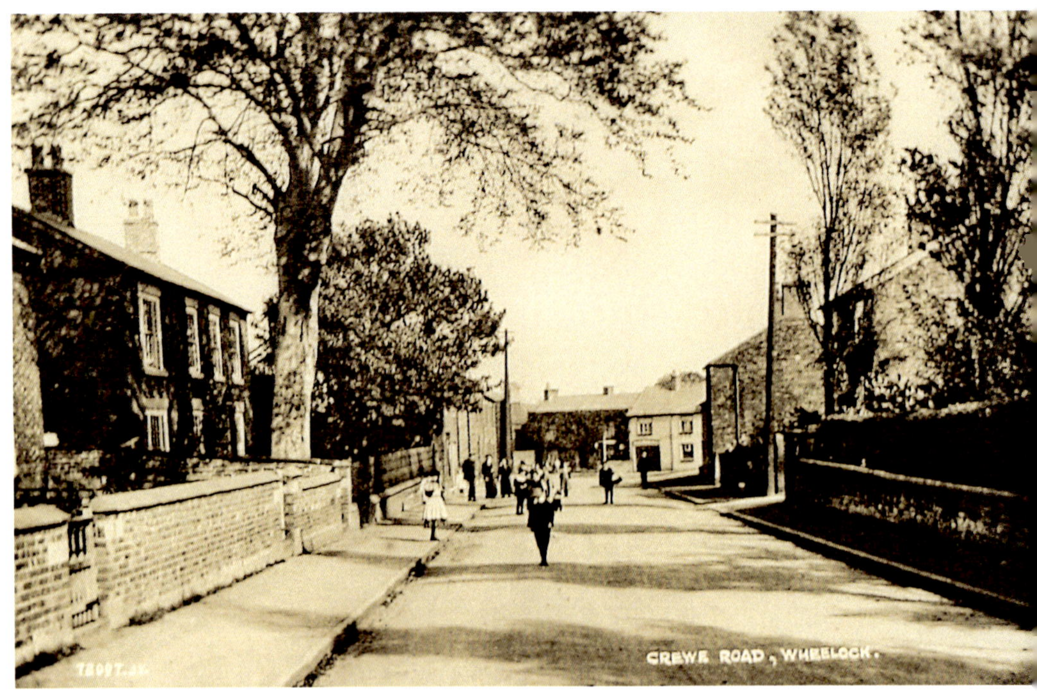

Crewe Road into Wheelock, Early 1900s and 2010

Back now towards the Nag's Head, which can be seen in the distance. The large house on the left is the one in the Brook Terrace set that has been turned from one to two dwellings.

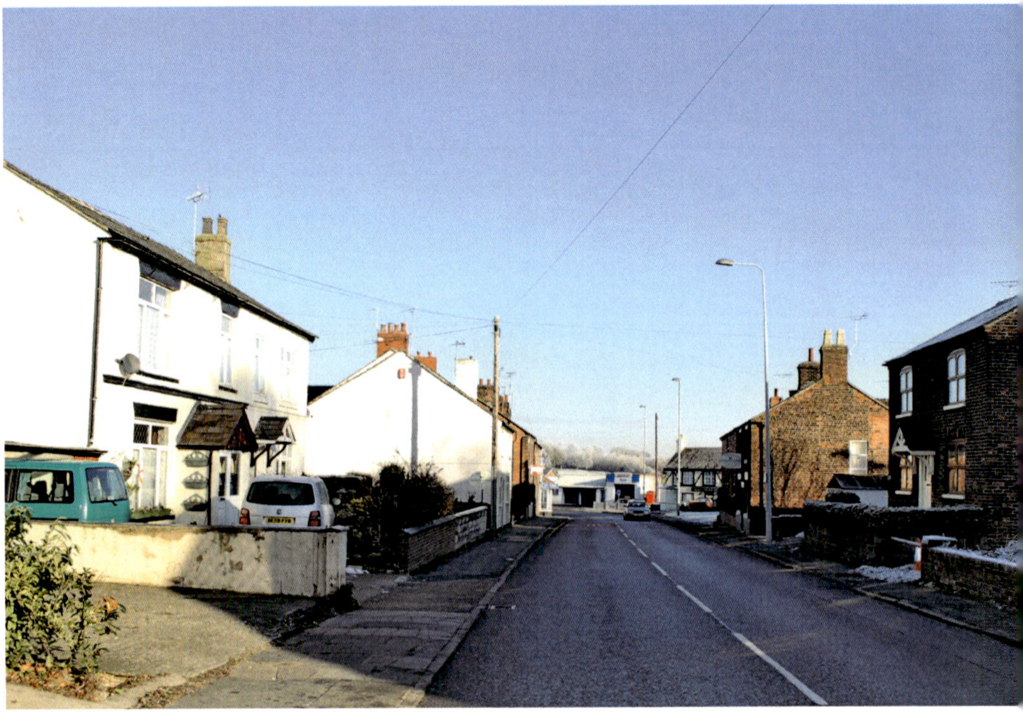

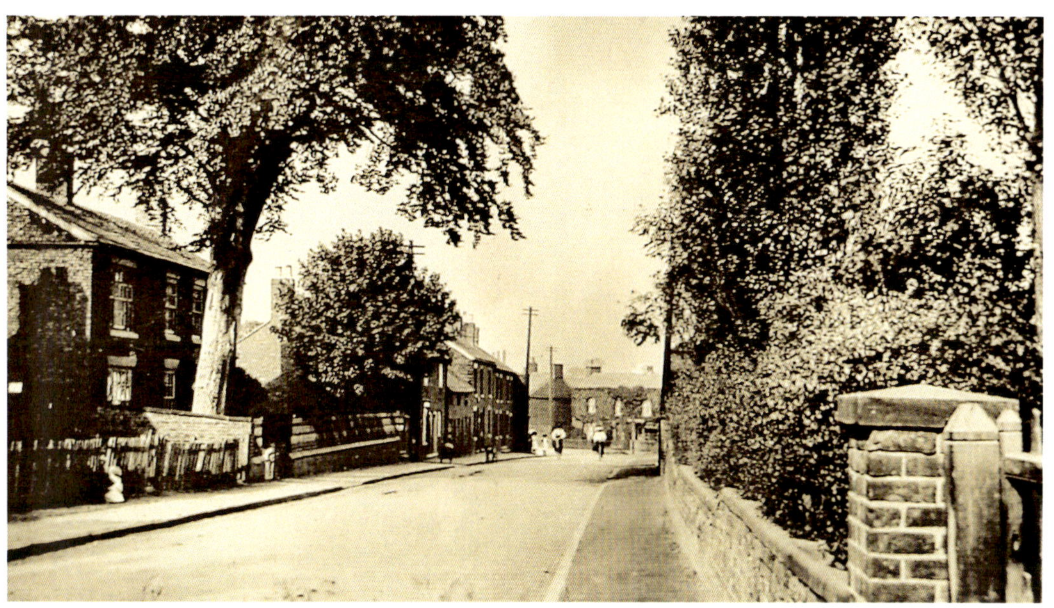

Towards Wheelock, Early 1900s and 2010

Here we are still in the same location but looking from a different angle. The large house next to the Nag's Head is covered in ivy and in the modern shot it has been demolished to make way for a garage premises. A lot of the flora from this area has gone over the years.

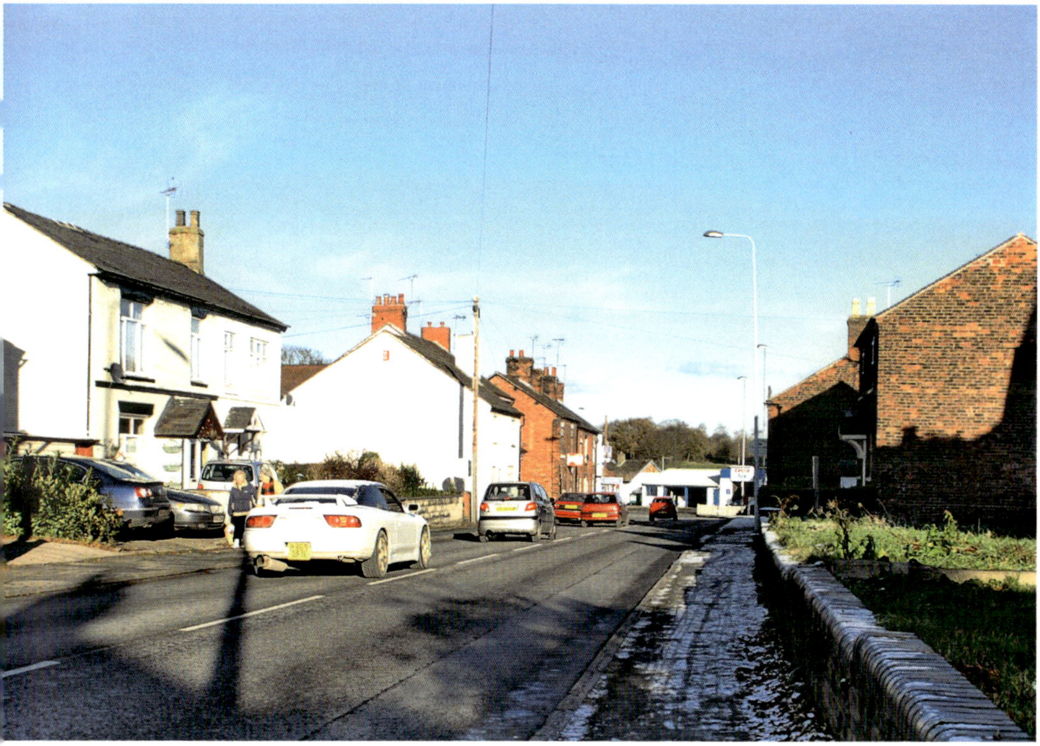

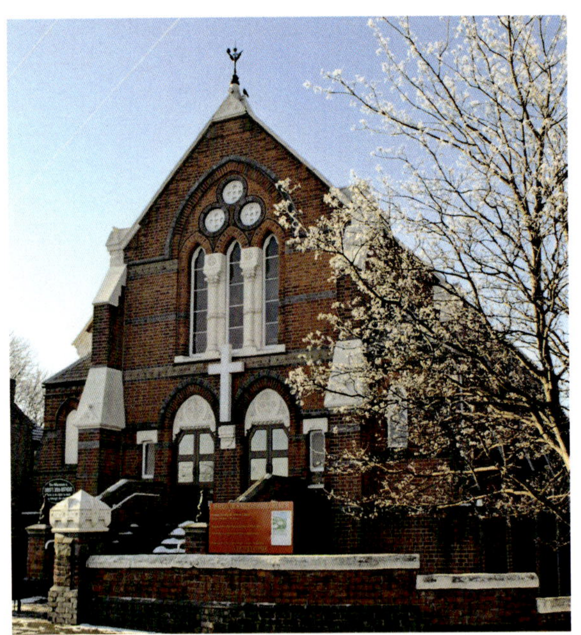

Wheelock Methodist Chapel, 2010 and Early 1900s

This chapel was rebuilt in 1874. During the Second World War it was severely damaged by a German landmine that went off nearby. It is currently home to a very active parish with Kim Stilwell as the pastor.

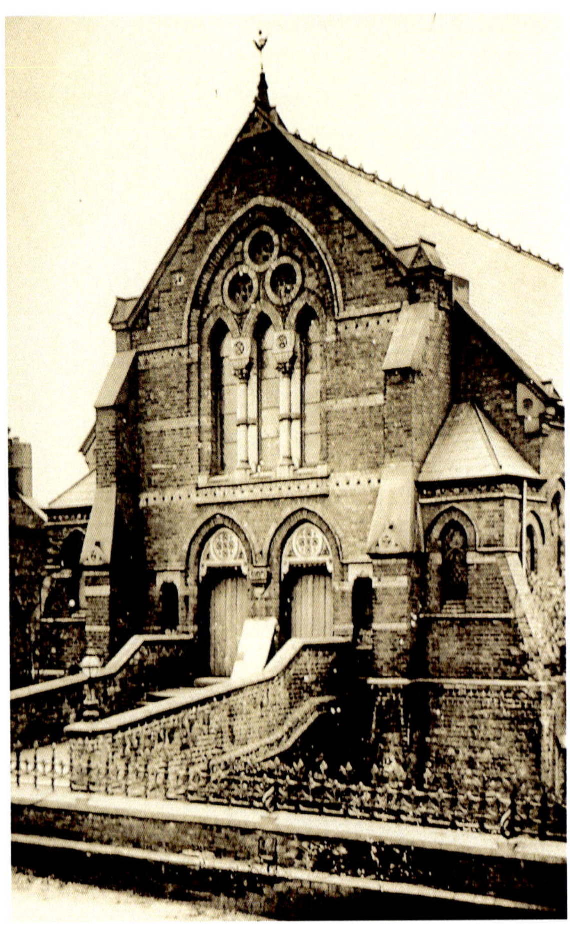

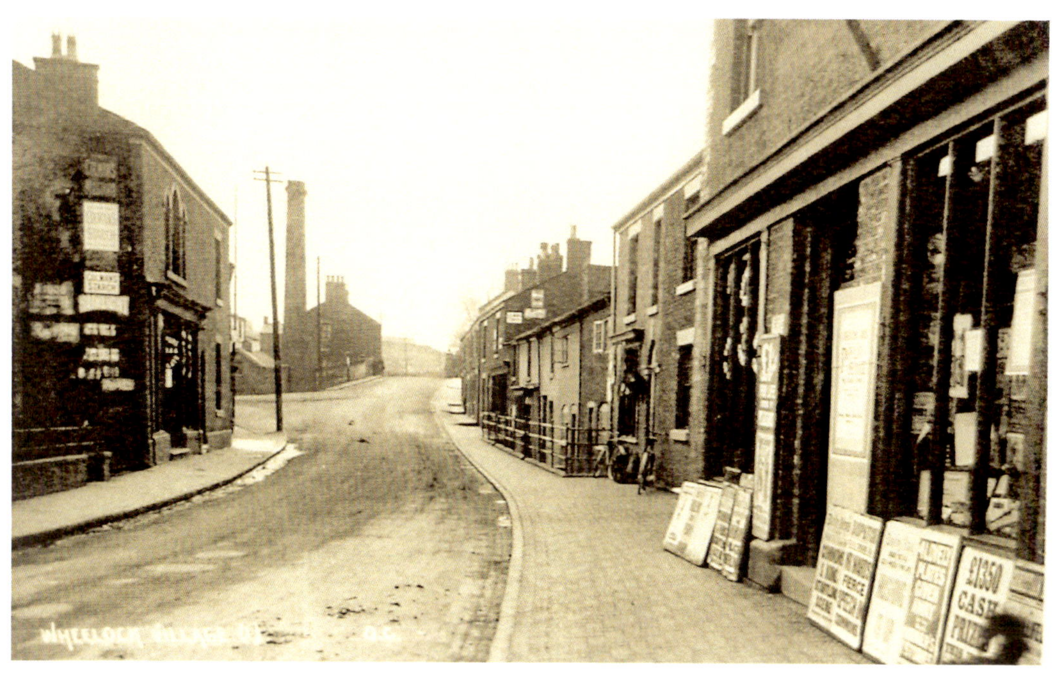

Last Look at Wheelock Village, Early 1900s and 2010

A last look at Wheelock village at the turn of the last century and as it looks today. The photographs here are self-explanatory and offer quite a good comparison. The post office was situated just behind the photographer, but it closed in 2010.

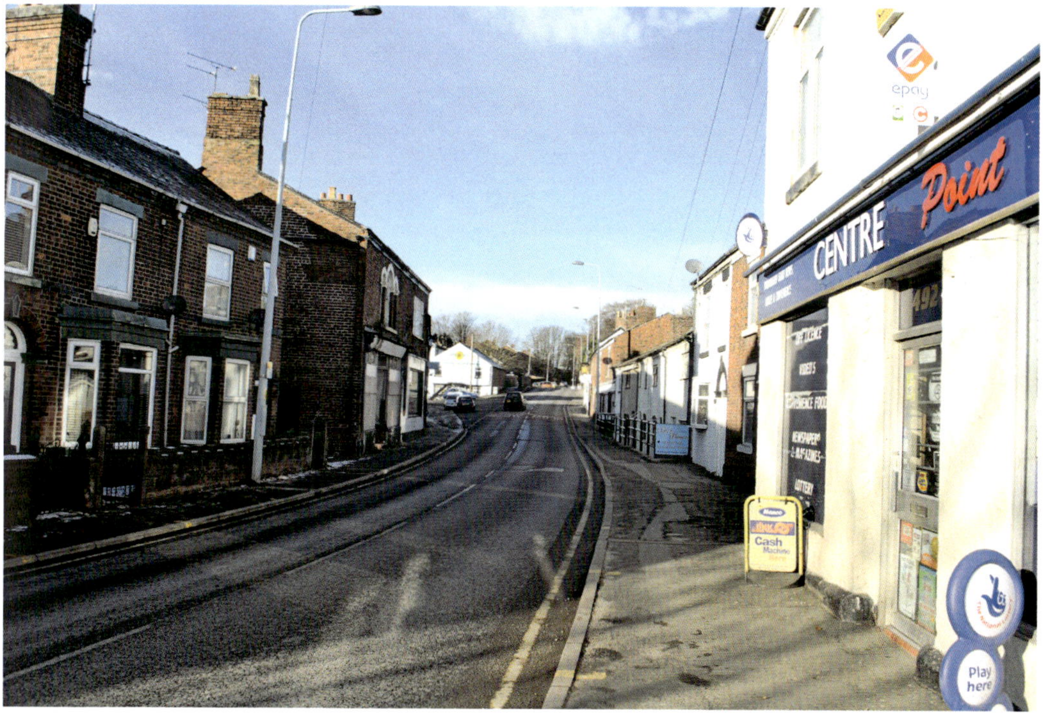

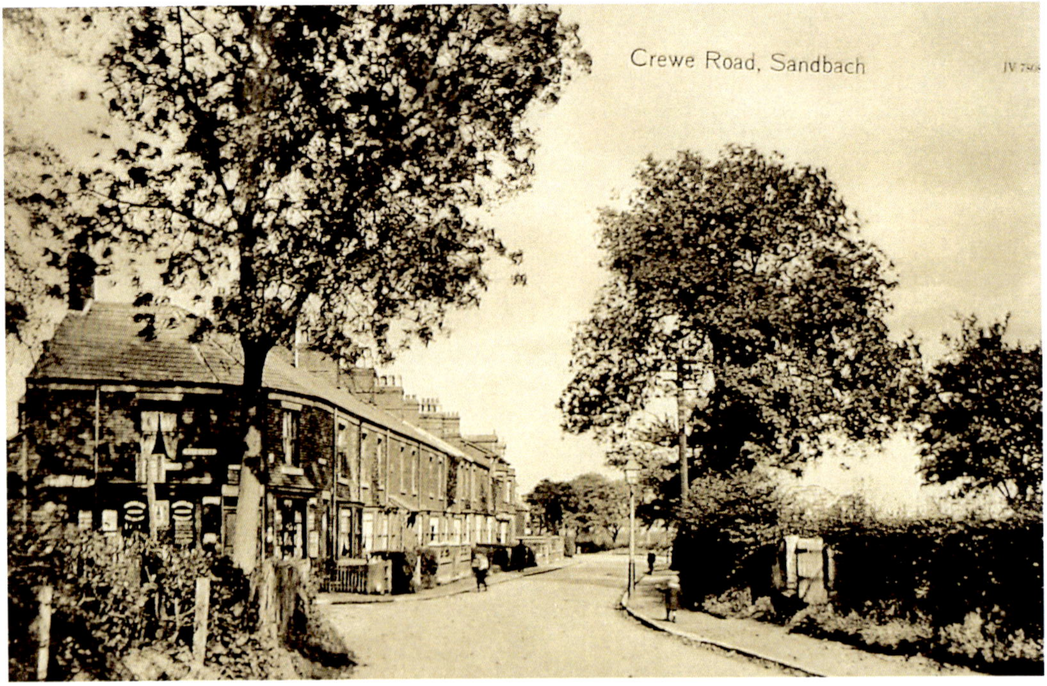

Crewe Road, Park Lane Junction, Early 1900s and 2010

As we travel back towards Sandbach, we come across the junction with Park Lane and the corner shop that has been there for many years. The junction has been widened here to make way for a bus stop, and some more houses have been built on the opposite side of the road. But other than that, there is little change.

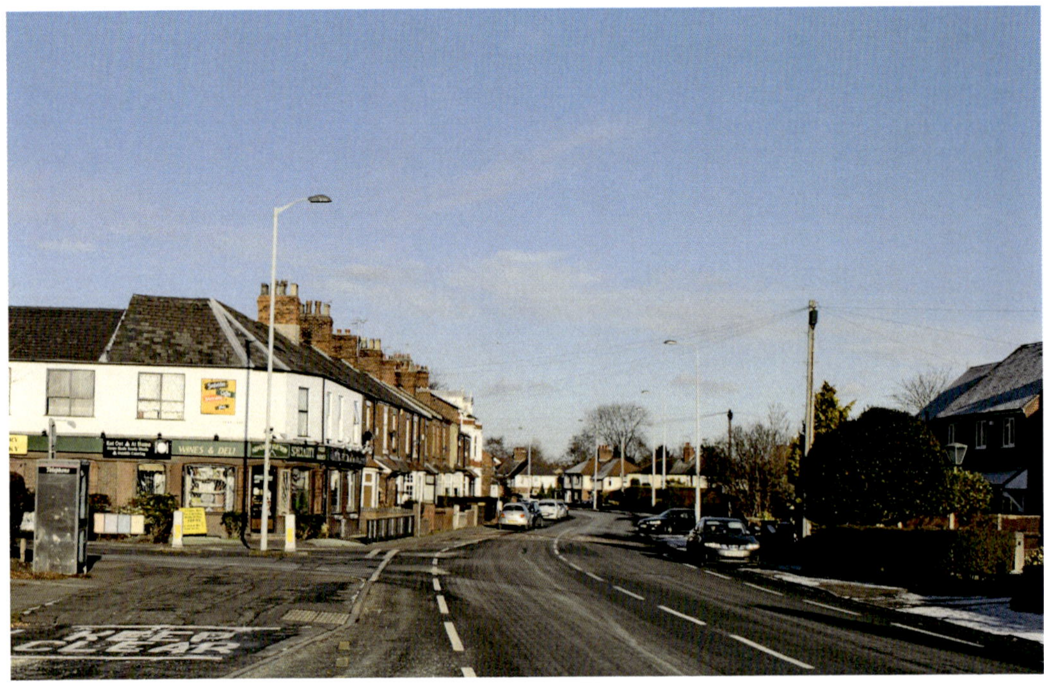

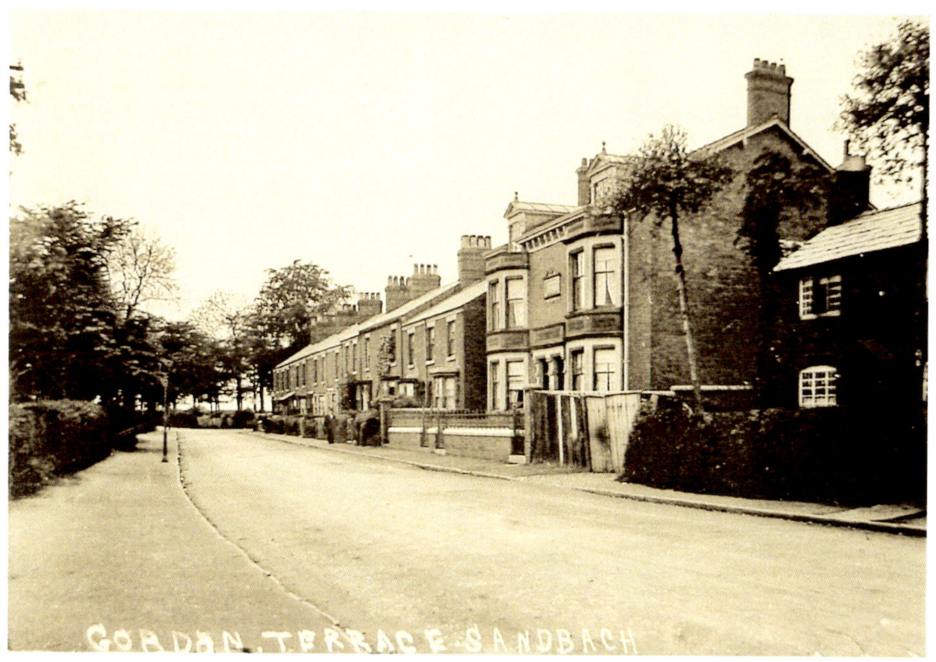

Gordon Terrace, Early 1900s and 2010

Passing the junction and looking back, we get a closer view of the terrace of houses known as Gordon Terrace. The road has been widened at this point but not a lot has changed in the intervening century or so. Outside, that is – inside there will have been a lot of changes. These houses will originally have had gas or oil lighting. The large detached house in the foreground may have had a few more luxuries, but the terraced row, even when built, would have been of good quality.

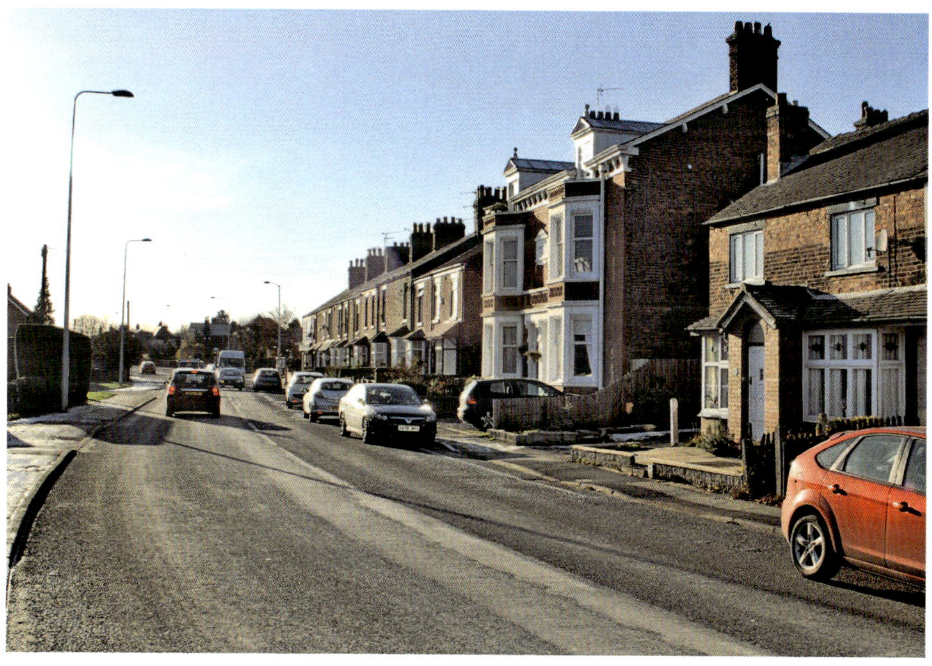

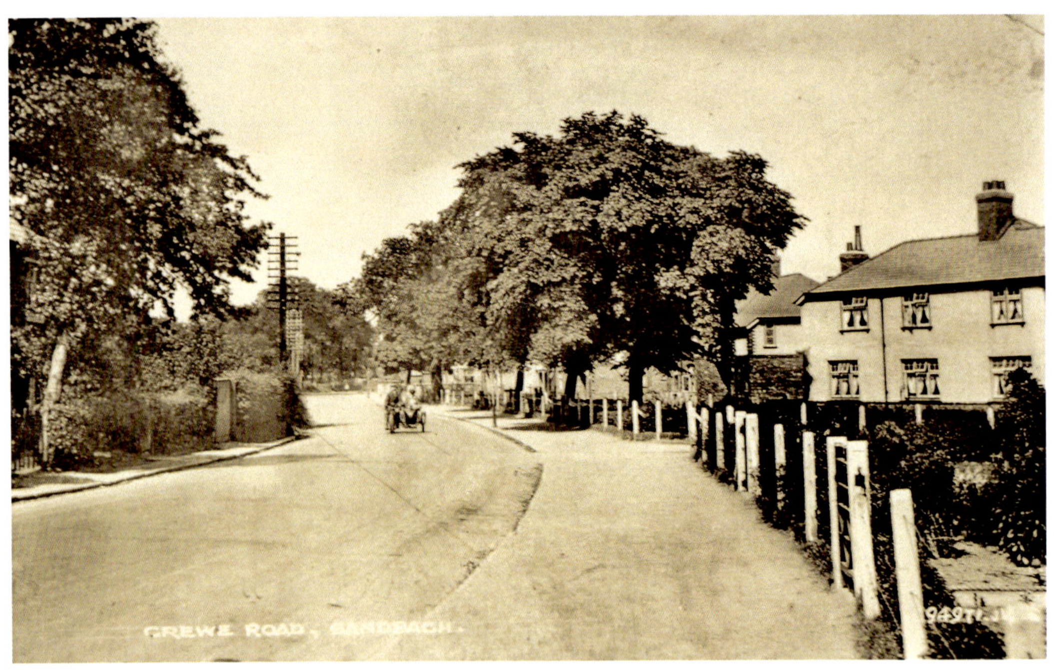

Last Look Along Crewe Road, 1930s and 2010

Just down from Gordon Terrace, we look towards Sandbach for the last time before exploring elsewhere. A motorcycle and sidecar makes its way leisurely down the centre of the road towards Wheelock. Again, a lot of the trees have since disappeared.

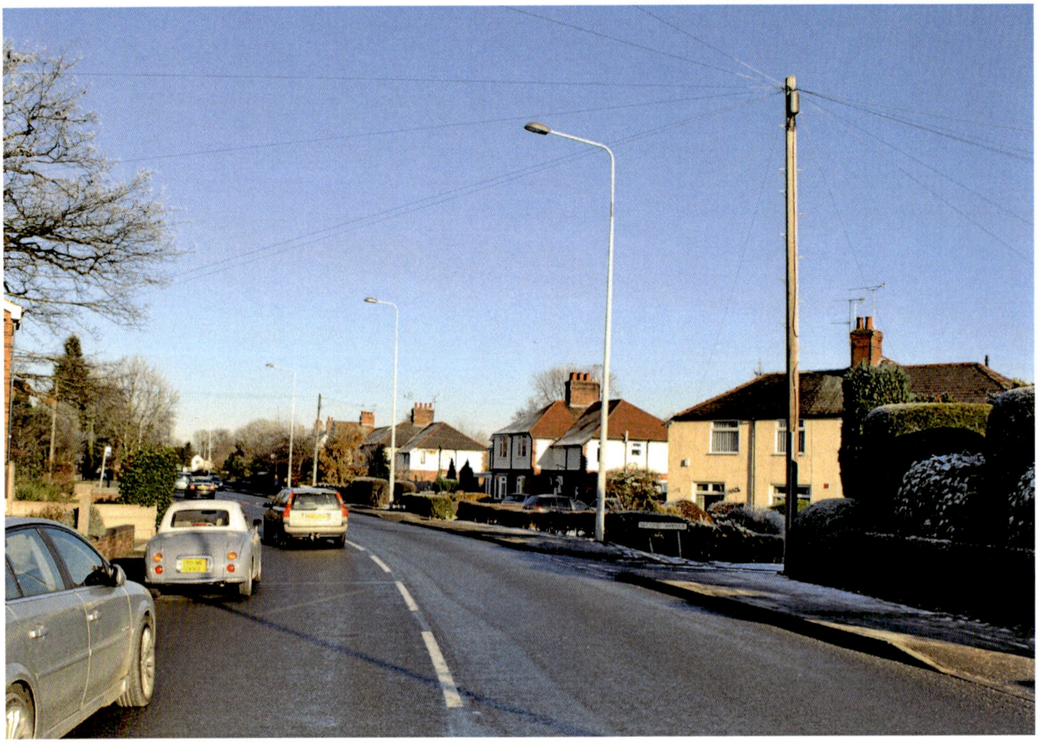

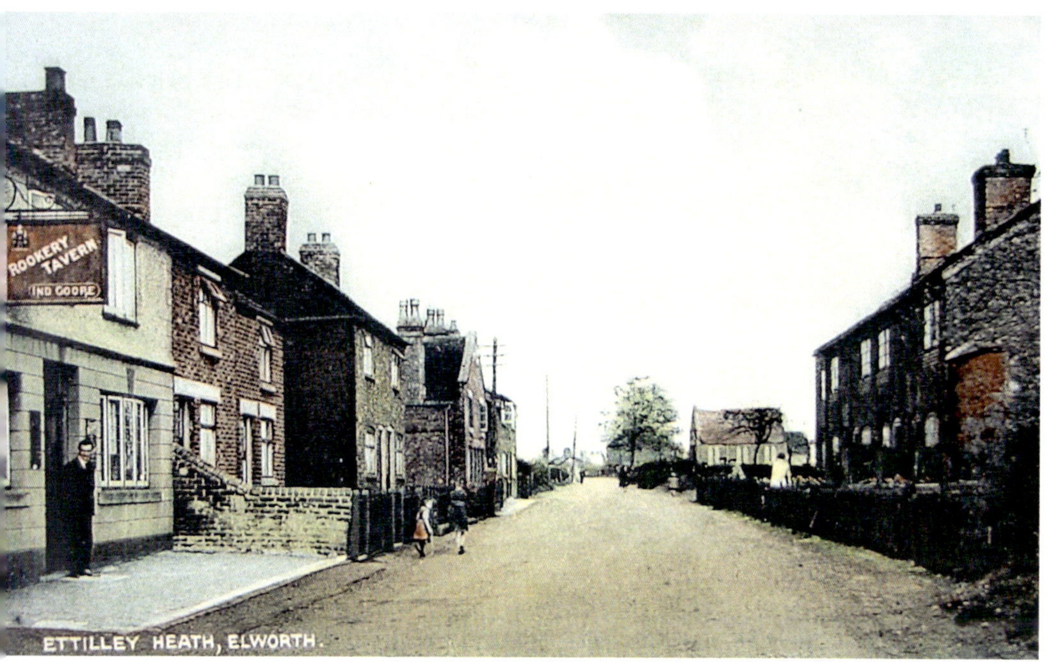

Ettiley Heath, 1930 and 2010

Now we take a walk to Ettiley Heath near to the Sandbach boundary and view the old Rookery Tavern that still serves the village. At the turn of the last century, William Dunning was the licensee and the pub will have seen the building of the Rookery Bridge salt works nearby; later it will have served the thirsty workers. These works are now an industrial estate. The old image is from a hand-coloured postcard with the name misspelled. There was also a goods depot here on the old Salt Line.

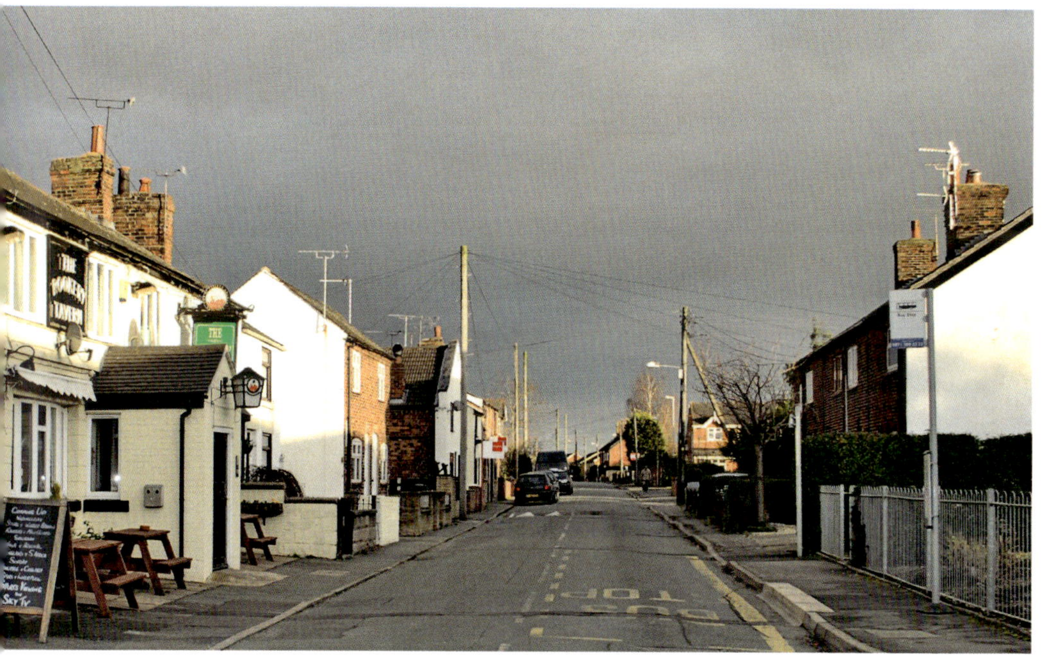

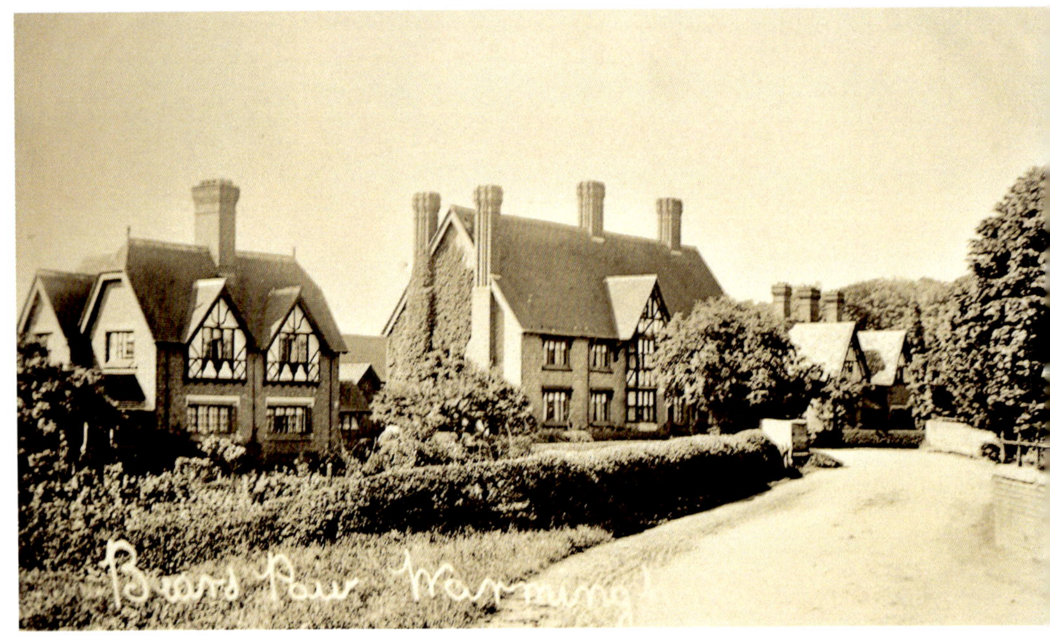

Bear's Paw, Warmingham, Early 1900s and 2010

Here we travel to one of the outlying villages; in this case it is Warmingham and we look towards the ever-popular Bear's Paw public house. The licensee was also a farmer and at the time of the old photograph it will have been John Broad. This is now the only pub in Warmingham; the one called The Crown became a farmhouse around the time that the church was rebuilt, while the other, the Old Rectory, was turned in the 1970s into a nightclub called Warmingham Grange. That closed in 2005.

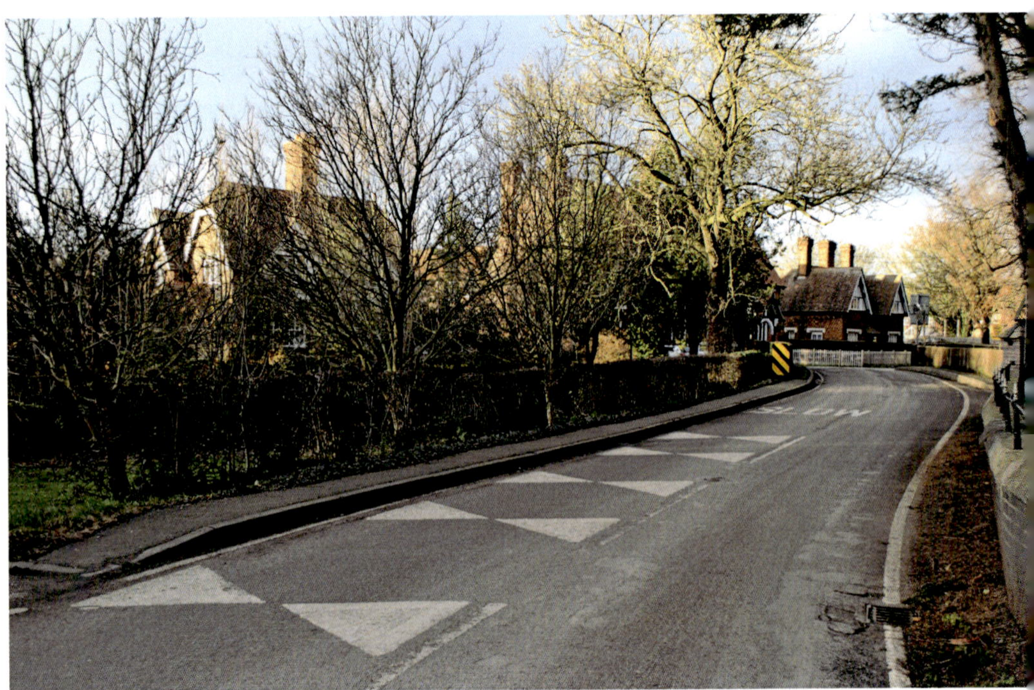

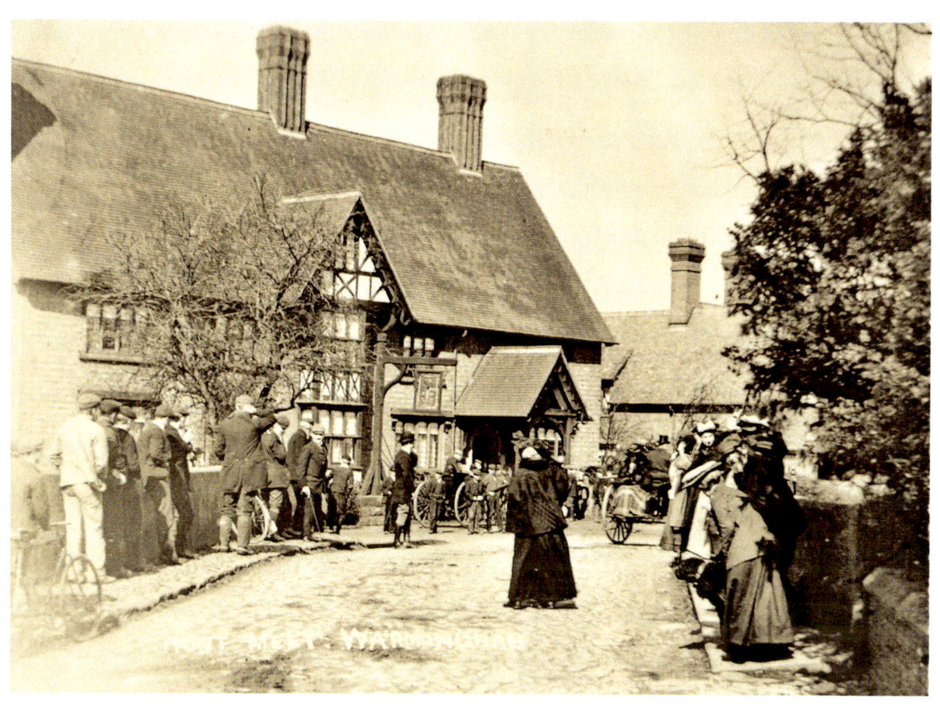

Warmingham Hunt Meeting, Early 1900s and 2010

At the turn of the last century this was a very popular public house and the same applies today when booking is usually required to secure a place to dine. In the old photograph we see people milling around as they await the fox hunters. This image is taken from the bridge over the River Wheelock, whereas for the modern shot I had to get closer due to the foliage.

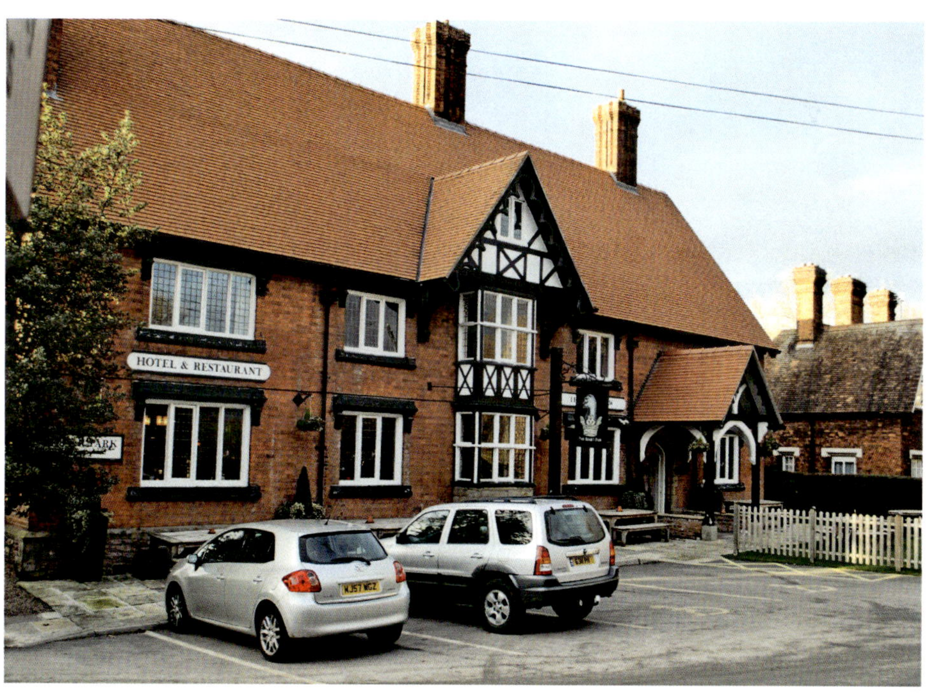

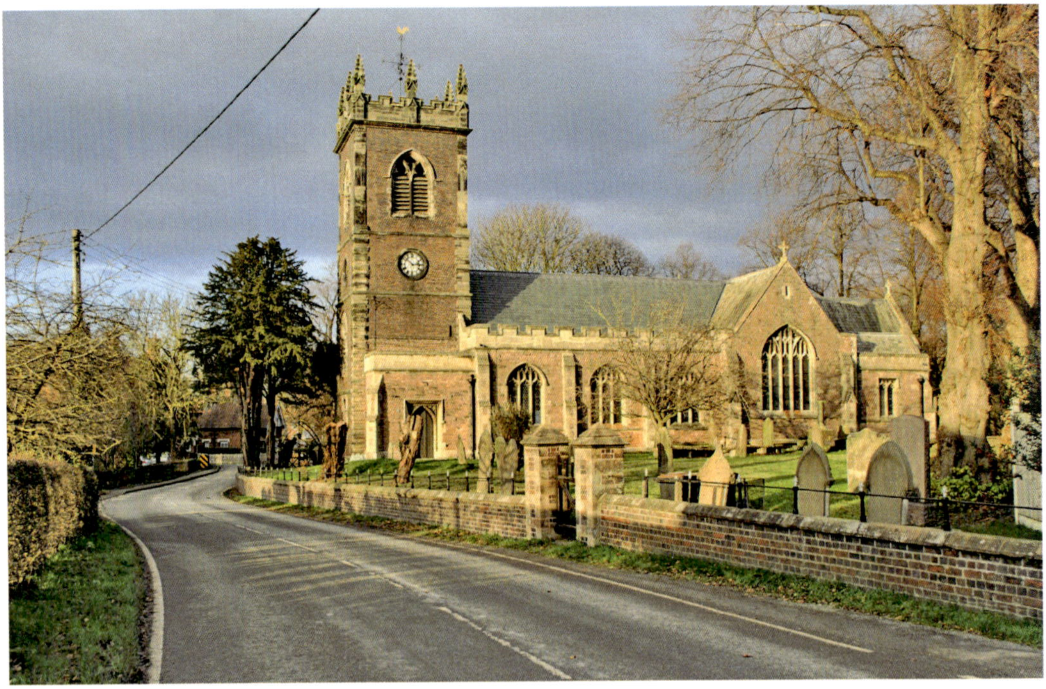

Warmingham Church, 2010 and Undated

In an earlier caption I complained of the poor lighting conditions at that particular spot, yet here we have the opposite. The sun has brought out the warm colours of this ancient church, bathing it in a soft glow. The church is dedicated to St Leonard and, like the church at Holmes Chapel, was originally timber-framed with a brick tower dating from 1715. The whole church was rebuilt in stone in 1870 by the architect Richard Charles Hussey. Twenty years later, the windows in the tower were replaced with windows in the Gothic style.

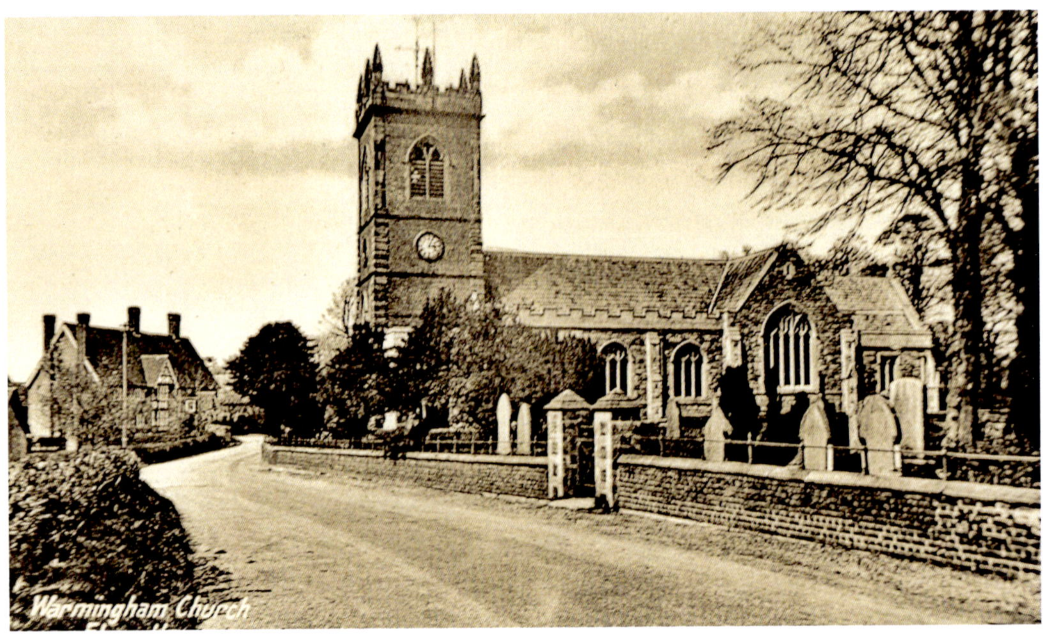